D1768271

The Vietnamese Communist Party's Agenda for Reform

ALSO BY LEWIS M. STERN

*Imprisoned or Missing in Vietnam:
Policies of the Vietnamese Government
Concerning Captured and Unaccounted For
United States Soldiers, 1969–1994*
(McFarland, 1995)

The Vietnamese Communist Party's Agenda for Reform

A Study of the Eighth National Party Congress

by Lewis M. Stern

McFarland & Company, Inc., Publishers
Jefferson, North Carolina, and London

For Mary, Eva, and Anna

British Library Cataloguing-in-Publication data are available

Library of Congress Cataloguing-in-Publication Data

Stern, Lewis M.
    The Vietnamese Communist Party's agenda for reform:
a study of the eighth national party congress / by Lewis M.
Stern.
      p.   cm.
    Includes bibliographical references and index.
    ISBN 0-7864-0487-6 (library binding : 55# alkaline paper)
    1. Đảng cộng sản Việt Nam. 2. Vietnam — Politics and
government—1975–   I. Title.
JQ898.D293S74   1998
324.2597'075'09048 — dc21   98-7535
                                                                         CIP

©1998 Lewis M. Stern. All rights reserved

*No part of this book may be reproduced or transmitted in any form
or by any means, electronic or mechanical, including photocopying
or recording, or by any information storage and retrieval system,
without permission in writing from the publisher.*

Manufactured in the United States of America

McFarland & Company, Inc., Publishers
  Box 611, Jefferson, North Carolina 28640

Contents

	List of Tables	vi
	Acknowledgments	1
	Introduction	5
1	Preparatory Meetings and Local Party Congresses	9
2	Basic-Level Meetings, Provincial and Bloc Congresses	29
3	From the Tenth Plenum to the National Congress	47
4	The Eighth Party Congress	69
5	Conclusion: The Congress and Change in the Vietnamese Political System	103
	Notes	115
	Bibliography	139
	Index	165

List of Tables

1	The Politburo Lineup: From the Sixth to the Eighth Congress	86
2	The Control Committee: From the Seventh to the Eighth Congress	87
3	Composition of the Seventh and Eighth Central Committees	93
4	Provincial Party Deputy Secretaries — Incumbents and Newcomers — Elected to the Seventh and Eighth Central Committees	94
5	Military Professionals in the Central Committee: From the Seventh to the Eighth Congress	95
6	The Security Ministries from the Seventh to the Eighth Congress	96
7	Ministerial-level Representation on the Central Committee: From the Economic, Social, and Security Ministries, 1991–96	97

Acknowledgments

The easiest part of any writing project has to be thanking everyone who helped in making the task a lot less difficult than it might have been.

I owe many personal and professional debts.

My family indulged my preoccupations, tolerating a proliferation of Vietnamese newspapers, document collections, and books piled high and in great disorder throughout the house. Importantly, I was allowed to compete successfully for computer time with a teenager come of age in the Internet era. My daughter Eva surefootedly surfed the Net to locate newspaper articles and other references for me. My daughter Anna reminded me that my first and second books had played useful roles in earlier show and tell sessions, in an effort to encourage me to complete this third writing effort. My wife Mary allowed me to haul parachute bags full of musty, mildewed, insect-eaten Vietnamese books into the basement after frequent trips to Hanoi, and listened patiently to arguments that these book-buying sprees represented real investments in documents of unquantifiable historical value. Mary's perspective suggested that the finds were more akin to baseball cards than Gutenberg bibles, and indeed they were frequently traded with like minded obsessive-compulsive personalities for other collectibles.

Frederick Brown, Nayan Chanda, Virginia Foote, Lim Hang Hing, Douglas Pike, Mark Sidel, William Turley, and Joseph Zasloff took an interest in the views I expressed and interpretations I offered, and were helpful with frank and valuable criticisms at various stages of the project. William Turley read an early version of this study and provided trenchant criticism, moral support, and a supply of his own valuable writings on recent developments in Vietnam. As usual, Doug Pike willingly offered the benefit of his long experience in analyzing the Vietnamese Communist Party, and added clarity to many confusing moments in recent party history. Fred Brown allowed me to try out portions of the arguments central to this book on his unsuspecting students at the School for Advanced International Studies in Washington, D.C., who put these hypotheses through tough tests of coherence and sensibility with their classroom remarks and questions. Fred's own responses to trial runs of my ideas were always extremely helpful as I sought to improve and clarify my thinking. Mark Sidel shared an obsession with how the Vietnamese political system works, and a matching interest in the personalities that drive that system. I am grateful for his willingness to introduce me to many of his Vietnamese acquaintances, and to share with me his own thoughts on Vietnam's government and the Communist Party.

My colleagues in government, including Joe Kinder, Dennis Harter, and George Thomas offered support and good ideas. Cecilia Minh-Hang Gillin was consistently helpful in locating articles and essays and in providing accurate and clever translations for seemingly inaccessible phrases. Bob Destatte allowed me to benefit from his unmatched tenacity in analyzing Vietnamese behavior, and his vast library of Vietnamese sources. Colonel Ed O'Dowd, our government's first defense attaché in Vietnam, shopped for the latest publications for me on the streets of Hanoi in a manner that was clearly above and beyond the call of duty.

Deputy Secretary of Veterans Affairs Hershel Gober, Deputy Assistant Secretary of Defense Kurt Campbell, and Deputy Assistant Secretary of State Kent Weidemann, among others, took an interest in my interpretation of Vietnamese politics and pummeled my views with provocative questions of their own that frequently sent me back to the drawing board. General John W. Vessey, Jr., the presidential emissary to Vietnam under the Reagan and Bush administrations, allowed me to burn up his fax machine with drafts of portions of this book and to drive many conversations toward the subjects treated in this writing.

Many Vietnamese Americans spent hours with me, poring over esoteric points of culture and history to help me understand decisionmaking, laying out their own analyses of leadership alliances within the Vietnamese Communist Party, and volunteering their own essays on the subject. Mr. Ha Van Dong was an especially good friend during this period, challenging me to travel beyond conventional wisdom in viewing the process of preparing for the congress, and despairing when I detoured down a path he thought unproductive. I learned a great deal from Mr. Dong, including some of the riches of the southern dialect. I apologize for dragging him into voluble arguments in his wonderful language that always turned heads in the Pentagon dining room.

I continue to benefit from Mr. Chau Kim Nhan's calm, confident, and consistent approach to the behavior of the Vietnamese leadership. Long discussions with Mr. Nhan and his colleagues on human rights, Vietnamese history and culture, and the pre–1975 government of South Vietnam have helped me to think through some of the puzzles I attempt to treat in this book.

Mr. Pham Duc Kien allowed me to draw him into lengthy debates about the fundamentals of Vietnamese history. I profited greatly from his interpretations and his friendship while formulating some of the earliest versions of the ideas embedded in this book.

I owe an extreme debt of gratitude to Ambassador Le Van Bang and to Mr. Ha Huy Thong, the deputy chief of mission of the embassy of the Socialist Republic of Vietnam in Washington, D.C., who shared their mission's library with me, allowed me access to newspapers, press releases, and press conference summaries, and were extremely helpful in locating recent publications and official statements on subjects of relevance to my study. Mr. Nguyen Xuan Phong of the Foreign Ministry's America's Department also graciously tracked down recent publications on party history for me. Their kindness and their abiding interest in dialogue were important to me throughout the course of this project.

Many Vietnamese government officials, party functionaries, academics, and students provided helpful comments, personal views, and compelling analysis during private conversations in Washington, D.C., Hanoi, and elsewhere that guided a good deal of my work, especially in the months leading up to the congress. Some of those views are reflected in these pages in a manner that affords them anonymity.

Deputy Foreign Minister Le Mai passed away suddenly and unexpectedly in June 1996. Mai was a consistently constructive force in U.S.–Vietnamese relations, a talented negotiator with a detailed understanding of the complexities of the U.S.–Vietnamese relationship, and a welcome partner in discussions of issues of mutual interest. His frank and accurate assessments of regional and bilateral issues were unfailingly the basis for positive meetings. Ambassador Mai always made visiting delegations feel at home and comfortable in Hanoi, setting a stage for cordial discussions on difficult issues. He personified Vietnam's real commitment to making rapid progress toward mutual understanding.

This study is offered in that spirit.

I alone am responsible for the contents of this book. The views expressed in this writing do not represent the positions of the Department of Defense or any part of the U.S. government.

Introduction

The Eighth Congress of the Vietnamese Communist Party (VNCP) convened in late June 1996, with the task of reviewing the process of reform initiated by the Sixth Congress in 1986. During the year leading up to the meeting, Vietnamese government officials and rank-and-file party cadre anticipated the national congress as a formal opportunity to reaffirm the course of reform, eliminate existing reticence about economic change and social transformation, and authoritatively make the political changes necessary to sustain the renovation process. By the last quarter of 1995, senior Vietnamese officials were privately making it clear that the Eighth Party Congress would be a major benchmark in the reform process.

To such officials, the Fifth Congress (1982) addressed exclusively organizational issues, and the Seventh Congress was concerned almost entirely with "housekeeping" matters. The January 1994 interim party conference focused on electing a new group of Central Committee and Politburo members. So the Eighth Congress would represent a major departure from the core agendas of the past several congresses. By the end of October 1995, senior government officials were saying that the Eighth Congress would be responsible for summing up a decade worth of economic renovation, and paving the way for the consolidation of economic reforms in the future.[1] A series of early December editorials in *Nhan Dan* underscored the responsibility for appraising a decade's worth of reform that would fall to the National Congress.[2] Senior- and middle-level Vietnamese officials expressed the view that the Eighth Party Congress would be responsible for extracting lessons from ten years' worth of reformist experiments, and for confirming this reformist path as the one the party should follow for the next five or more years. According to senior officials, the key agenda item for the national party meeting would be the comprehensive review of renovation, which would determine the pace and scope of future economic and political changes and make the most fundamentally difficult choices on matters such as divesting state enterprises and implementing a market–based economy in a thorough and unhesitating manner. One senior diplomat commented that the congress would do an even more thorough job of debating and reviewing the specifics of reform policy than the last several Central Committee plenary sessions, which themselves had been profound assessments of the course of the reforms in agriculture, culture, and industry.

During the last quarter of 1995, senior Vietnamese officials privately made the case that issues such as land reform and privatization were likely to get a thorough airing, especially issues where narrow ministerial equities had been able to dislodge reformist undertakings. The willingness of ministers to seek exceptions to policy, to question the wisdom of reformist plans, or to act to defend their own narrow interests blunted reforms and made it possible for a single minister to undermine the party's sworn goal. The Eighth Party Congress would seek to limit the extent to which the conservative ministerial interests were able to pose obstacles to reforms. The congress, senior officials opined, would go far toward recognizing that market economics could not work if measures were allowed to go only halfway toward a nonplanned economy. The Eighth Congress would address strategic issues for the first time since 1986. The party would undertake a thorough inventory of ideological and developmental issues. Middle- and senior-ranking officials felt that the congress's review of ideological issues was likely to focus on the consequences of the move to a market economy, the influence of capitalism on Vietnam, and the worries of the "old people" regarding the difficulties of reconciling marketization and economic reform with nationalism and Vietnam's continued commitment to socialism. The Eighth Congress would also represent a critical moment in generational change. Younger leaders who supported continued reform would play an important role in discussing these issues and adopting the authoritative resolutions defining the party's goals for the next five or ten years.

In the end, though, the Eighth National Congress fell far short of the expectations held by the strongest supporters of reform, and instead reflected lingering party suspicions regarding the consequences of unbridled change for Vietnam's stability and the party's political future. The congress restated the core values of Vietnamese communism, and reminded the party of the need to practice caution, preserve stability, and implement change prudently.

This book focuses on the preparatory process in advance of the congress — from the local party congresses that convened beginning in late 1995 through the provincial and party bloc congresses that met up to the eve of the National Congress — to assess the means by which the party center attempted to guide and control that process. It examines the effort to elicit local commentary on the key draft policy documents — the political report, the revised party statute, and the socioeconomic plan — prepared for presentation to the congress. The study concludes with an analysis of the national meeting, the documentary record it generated, the leadership changes it put in place, and the policy courses it criticized, reshaped, and ultimately blessed.

1

Preparatory Meetings and Local Party Congresses

Preparing for the Eighth Congress: Basic Party Committee Meetings

The process of preparing for the 1996 Party Congress differed from the steps taken to advance the 1991 Congress. In anticipation of the Seventh National Congress, the party began making plans for convening congresses in early January 1991. Key cadre conferences discussed the goals for local preparatory congresses, including the election of delegates to attend higher-level meetings. Preparations for local congresses took place alongside campaigns to "purify" party membership, oppose corruption, and improve recruitment practices and production plans. The first round of grassroots party organization meetings, held during February and March 1991, were not particularly well organized and were poorly attended by younger groups. Efforts to elicit critical comments on and contributions to the draft political report yielded meager results. By late February some provinces could report only partial completion of the initial round of local congresses. Some provinces held cadre meetings to review local party sessions and offer midcourse corrections to the process. Early March projections suggested that the grassroots meetings would continue through April. However, by late February the original May date for the convening of the Seventh National Congress slipped to June and later July as the result of the disorganized state of local meetings and the intensity of debate over the draft documents.

Southern party meetings preparing for the Seventh Congress

proceeded at a more casual pace than sessions in the center and the north. By mid–March party chapters and grassroots organizations had completed the first round of congresses, the selection of delegates, and the compilation of critical views and opinions on the draft political report. At that time, municipalities directly subordinate to the center conducted experimental, first-round congresses in grassroots organizations. The first district congresses were reported in the media in late March, and provincial committees convened to review the first-round congresses in mid–March. During March and April, ministries and military region party organizations convened their first round congresses. Provincial party organization congresses were under way by the third week in April.

Local party structures experienced similar disorderliness and confusion in the grassroots sessions and experimental congresses that prefaced the Eighth National Congress. However, in 1995 the party center was careful to limit the rounds of congresses that were convened by lower level organizations, in order to minimize the number of oversight sessions conducted by superior echelons charged with reviewing local party committee congresses, and to involve Central Committee members in providing guidance to local experimental congresses at an earlier stage and in a more public manner. In spite of earnest efforts to manage the process, local committee debates sprawled across issues in an unfocused manner, comments on the draft documents lacked the punch and specificity that was sought by the Central Committee, and initial drafts of party committee political reports did not meet Central Committee standards.

Beginning in mid–1995 two entwined processes reviewed institutional strength and policy direction in anticipation of the Eighth National Congress. First, by the end of the first three months, selected provincial and city party committees had completed an appraisal of grassroots party organizations and an assessment of members that had begun in late 1994. The national goal was to hold the number of weak party entities to 5 percent of the national total, lowering the number of cardholders who violated disciplinary standards, and adding to the ranks of "outstanding members."[1]

Second, at roughly the same time, provincial party committees were conducting expanded conferences of district and city secretaries to review the groundwork for the upcoming party congresses and to nominate delegates to attend those sessions. Local congresses were to be prefaced by a round of local meetings that would review the Central Committee Plenary resolutions, issued between June 1992 and January 1995, and pay special attention to the party's faithfulness to the provisions of the Third Plenary Resolution, which reiterated the importance of repairing critical aspects of party organization, membership policy, and leadership practices. The third resolution also spelled out the principles that the party leadership wanted enshrined as the guide to foreign policy formulation during the course of preparations for the National Congress.[2]

The preparatory congresses progressed in fits and starts. Basic-level organizations encountered difficulties in working the kinks out of the documents for the National Congress and in managing the process of local leadership selection. According to a Central Committee directive (07/Ke Hoach/Trung Uong), the grassroots-level congresses were to run from June to September 1995, and district, precinct, and provincial congresses were to convene from November to December. During that time, the local party organizations would evaluate past achievements and current weaknesses of the party, extract "management experiences" from the performance of past committees, define targets and duties for the next party committee, and discuss the process of contributing ideas to the draft documents for the National Congress.

In mid–May visits to the provinces, senior party and government officials reviewed local efforts to implement the resolutions of the Seventh Party Congress having to do with economic policy, social development, security, and party building. These were the first indications that a comprehensive review of party leadership and national economic performance was in the offing.[3] By late May all provincial and municipal party committees had held conferences to discuss plans for conducting local party congresses in accordance with the Secretariat's Directive 51. The conferences also reviewed the Central Committee Organization Department's five year manpower plan for provincial, city, precinct, and district executive committees. By late May 1995, 38 provincial and city party organizations had reviewed a version of the draft report on party building work.[4]

These conferences continued through at least mid–June, by which time subordinate party entities had begun to prepare reports for presentation to the precinct congress, and precinct-level party committees had begun to organize subcommittees to draw up agendas and select delegates for the precinct congresses.[5] Precinct committees summarized the last stages of the review of the Third, Seventh, and Eighth Plenary resolutions as well as two resolutions on mass mobilization work (Resolutions 8B and 07-08 BCT).[6] During the first week of June, General Secretary Do Muoi visited Gia Lai, Kon Tum, Dac Lac, and Lam Dong to review progress toward implementing all the resolutions of the Central Committee from 1991 to 1995, including emphasizing the central goals of agricultural industrialization, administrative reform of the state-operated enterprises, infrastructure development, and cooperation between the highlands and the mountainous areas. In early June Dao Duy Tung joined Do Muoi in a visit to a model district in Dac Lac Province to measure the results of rural economic renovation and administrative reform. Both visitors urged provincial-level party organizations to devote serious efforts to preparing for the congress.[7]

In June the Central Committee Organization Department circulated Guidance 06-HD-TC/TW, which authorized all provincial party committees, municipal party organizations, and party organizations subordinate to the Central Committee to reformulate plans for guiding congresses at all basic levels in accordance with new issues and imperatives. On the basis of the Secretariat's instructions, provincial and municipal committees focused on cadre issues, established guidance committees to monitor the preparatory process, and concentrated on directing pilot congresses in a number of basic organizations representing village, street, and enterprise party organizations.

By mid–June precincts had conducted preparatory seminars on socioeconomic issues, cultural development problems, national security matters, and system reform.[8] Precincts had also conducted evaluations of special developmental projects and focused on distilling lessons from those efforts and from attempts to implement Resolution 8B on mobilization work for presentation to the precinct congresses.[9] Politburo members visited various regional gatherings of provincial committees organization department cadre in early July, following reviews of pilot district congresses. At a meeting of cadre from the city of Haiphong, and Nam Ha, Hai Hung, Ha Tay, and Thai Binh provinces, Le Phuoc Tho, director of the Central Committee's Organization Department, analyzed the results of pilot congresses conducted in three districts in Thai Binh Province. Tho emphasized economic development issues and party to people relationships as two key objectives of the grassroots congresses, and showed that security matters and "peaceful transformation" themes would be a central part of the local congressional agendas.[10]

By mid–July provincial military party committees had commenced preparations for holding party congresses. The Khanh Hoa Province Military Party Committee, for example, set up subcommittees to deal with personnel and agenda issues, selected delegates to the congresses of superior organizations, and prepared for the election of a new executive committee. The People's Army of Vietnam (PAVN) general departments appear to have conducted preparations for their congresses in mid–August. At its congress during the second week in August the Army General Technical Department reviewed the implementation of the Third Plenary resolution and inventoried the performance of its various chapters, dissecting the organization's record in the area of membership recruitment.[11]

In mid–July the Central Committee's Secretariat issued a piece of official correspondence (no. 266/CV-TRU, 12 July 1995) that called upon basic-level party committees to conduct congresses "to discuss reports of the upper-level party organization congress, determine the direction of the mission in the coming term, elect delegates to attend the upper-echelon party congress, and elect new executive committees."

By late July, in preparation for basic level congresses, district party committees had begun the work of reviewing local production levels, assessing the implementation of Central Committee resolutions, and establishing the committees that would draw up local political reports, review draft documents, conduct congress-related activities, and coordinate party committee elections and personnel decisions. At the same time party organizations in provinces and cities subordinate to the center promulgated documents implementing the Secretariat's instructions, and formed preparatory committees under the auspices of the provincial party organizations. Provincial committees directed districts and city organizations to appraise the implementation of Central Committee and Politburo resolutions, and to conduct party membership recruitment at the basic levels. For example, from 21 to 22 July the Ha Tay Provincial Party Committee convened a key leadership conference — drawing representatives from all offices, branches, districts, and villages — with the goal of recapitulating three years' worth of work on Resolution 3, five years of efforts to implement Resolution 8b, and Politburo Resolution 4 on party-people relations, mass work, and party responsibilities. The province meeting emphasized the importance of recruiting specialized, educated, and youthful members; expressed concern over the manner in which party entities in private enterprises had developed; and focused attention on consolidating women's organizations from the basic organization level to the provincial level in order to confront continuing social problems and political issues relevant to women.[12]

The municipal documents laid out yet another schedule that called for trial basic-level congresses to be held between late July and 20 August, and for the schedule of basic-level party organization congresses to begin in late August and run until the beginning of December. District-level congresses would begin between November and December and conclude no later than mid–February, at which time municipal party congresses would commence.[13] Essentially, the new schedule sought to shave a month from the plan that was sketched in mid–May.

PARTY ORGANIZATION CONGRESSES IN THE LAST QUARTER OF 1995

Even with advanced planning, focused Central Committee–level scrutiny of the process, and the revised schedule, party organizations below the provincial level were not completely successful in their efforts to convene congresses during August and September. Many provinces publicly acknowledged problems that confronted the basic organizations and influenced the quality of the meetings. An early August *Nhan Dan* article described the failure of basic level organizations to draft political reports and the resulting chain reaction that

1. Preparatory Meetings and Local Party Congresses

left progressively higher-party echelons unable to write their own reports without first having received the work of subordinate entities. The article also pointed to the excessive length of the reports of some basic-level organizations, and the failure of superior echelon cadre to comment on political reports from lower level organizations in a timely manner.[14]

For example, early August media reports suggested that the Tien Giang Province district and municipal committees had faltered in "applying past experiences" during preparations for upper-echelon meetings, and that basic-level party entities had demonstrated weaknesses in readying local documents for presentation to the congresses of superior level party committees. The province's local parties were seriously off schedule. Through late July approximately 12 percent of the total local committees in Tien Giang Province had conducted congresses. By late August this had only improved to 38 percent. Media reporting on the Cao Bang Province meetings criticized haphazard preparations for the local congresses. Indeed, by early September the media was only willing to give Cao Bang Province credit for having conducted the congresses in a generally satisfactory manner.[15] Twenty primary party chapters and branches in Ninh Binh Province representing village, government-office, and state-enterprise party organizations conducted meetings by early September. Two weeks later a total of 22 out of the 53 local party organizations in the province had completed their congresses. The local committees had encountered "numerous difficulties," and had not yet approached completion of the chapter meetings.[16]

In Binh Thuan Province initial experimental grassroots congresses were not conducted until the third week in September. Only 25 percent of the Binh Thuan basic-level chapters and committees had completed their party meetings by late August. In early September less than 33 percent of the 68 grassroots party organizations selected as pilot units in Ho Chi Minh City had conducted their congresses. A 7 September meeting of the municipal Party Committee Guiding Committee spoke of shortcomings that the districts and precincts experienced in managing these pilot meetings, including inadequate and untimely guidance from above, low quality discussions regarding party congress documents and faulty elections of delegates to higher-level party congresses, and a generalized confusion regarding procedural steps.¹⁷

The party attempted to fix these problems. Circular 09-TT/TU, issued by the party Secretariat in September, decreed that all party congresses of lower-level organizations should be completed by May 1996. Another mid–September circular (266-CV/TU) provided additional guidance to lower-level party entities on conducting congresses at the grassroots levels, at district and precinct levels, and at province, city, and centrally managed party committee levels. That circular also commented on the formulation of suggestions regarding draft documents, the communication of criticisms to progressively higher echelons, and the responsibility of integrating recommendations made by party chapters into grassroots-level political reports. Provincial and municipal organizations offered specific guidance to their subordinates. For example, in early September the Guiding Committee of the Ho Chi Minh City party instructed grassroots units to focus on essential issues only, to allot adequate time to discussing the draft documents, and to be thorough in composing their contributions to the draft documents so that the final products reflected lessons derived from the duties performed by the units, and agreed with the draft reports compiled by higher-echelon committees. The Guiding Committee issued a directive calling for pilot congresses in universities, high schools, cultural organizations, and certain businesses, and the selection of additional pilot committees at the precinct and district levels. The directive noted that the Party Congress Guiding Committee would conduct review sessions in each party bloc during this pilot phase.¹⁸

In order to sharpen the capabilities of leaders responsible for managing the local congresses, in mid–September the Ho Chi Minh National Political Institute initiated the first course for senior cadre especially designed to prepare them for drafting the political report and facilitate basic-level party congresses. Such classes investigated the process of implementing resolutions, surveyed current reform issues, and assessed local preparatory meetings. The course of instruction was closed ceremoniously in mid–November with a speech to the class by Do Muoi.¹⁹

These attempts to reconfigure basic party organization approaches to their congresses had minimal impact during the last quarter of the year. According to a party assessment issued in October, the action programs and critiques of the draft reports completed by local party entities during September and October were lifeless documents and irrelevant exercises that did not draw on the practical knowledge and experience of local committees in eliciting criticisms of the draft documents. Additionally, the local party structures had not disseminated the draft documents in a systematic way. The central party officials made it clear that local organizations had failed to convey the view that challenges to internal stability posed by hostile forces represented but one danger to the renovation process, and that the most complex aspect of the next step in the reforms would involve sustaining rapid economic growth and making strides toward industrialization. Local parties had also failed to propagate the view that economic reform exerted a significant impact on foreign relations and defense matters. Authoritative critiques asserted that until these standpoints were communicated throughout the system, party congress participants would be unable to offer meaningful contributions to the draft documents and effective criticisms of policy approaches.

Party critiques of precongress preparations issued in October (after the promulgation of Central Committee midcourse corrections), pointed out that most of the plans submitted by local committees did not include effective reviews of the party committee's overall performances and, in addition, dealt inadequately with personnel issues. Party committees misunderstood election procedures, and committed violations of existing party regulations in their attempts to orchestrate elections. Some party committees were simply unable to find a sufficient number of delegates to attend the congresses of higher echelons, even after conducting several rounds of elections.[20]

In early November the leaders of the party committees from seven southern provinces convened in Ho Chi Minh City to take stock of the efforts to implement the Seventh National Party Congress resolutions in anticipation of the next national meeting. In late November the secretary of the Hanoi Party Committee chaired a conference of key cadres to study the implementation of Resolution 8B in order to prepare for the upper-echelon party committee congresses. A similar meeting took place in Yen Bai Province from 28 to 29 November, attended by Politburo member Vu Oanh. From 22 to 24 November the Central Committee's Inspection Committee organized a conference on senior-echelon inspection committee activities during 1991 to 1995, which dealt with the issues of party building in the new period, raising performance and quality standards of party members, eliminating corruption and smuggling, "concretizing" party-state relations, and replenishing the ranks of party inspectors in anticipation of the Eighth Congress.[21]

Party Military Congresses

In late September the Defense Ministry's General Political Department convened a conference on preparations for the National Congress. Over 300 representatives of the military regions, corps, political commands, military institutes, and Defense Ministry researchers participated in the meeting, which was addressed by Politburo member and party secretary General Le Kha Phieu, representatives of the General Political Department, and Central Committee Ideology Department director Ha Dang. Chief of Staff General Dao Dinh Luyen previewed the draft political report, summarized key points in the draft document, and surveyed defense achievements over the past five years. He gave the military's preparatory efforts high marks.[22]

In early October the party sought to set the schedule for grassroots party organizations in the military, which were to begin in December and end in mid–January. The General Political Department convened a key cadre conference to study directives issued by the Secretariat and the Military Committee on compiling end-of-term evaluation reports by party committees, electing committee members, and organizing party congresses.[23] However, up to that point local military party committees had turned in uneven performances. An editorial in the October issue of the military party committee's journal indicated that though progress had been made, the process had not been completely rationalized. Much work remained to be done. Debate over the key documents tended to be diffuse and failed to focus on key problems. Local congresses had demonstrated an inability to conduct thorough discussions of central issues. Clashes of opinions were resolved by local committee personnel in a manner that failed to clarify issues. The editorial described how individual party committees should compile their own political reports, and spelled out the rules governing the selection process for new committee members.[24] An editorial in *Quan Doi Nhan Dan* on 8 November urged that local committees submit their political reports early, dispatch those reports rapidly to subordinate chapters for critical review, draw up as many "supplements" to correct the performance of chapter-level party leadership as were necessary.

Toward the end of 1995, Defense Ministry general departments began taking active steps to put subordinate organizations back on track. For example, in mid-December the General Political Department called a meeting of party committee secretaries, youth organization secretaries, labor and women's organization chairs, and school and factory authorities to review the implementation of both Resolution 3 and the Central Party Military Committee's Resolution 79 on reform and party renovation, as well as Resolution 8B. The meeting focused on ways to strengthen the training of party secretaries, upgrade inspection activities, sharpen leadership skills, and improve relations with committee members, local administrations, community organizations, and local populations in the vicinity of army billeting areas.[25]

In mid-December regimental commands began reporting the results of meetings to review the draft documents for the National Party Congress. For example, the 141st Regiment of Division 312 reported extremely high levels of party membership participation in research concerning the substance of the draft political report, the socioeconomic plan, plus the party statute amendments.[26]

The newspaper account of the 141st Regiment's party organization congress noted that the majority of opinions voiced at the meeting focused on the preservation of political stability as the primary condition for creating a developed economy. A number of opinions suggested that the party was being tested by complex global transformations and that the party's "positive creativity" (*vung vang sang tao*) would navigate the nation through these challenges. "Many ideas" offered "concrete" analyses of the national economic situation in order to "clearly affirm" the country's economic standing and establish firm plans for the economy. Some members of the regimental party organizations raised questions regarding national unity, and a number expressed ideas on how to confront corruption and social problems. Those members supported the party's approach to such matters, but offered specific criticisms of the methods employed to achieve certain social and economic goals. The 141st Regimental Party Congress also debated the extent to which worldwide changes and challenges, the threat posed by "peaceful transformation," and the internal choices regarding Vietnam's socialist orientation independently worked to galvanize the system to protect itself and guarantee the stability of socialist Vietnam. In the end, the news account stated, the regimental congress concluded that the conditions and circumstances that contributed to the protection of the party and the preservation of social order were "the most important factors," an observation which offered no real insight into an issue that would have an influence on security strategy and military resources. The 141st Regiment's congress represented the climax of the effort to solicit criticisms and views regarding the draft political report from subordinate military units, but that process generated incomplete, unconvincing, and vague views (*chua duoc chuan bi ky luong, chua co tinh thuyet phuc, con chung chung*). According to the newspaper account, practically all of the ideas contributed to the debate over the draft documents at the basic levels failed to offer objective assessments of the practical aspects of party work in the units. Moreover, views regarding national defense tended to be ill-formed.[27]

THE NINTH PLENUM

The Ninth Plenum convened from 6 to 14 November to vote on the contents of the draft political report, the socioeconomic plan for 1992 to 2000, and the revision of the party statutes prepared for the Eighth Party Congress. The Ninth Plenary closed out the round of preparatory party meetings and prefaced the first local congresses that were to begin in November or December 1995 and continue through

1. Preparatory Meetings and Local Party Congresses 21

January or February 1996, at which point the municipal meetings, followed by the provincial and party bloc congresses, would begin, according to the party's schedule as it stood in the last months of 1995.

The Ninth Plenum communiqué, issued on 15 November, observed that after six days of debate, and nearly 400 speeches delivered by participants — presumably including non–Central Committee specialists — the plenary reached agreement ("high unanimity") on the contents of the draft reports, and on the achievements of the efforts to renovate the system of governance and reform the economy. The communiqué stated that the tasks defined by the Seventh Party Congress had been fundamentally completed, and a socioeconomic crisis had been averted, although in some sectors this had not been accomplished in a tidy, thorough manner. The country had achieved the prerequisites for national industrialization and was moving into a new period, which would feature the acceleration of industrialization and modernization.[28] The communiqué also stated that Vietnam must preserve the socialist character of the system; combine economic and social reform; shape an effective, correct relationship between economic and political change; broaden participation by expanding the "national unity bloc"; sustain efforts to diversify foreign relationships; and "maintain the leadership role of the party."[29]

The plenary accorded primacy to the tasks of rescuing Vietnam from impoverishment and underdevelopment, accomplishing basic national security responsibilities, and confronting lingering social issues. This suggested that the debate over which comes first, stability or economic growth, resulted in a Central Committee judgment to continue to focus on multiple priorities. The ninth session concluded that while the reforms had built up sufficient energy to propel the party to a new stage of intensified industrialization and modernization, some of the key problems and threats to stability identified by the conference participants had not yet been thoroughly eliminated.[30]

The Central Committee concluded by noting that the party statutes would be published and circulated "among various echelons and sectors for public views" following some revisions resulting from discussions among plenary participants, and that the Politburo would refine the various draft reports in accordance with the voting conducted during the plenum on unspecified issues of substance. The plenary resolution reflected the Central Committee's decision to assign the responsibility of reviewing the draft documents prior to circulation to the Politburo, and called for "wide efforts" among party and population to review and criticize the penultimate products prior to setting the reports before the National meeting.[31]

In his speech Muoi told the plenary session that because of the benchmark nature of the Eighth Congress — which would define the stage of industrialization and modernization — the preparations for the congress were especially important. He pointed out that in the short time before the congress the party had much work to do. Muoi instructed party officials at all levels to implement the Secretariat's directives and the contents of the Ninth Plenary documents in the course of preparing political reports at all levels. He stressed that the Fatherland Front, community organizations, and social organizations (*mat tran to quoc, cac doan the va cac to chuc xa hoi*) had to be involved in debates over the draft documents because the preparations for the congress should not be the exclusive responsibility of the party.[32]

Muoi dwelt on the negative effect corruption had — its symbiotic relationship with smuggling, tax evasion, and wastefulness — and urged strong party efforts to eliminate these internal infections. He told the Central Committee that punishing violations of discipline and transgressions against the party statutes must be a primary mission of all levels of the party in the course of conducting local congresses.[33]

Much of the discussion at the Ninth Plenary session was devoted to the issues that had emerged during the conduct of the basic level preparatory congresses through late 1995. Though the documents and speeches from the plenary reflected optimism about the process, the party leadership noted that a lot of preparatory work remained unfinished, and that in some instances the groundwork that had been laid was spotty and unsatisfactory.

Post-Plenary Progress and Lapses

Early December editorials in the party's daily newspaper reviewed the tasks that confronted the basic party organizations as they readied themselves for the preparatory congresses, and invoked the authority of the Central Committee and the Secretariat in restating the goals that would guide this process. The preparatory congresses were to pay as much attention to security, defense, local leadership, and party renovation as they were to defining economic aims and social development goals. The meetings were also to concentrate on defining the role of basic party organizations, explicating leadership methods, and apportioning responsibilities to the party rank and file for combating bureaucratism, corruption, and alienation from the people. Finally, local levels were to focus on organizing basic party committee elections, ensuring standards for party committee electoral hopefuls, and managing the leadership succession issue.[34]

By the first week in December about 7 percent of the basic party organizations in central Vietnam and the highlands had concluded their congresses. In the majority of provinces, including Quang Nam-Da Nang, Quang Ngai, Phu Yen, and Khanh Hoa, pilot meetings continued to be looked to as the models for district-level preparatory work, which by early December had been only partially completed. Provinces such as Quang Ngai had yet to convene more than a handful of congresses at the district level. For the most part, according to criticisms carried in the party-controlled press, preparations for local party meetings had been weak. Many localities had only provided pro forma comments on the political reports compiled by district and precinct party committees and had only responded to the reports of echelons immediately above their level. The quality of debate over the content of the reports was uneven. Early December articles in the party's daily newspaper stated that in some unspecified instances basic party organizations submitted incomplete and unsatisfactory political reports, sometimes prior to the deadline for submission, which suggested that the entire exercise was handled in a perfunctory manner. Reports tended to be confused, standards for reporting were ignored, instructions lacked clarity, and final products often bore no relationship to local realities, either misrepresenting or inaccurately depicting local situations, accomplishments, and problems.

This was not to say that the process was in total disarray. Some basic party organizations in provinces such as Quang Nam-Da Nang, Khanh Hoa, Gia Lai, Binh Dinh, and Dac Lac succinctly and accurately captured the status of agricultural production in various specialized growing areas, according to party commentaries. However, the majority of party organizations in villages and enterprises assembled reports that lacked focus, specificity, accuracy and depth. The proportion of party members who participated in criticizing draft reports remained small, and many members simply accepted the contents of reports under review, yielding a meaningless unanimity of views or the shallowest and most fragmentary of criticisms.[35]

Through the end of the year party organizations suffered a chronic inability to capture details regarding local situations precisely and succinctly in their reports. Many pilot units compiled excessively lengthy draft reports that failed to live up to party expectations. Personnel issues had been poorly managed, resulting in lapses in the process of selecting election ballots for party committees and ineffectively conducted elections for executive committees. Basic levels had failed to recruit females and youths. Party chapters of more than 200 members — where 30 percent of the members were women — had not selected any women delegates to their congresses. Much of the personnel work and preelection matters that should have been handled by preparatory meetings were left unfinished and had to be managed by basic congresses.[36]

Getting Back on Track Again: Guidance for Conducting Congresses

A mid–December summary of Central Committee, Secretariat-level correspondence and directives sought to strike a balance between economic development issues and security and defense concerns, redirecting the attention of basic level party organizations to global issues, foreign relations, threat perceptions, and regional matters that would impact on Vietnam's well-being.[37] The summary noted that, whether or not the terms of office of grassroots organizations had expired, congresses should be conducted in accordance with the Central Committee's mid–July correspondence on the subject (266-CV/TU, 12 July 1995), suggesting that some local party committees were delaying the convening of congresses because they were nearing the end of their tenure. Additionally, the summary said that basic organizations that had encountered difficulties should reduce the focus of their congresses to the discussion of the draft documents and the selection of delegates to higher-level congresses, and delay the work of defining orientations and responsibilities and electing a new executive committee until after the district- and precinct-level congresses had concluded. This provision seemed to imply that basic organizations continued to became bogged down in unresolved debate over local issues, or conducted only the weakest of discussions concerning key issues that threatened to invalidate the efforts of basic organizations to synthesize critical views of the draft political report. Those party entities seem to have resorted to deferring issues until the new executive committee was seated, an alternative that was not acceptable to the party probably because of the damage it did to the projected calendar for local congresses.

The summary of Secretariat directives provided an authoritative schedule for the remaining congresses. Grassroots meetings would take place from December 1995 to January 1996, district and precinct party organization congresses would be held during February and March 1996, and provinces, municipalities, and centrally managed departments would convene their congresses from 1 April to 10 May. Party officials authorized provincial and municipal congresses to issue specialized reports (*bao cao chuyen de*) exclusively focused on socio-economic development issues for the years 1996 to 2000, a hint that some party organizations would not be deterred from fixing their attention entirely on economic matters, even after months of criticism for neglecting other issues. The Secretariat's instruction that local organizations should ensure that their reports reflected the real circumstances of the local scene was repeated, a circumstantial indication that through mid–December the party center continued to see abstract, remote, or perfunctory approaches to compiling political reports. The Secretariat set limits for the total number of executive committee members for provinces, cities, districts, and precincts; defined the parameters for the selection of delegates to the National Congress from the various levels of party committees; and spelled out the maximum length of congresses at all levels.[38]

The party put in place unique ways of correcting local party errors. By early December district-level pilot congresses in Hai Hung Province had established guidance committees to usher all levels of subordinate party chapters through the process of preparing political reports, in accordance with the directions of the Central Committee's Organization Department. In a number of unspecified areas, mass organizations helped in compiling basic organization political reports, which reportedly had a positive impact on the cultivation of party-to-people relations. Just before the end of the year the Ho Chi Minh City party apparatus singled out several basic party organizations that had conducted successful meetings as models to be emulated by subordinate levels that had yet to convene their congresses, presumably to help the local party structures get beyond the inadequacies in the process of reviewing draft documents.[39]

On 27 December the Secretariat issued an instruction (*chi thi*) on the formation of a nationwide movement to advance the goals of the Eighth National Congress, including the review of 10 years' worth of reformist activities. The instruction stated that these tasks could be fulfilled if each province, city, and party committees at all levels established a "concrete plan," galvanizing the leadership to undertake party building, oppose corruption, and end embezzlement. The instruction further stipulated that the Central Committee's Ideology and Culture Department must play a critical role in this process, and directed the components of the party system, mass organizations, and economic and social organizations (*to chuc kinh te, xa hoi*) to organize preliminary summaries for the Secretariat.[40]

Following the dissemination of this instruction, on 30 December the Secretariat convoked a meeting for cadre in Hanoi that featured the general secretary, who provided guidance regarding the continuing basic-level party congresses.[41] Muoi was clearly disturbed that almost none of the basic organizations whose performances had been reviewed during his mid–December travels through Hanoi, Ha Tay, Thai Binh, Hai Hung, and Haiphong had taken up the issue of rural industrialization and modernization. He pronounced that without industrialization it would not be possible for the country to protect the very basic economic advances it had achieved, or to resolve the problems associated with sustaining an improving level of annual national income. The country would not be able to become rich and strong, and whole areas would continue to lag behind in basic agricultural practices and industrial technology. It was therefore necessary that party organizations at all levels get to the heart of the issue of rural and agricultural industrialization. To Muoi, this would involve nationwide debate over microstrategies and choices for rural development: from decisions regarding what crops to plant and livestock to raise to which production methods to utilize. In Muoi's view it would be wrong to focus exclusively on developing production in a select few areas because fundamental questions such as the means of guaranteeing sources of raw material continued to represent potential problems for very rudimentary industries that were basic to the rural development strategy. The country needed plans to rehabilitate, reform, and renew industrial equipment, and replenish organizations and cadre, as well as expand the sources for basic raw materials and enlarge the market for consumer products. These very basic matters must be seriously discussed throughout the party system. Muoi argued that through late December the role of state economy, cooperative economy, and individual economy, as well as joint economic entities, had not been the subject of any clarifying discussion at the basic-level congresses. Key questions of cadre development had also been neglected at these meetings.

Muoi stated that investment remained the single most important variable in the launching of an industrialization drive. Without it, the business of achieving industrialization was nothing more than a dream. Therefore, it was a subject that should have been on the agenda of the basic-level party meetings. He outlined an approach to investment that began with domestic accumulation and strenuous efforts to foster savings, and warned that though external sources of capital were important, the risk of overdependence on foreign investors was serious. The general secretary also cautioned against becoming a debtor or the "hired laborer" of capitalism (*lam thue cho chu nghia tu ban*), and implied that industrialization could be funded by diverting funds and resources that were squandered by the current system on rural development—a rather simplistic proposal but an effective soundbite, intended to underscore Muoi's continued frustration over corruption. In his view some very simple fixes could repair the economy and free up the resources necessary to push ahead with reforms and make substantial economic progress.[42]

2

Basic-Level Meetings, Provincial and Bloc Congresses

INTO THE NEW YEAR

During the first months of 1996, the party inveighed against social evils, stressed the state's role in managing the economy, and emphasized the mission of defending Vietnamese sovereignty in the face of a more intrusive world, a more open economy, and uncontrolled communication and information flows. The party acknowledged the weaknesses of the state owned enterprises and the inefficiencies that marred the state's performance as an economic manager. Alternatives — such as allowing private enterprises to fully dominate the economy or moving the state out of the strategic sectors (energy, transportation, and infrastructure) — were unacceptable to the party, which believed that withdrawing the steady hand of the state from critical strategic sectors was a recipe for instability and economic collapse.

A decidedly more conservative and "strict constructionist" tone about economic reforms emerged in the weeks before the Tet celebration.[1] During this period the party was closely attentive to the impact of new realities on the organization. An early January meeting in Ho Chi Minh City under the auspices of the Central Committee's Organization Department considered the establishment of grassroots-level party entities in the nonstate business sector and reviewed the Secretariat's directive on party work in cooperatives and joint ventures with foreigners. According to a *Saigon Giai Phong* account of the meeting, business representatives participated in the sessions and provided their views on how to shape party organizations in this new and unique environment. A mid-January Politburo resolution (12/NQ/TU) clarified the party's thinking about market development, the preeminent role of the state in trading activities, and the party's distrust of private traders, especially in rural markets.[2]

During a January visit to Ho Chi Minh City, Muoi asserted that industrialization and modernization were core concepts for the basic party congresses and a strategic responsibility for the coming period. Muoi told the gathered party cadre that the Fifth and the Seventh Plenary resolutions, and the resolutions of the interim conference, established the requirements, direction, and responsibilities for the modernization and industrialization processes, especially in the countryside. The draft document for the Eighth Congress stressed that these processes must be pursued in order to build socialism's material and technological foundation. Muoi particularized the message for the Cuu Long Delta, noting the importance of confronting land use issues and hunger.[3]

These authoritative clarifications were important for what they omitted as well as for what they said. While speeches and articles explicated the core meaning of modernization, reminded the party of the critical importance of resolving lingering quality-of-life issues, and restated principles underlying the development of a socialist market economy, they omitted consideration of some of the tougher questions such as enfranchisement of private businesses, the limits of political participation for the new social interests and economic structures that emerged from the reforms, and the disposition of state-operated enterprises that had come to burden economy.[4]

SHAPING THE DRAFT REPORT DEBATE

The party continued its efforts to shape the debate over the draft report and the revised statutes by reviewing the proceedings of basic organization congresses, offering criticisms of the preparatory meetings, and intervening in local debates, especially when the local organizations failed to provide a conscientious evaluation of the draft socioeconomic plan and political report anchored to local economic and reform issues. The party cautioned members to stick to the most important issues in registering opinions regarding the draft documents, and to avoid drifting toward overly generalized discussions. Grassroots level organizations, especially in the rural areas, were instructed to develop concrete targets with local relevance and to focus on the rural dimension of industrialization. Party organizations in enterprises were told that they must devote their attention to the practical aspects of improving business and trade, increasing competitiveness, and enhancing capital efficiency. Party cells in administrative agencies were instructed to improve their performances. All party entities were ordered to turn their energies to national defense and economic development, and invest their resources in resolving intractable social issues (such as hunger and poverty), curbing bureaucratic excesses, and preventing extra-legal activities of members. Party organizations were instructed to place a premium on the successful implementation of policies concerning land use, capital construction, joint ventures, import and export activities, and public assets and social funds.[5]

In late January Do Muoi visited districts and spoke with party secretaries about preparations for the local party organization meetings that were to begin during the first two weeks of February.[6] During the working sessions with district party's committee and people's committee chairs from Hanoi's Giai Lam and Dong Da districts, Muoi made it clear that the upcoming National Congress would define the means by which the nation would achieve industrialization and establish the material and technical bases for socialism in Vietnam. The district-level party committees were responsible for articulating "practical tasks for relevant sectors to carry out the socioeconomic development plan for the next five years, centering around the theme of industrialization and modernization." The message appeared to be that basic-level party organizations had veered off course in preparatory sessions that should have focused on the renovation and consolidation of production relations, the role of the state and cooperatives in the economy, and industrial, agricultural, and service sector relationships.[7]

Following those visits, Muoi spoke to a conference of party officials in Hanoi on the local and branch party meetings. He summarized the generally positive indicators of socioeconomic development on which basic party organizations had based their assessments of economic growth and pointed out weak points including labor force redundancy, job creation problems, and income difficulties at village and precinct levels. He told the gathered party officials that the local organizations must work out practical measures to implement agricultural and rural industrialization at their levels. During the third week in January, Politburo members Dao Duy Tung and Nguyen Duc Binh joined Muoi in delivering the same messages to a ten-day class on party policies for intellectuals and art and literary workers organized by the Secretariat and the Ho Chi Minh National Political Institute.[8]

Mid-January also saw several major inspection tours of provincial and municipal party organizations to review the record of basic party congresses. Le Phuoc Tho traveled to Tien Giang, Song Be, and Minh Hai in the south, where he found that basic party organizations had quickly convened congresses in late 1995. In other provinces, such as Binh Thuan, Dong Nai, Ninh Thuan, and Lam Dong, significantly fewer basic organizations had completed their congresses by the last months of 1995. Tho concluded that the basic organizations had effectively implemented instructions and official guidance from the Secretariat and the Central Committee Organization Department regarding cadre training, membership education, and the overseeing of pilot projects. Although he was impressed with the "spirit, democracy, and unanimity" achieved in most basic-level organizations, their close adherence to appropriate statutes governing personnel policies, and improvements in the quality of specialized political and cultural cadre, he did observe an unevenness in the quality of various organizations. Tho found fault with the manner in which ideological principles in the party documents prepared for the National Congress had been only slowly and incompletely communicated to cadre and members. He repeated earlier criticisms to the effect that concrete issues and real local problems had not been treated effectively in local committee political reports. Many areas had generated poor-quality reports, suggesting a lazy approach to this exercise. Tho also lamented the failure of the basic-level party organizations to recruit women and minority ethnic and religious members in greater numbers.[9]

By mid–January the party center had issued Central Committee Guidance 51, Correspondence Number 266, and Circular Letter Number 09, and had distributed summaries of Do Muoi's two key cadre conferences in the north and the south in order to spread the word on the midcourse corrections.[10] In late January, following the flurry of directions from the party center, the media commenced carrying stories on provincial successes at completing the basic organization meetings.[11] One typical article noted that all of Can Tho's basic party entities had completed their congresses, though not without a certain amount of confusion in many unspecified locations that strayed from the model for such meetings, did not keep to the course of industrialization and modernization, and were unfamiliar with the fundamental problems of rural modernization in spite of provincial committee-level meetings aimed at clarifying these themes.[12] In his talk to the Cam Binh District Congress in Hai Hung Province, held from 23 to 25 January, Dao Duy Tung reviewed the district's productivity and its exertions in agricultural development.[13] At roughly the same time, Foreign Minister Nguyen Manh Cam attended a meeting of the Thanh Hoa Party Standing Committee as a representative of the Politburo. He took stock of provincial socioeconomic progress and reviewed development plans through the year 2000, with the goal of prompting preparations for the provincial party congress.[14]

In late January higher-level basic party organizations began to publicize the election of new executive committees. By the first week of February, according to press accounts, approximately 63 percent of the basic party organizations in Thai Binh, nearly 80 percent of those in Quang Nam-Da Nang, and nearly 90 percent of those in Yen Bai had completed their congresses. In Yen Bai 75 percent of the basic-level organization committee members were reelected, but the newly elected members tended to be more specialized and better educated than the incumbents. About 30 percent of the new committees were minorities, 10 percent were women, and the newly elected members were 1.5 years younger than the committee members they succeeded. In Thai Binh 75–80 percent of the incumbents were reelected to basic organization committees. Their average ages were 37–38, and their levels of education exceeded those of the committee members they replaced.[15]

THE CONDUCT OF THE BASIC-LEVEL CONGRESSES

Provincial vigilance over the system of basic party congresses intensified in early January, following the dissemination of Central Committee Secretariat Circular Number 11 urging reinvigoration of the basic organization efforts to solicit views regarding the draft documents. Provinces made special efforts to assist basic party entities to organize their meetings in accordance with the spirit of the Secretariat's directives. For example, the Ha Tay Committee convened enlarged meetings of party secretaries of subprovincial committees to review internal issues raised at basic party organization congresses, and dispatched three or four committee members to districts and villages to provide guidance for basic party meetings. At about the same time Central Committee departments — for example, the Ideology and Culture Department — began to scrutinize preparations for the National Congress, and to offer guidance aimed at keeping the process focused and on schedule.[16] In mid-January provincial party committees ordered subordinate organizations to summarize what they had accomplished in attempts to implement various plenary resolutions and other party directives dating to the Sixth Congress. Local organizations were also instructed to step up inspections of party organization compliance with statutes.[17] Larger cities began convening their congresses in mid-February. For example, the Ha Long party organization's twentieth session, which was attended by Central Committee Secretary Hong Ha, concluded on 11 February. The meeting drew attention to municipal weaknesses in the area of administration and township management, the unimpressive quality of state enterprises operating in Ha Long, local poverty, and onerous tax burdens.[18]

During the latter half of February, senior leaders paid working visits to select provinces where they evaluated basic economic performances. The leaders urged the provincial party organizations to undertake accurate appraisals of the local situation and to debate the political report and the party's resolutions, with the goal of making critical improvements to the draft documents. Vo Van Kiet toured Lam Dong Province on 14 February.[19] Le Duc Anh led a distinguished group of party officials to a meeting of representatives from 10 Mekong Delta provinces held in Can Tho in mid–February, under the auspices of the Secretariat. The meeting reviewed preparations for provincial-level congresses and studied the contributions to the party's draft documents that had accumulated during the course of basic-level meetings.[20] In mid–February Le Duc Anh led a group of senior party officials on a swing through eight southern provinces to reaffirm party building goals and to stiffen the resolve of the southern party organizations to pursue industrialization and modernization by sticking to the script for agricultural and rural economic improvements in the cooperative, manufacturing, and farming sectors. At about the same time, a Politburo-level delegation traveled through Ha Tinh and Nghe An on an inspection visit in advance of the convening of the provincial congresses. In Nghe An and Vinh two members of the delegation, Le Kha Phieu and Nguyen Ha Phan, stressed that industrialization and modernization were not merely economic processes but rather a means of moving to a new level of economic growth and development.[21] Vo Van Kiet spent two days in Pleiku in mid–February conferring with Gia Lai, Kontum, and Dac Lac Province officials on development plans for the economy of the highlands and preparations for the Eighth National Party Congress.[22] Vo Van Kiet also paid a visit to Da Lat, Lam Dong Province, where he reviewed the province's record of agricultural production, rural investment, and resolution of local social issues, as well as Lam Dong's preparations for the congress.[23] On 14 and 15 February Politburo members Dao Duy Tung and Nong Duc Manh and party secretary Hong Ha visited Hoa Binh, Son La, and Lai Chau to review preparations for the congress and to take stock of basic provincial-level economic performances.[24]

Between early January and late February the general secretary consulted with the standing committees of 14 provinces regarding preparations for the provincial congresses and the national meeting. He was assisted in this work by an assortment of Politburo members, including Vu Oanh, chairman of the Central Committee's Inspection Committee Do Quang Thang, and party secretary Nguyen Dinh Tu, as well as numerous Central Committee members and ministerial officials, including planning and investment, finance, and state banking officials. Do Muoi previewed the provincial political reports and listened to the provincial secretaries on the conduct of basic party congresses and plans for economic development. An early March report suggested that Muoi focused on provincial-level use and development of human and natural resources, supported the idea of featuring a broad spectrum of light industry development in rural areas in order to produce consumables for the local population and for export, and urged cooperation with the center in short- and long-term plans for urban and rural infrastructure development.[25] During his New Year's visits to select provinces, Muoi reiterated the need to control corruption by — among other things — punishing companies that operated beyond the pale of the law, and spoke strongly in favor of managed, regulated markets and "consolidated" relations of production, plus a continued state role in economic oversight.[26]

In late March and early April district, municipal, and provincial party committees organized conferences of nonparty personnel representing Fatherland Front interests, including political organizations, social groups, intellectuals, artists, religious and minority groups, and private enterprise interests, in order to elicit these organizations' share of views on the draft documents. In these meetings the senior echelon would select a reporter (Bao Cao Vien) to introduce and clarify the contents of the political report in order to facilitate debate and to synthesize the contributed views, as well as to summarize the results and accomplishments of such sessions. Such meetings generally lasted one day, though in larger cities they sometimes continued for up to two days. The party echelons were responsible for concluding this process by 9 April through the mechanism of propaganda committees that reported results to Secretariat level. The propaganda committees guided the reporting process, and were charged with selecting the highest quality and most spirited views for publication and broadcasting, in order to introduce a representative example of how various problems were treated in party-organized debates over the draft reports. The party committees and the subordinate propaganda committees were responsible for forwarding a report singling out the most important views to the higher echelons, and transmitting the viewpoints of the people to the Central Committee's Department for Ideology and Culture. The Central Office for Guidance (Van Phong Trung Uong Hung Dan) set the standard for the orderly transmission of reports on the viewpoints expressed in this process through the appropriate party organization chains of command.[27]

A Post-Mortem Assessment of Basic Party Congresses, March 1996

On 23 March the party's daily newspaper proclaimed the essential completion of the basic level party congresses. The article stated that the congresses of basic-level organizations had conducted a great deal of debate concerning the party's leadership role, the role of people's organizations, and the process of organizing party chapters. However, many basic entities had not clarified the main tasks for the five year planning period, 1996–2000. Basic organizations remained confused about such critical matters as the means of achieving industrialization at the unit level. Additionally, according to the press report, a number of local party organizations relied on the views of senior echelons and failed to generate political and socioeconomic reports based on local circumstances, ignored party building tasks, were not capable of defining roles for specially trained party leaders at the basic level, and in a number of instances conducted discussions without real debate, flaccidly accepting all views offered, and in some areas confusing the responsibilities of the party and state authorities.

Press reports suggested that for the most part basic organizations successfully conducted elections for executive committees. Candidates elected to party offices generally had wide support.

Incumbents were reelected in the majority of party chapters. In all, a range from 20 to 28 percent of the party committee members were new, and of those the majority were young, technically educated personnel with "appropriate" cultural and "theoretical" levels. Many committees selected women and minority group representatives.[28]

By early April, as district-level party organizations began to report their congresses, it was clear that some debates had not been resolved. For example, the Mo Duc District Party Committee in Quang Ngai Province debated the relative importance of agricultural production, the means of coordinating agricultural and industrial cooperation, and the impact of sectors such as animal husbandry and forestry on agricultural production and rural services. Delegates to the Tieu Hai District Congress in Thai Binh Province debated the practical aspects of implementing industrialization plans, and the development of cooperatives in the immediate future.[29] Other district congresses aired differences over incomplete economic transformations, the role of cooperatives, and the low level of employment for educated workers.[30] Municipal-level party meetings reflected preoccupations with the full employment issue, the relative authority of the state over economic matters, local efforts to raise productivity, and the customary social issues including housing, environmental degradation, and education.[31] Parish visits by senior party personnel in March also addressed a number of these unsettled problems, including the management of social issues, the portion of the economy that should be state controlled, administrative reform, social issues, and agricultural development plans for the delta region.[32]

Ministry and Central Party Bloc Congresses

By early February the party organizations of specialized national-level institutes had begun to convene their congresses. Ministries and central government and party institutions commenced their party meetings in late January.[33] For example, the party organization of the Ministry of Education and Training held its second congress of representatives in late January. Party Secretary Nguyen

2. Basic-Level Meetings, Provincial and Bloc Congresses 39

Dinh Tu and Minister Tran Hong Quan attended the meeting that reviewed the educational scene and drew connections between training and educational levels and the goals of industrialization and modernization.[34] The Finance Ministry Party Organization met in mid–February and reviewed the steps necessary to create an environment conducive to stable budgetary processes, effective monetary policy, inflation control, and specialized cadre development and training.[35]

Many ministerial level party organizations did not convene their congresses until late March. For example, from 25 to 26 March the party organization of the Ministry of Agriculture and Rural Development held its congress, and vigorously debated questions concerning slow export development levels that had not kept pace with accelerated agricultural production, continued and troubling population increases that outpaced agricultural growth, and the failure of the system to translate parallel increases in gross per capita income and agricultural production into substantial quality of life improvements for the population.[36] The early April meetings of the ministries of Finance and of Industry echoed the generalized enthusiasm for reforms. The representatives of the Ministry of Industry dealt with the issue of developing party cells in general companies, and described their roles as those of command structures for the party and the state in the effort to industrialize and modernize Vietnam. The Finance Ministry representatives endorsed the early promulgation of a law on financial policies.[37]

Central Committee bloc meetings began in late March. For example, from 26 to 27 March the 166 delegates representing the Central Committee's foreign relations bloc met for their fourth party congress, which underwrote the open door foreign policy, reiterated the importance of sustaining party-to-party relations globally, and emphasized the centrality of relations with the Association of Southeast Asian Nations (ASEAN) members and the international financial institutions, and with sustaining healthy, robust economic ties with all countries.[38] The ideology and culture bloc unreservedly endorsed continued reform at its early April meeting.[39] Muoi addressed the central economic bloc's party congress in late April. He reiterated the importance of building a material and technical basis for socialist development, and spoke of the need to consolidate the union of agricultural, industrial, and intellectual workers. In addition, Muoi stressed the critical importance of clarifying administrative and managerial responsibilities for leading cadre in a new and unfamiliar market environment, and restated the leading role for the state economy.[40]

Military Congresses

Through the first two months of the year the military remained very blunt about lapses in the process of preparing for the congress. An editorial carried in the army's daily newspaper on 1 February stated that many basic party organizations had failed to grasp the concept of industrialization and modernization, and had lagged behind expectations for local development. Moreover, a significant number of party members in positions of power had been captured by the allure of money and had become corrupted in a way that seriously undermined public trust in the party and besmirched the VNCP's reputation. The military warned that two main threats confronted the nation: economic backwardness and a degenerated ruling party.[41]

The Naval Party Congress was convened from 29 to 31 January under the leadership of Defense Minister Doan Khue.[42] The congress raised readiness issues, discussed requirements in view of the situation in the South China Sea, and reviewed training needs.[43] The Ho Chi Minh City Military Party Committee's Seventh Congress, which concluded by 10 February, stressed training requirements. The congress of the Military Transport Department's party organization placed strong emphasis on developing technical military capabilities.[44] The Air Force Party Committee conducted an inspection of party members, focused on training levels and performance, and on decreasing the number of infractions against party rules committed by members. Basic level party organizations within military regions finished their congresses by the third week of February.[45]

Most of the senior echelons' Military Party committees repeated the political and economic themes that were given play in the congresses of basic-level, district, and provincial committees. The provincial Military Party committees of Ha Giang and Ha Bac provinces held their congresses by 2 March. The Ha Bac congress emphasized local military development projects. The Ha Giang Military Party Committee concentrated on the issue of nurturing high-quality, creative party members.[46] Ninh Binh Province's Military Party Committee convened its sixteenth congress during the first week of March, and covered the issue of "peaceful transformation" as a threat to security. Lam Dong Province's Military Party Committee, which concluded its seventh congress at roughly the same time, spoke to the issues of developing the provincial armed forces, perfecting local commands, building a provincial armed force, and addressing difficulties experienced by cadre, party, and youth-union members.[47] By the end of the first week in March the Capital Military Region party organization's basic levels had almost completely concluded their congresses.[48]

Throughout March and April, military units, Defense Ministry subordinates, and provincial and regional military party committees held congresses that aired military concerns regarding training, readiness, defense capabilities, technological levels, national and local defense strategies, and threats to security and stability. Delegates to the early March party congress of the general staff criticized the theory that a strong economy engendered a vigorous defense, countering that economically strong areas did not necessarily have matching security, though it was stipulated that independence and stability were generally the product of modernization and industrialization. The media summary of the General Staff Congress noted that many ideas raised during the party meeting spoke to the importance of developing a body of educated, specialized cadre who could manage the affairs of the general staff. General Dao Dinh Luyen, a standing member of the party's Military Committee, told the congress that the character and quality of cadres and party members had not yet been stabilized, and that there were many areas in which party officials did not meet national standards. State management was still weak, and the party had not yet achieved a full measure of success in its leadership role.[49]

In his address to the party congress of the National Defense Academy in late March, Defense Minister Doan Khue singled out training as a critical defense requirement, and reminded the party of the task of drawing up comprehensive local security plans involving economic as well as defense components.[50] The Ninth Congress of Military Region One's party committee, which met in mid–March under Doan Khue's leadership, discussed the unresolved issue of the party's responsibilities in creating regional defense forces in the northern zone. Many delegates, according to the media account of the congress, raised the issue of Military Region One troops combining with local party organization assets, provincial administration personnel, and the minority ethnic population of the Viet Bac area to guard against subversive threats posed by peaceful evolution, a point that was echoed in Doan Khue's speech to the gathered delegates.[51]

The Military Political Academy Congress, convened in mid-March under the guidance of Politburo member Le Kha Phieu, director of the General Political Department, discussed the complexities of changes in training regimes for rank and file party cadre serving in the military, recognized the strains that training obligations imposed on the PAVN, and explored the military's role in industrialization and modernization.[52]

The Ninth Military Region's Party Congress in late March brought up the economic difficulties confronted by the Delta area, and resolved to stabilize border areas and fulfill basic local defense duties. The congress discussed the cultural and political level of soldiers and military intellectuals, the deficiencies of platoon-level party members, and the disappointingly low quality of new soldiers in terms of their minimal leadership capabilities and low level of education.[53] The early April congress of the Seventh Military Region's Party Committee focused on lapses in military educational levels and leadership skills, and diminishing party membership.[54]

The party organization for the Seventh Military Region conducted its congress in early April. Le Kha Phieu stressed very basic security themes, and concerted efforts to thwart peaceful evolution schemes in his address to that meeting.[55] Military Region Three's party organization conducted its session at roughly the same time,

2. Basic-Level Meetings, Provincial and Bloc Congresses 43

and endorsed efforts to improve national defense capabilities, defense education, and internal security measures against peaceful evolution conspiracies against Vietnam.[56]

The General Political Department's party mechanism met in early April, reaffirmed the commitment to reform, refocused attention on the twin processes of industrialization and modernization, and restated the critical role of ideology in the country's current stage of development.[57] The General Department for National Defense Industry and Economics held its party organization meeting in mid–April, and placed a primacy on creating an environment in which industrialization and modernization of defense production could take place in tandem with overall national economic development, in accordance with the political report to the Military Party Committee.[58]

Do Muoi addressed the All-Army Party Organization Congress on 5 May, making the case for an integrated defense strategy that accomplished nation-building tasks as well as fulfilling security responsibilities. He echoed the Army Party organization's concern for reorganizing and strengthening the military's party structure, for cleansing the current leadership of the party, and for imposing high standards for future leaders. Muoi repeated the party-wide admonition to defeat the schemes of hostile forces aimed at "spontaneous evolution," especially by preserving the party's preeminent political leadership role. He acknowledged the abandonment of the military council system (*che do Hoi Dong Quan Su*), and noted the restoration of the party committee system that he saw as a more suitable means of accomplishing national defense policy management.[59]

Broadcast news items suggested that there was only partial support for an integrated defense approach that levied requirements on all ministries, localities and state bureaucracies, though much broader agreement with the more general proposition that the All-People National Defense System must be improved. Many delegates viewed efforts to enhance the military's political quality as the key to improving all dimensions of the defense and security capabilities.[60]

Unresolved Debates

Beginning in February and lasting through April, the party's theoretical journal, *Tap Chi Cong San*, ran three to four articles in each bimonthly issue in preparation for the national congress. The articles, generally written by academics associated with universities or research institutes or middle-level government and party officials, focused on the continued relevance of Marxism and Leninism — as well as the timeless strength of Ho Chi Minh's teachings — and offered a defense of Vietnam's past strategic choices and developmental decisions. The articles paid homage to classical socialist theory and restated the strong association the Communist Party drew between independence, development, and national strength on the one hand and "the socialist orientation" on the other. Abandoning socialism meant condemning Vietnam to uncertain rule, a perpetually primitive economy, and unrelieved social distress: inequality and class imbalances such as that which, in the view of party orthodoxy, characterized the American-supported Republic of South Vietnam.[61]

The wavering convictions of a number of doubters about the wisdom of pursuing a socialist course was traced to the collapse of the Soviet Union in various articles. The proverbial minority — "a number of people" — argued that, by electing a socialist course, Vietnam had chosen the wrong road and needed to select another direction for the nation: the capitalist road to development or — as another alternative — the road of social democracy.[62] The articles did not take the threat of peaceful transformation as the most insidious form of antiregime thought, but the authors did not discount the challenge posed to the regime by such views. Rather, they suggested that a panicked post–cold war view of Hanoi's options, erroneous thinking about the lessons of history, the realities of local, regional, and global change, as well as a drift away from the original Marxist standpoints, all combined to instigate questions — in some instances with support from overseas Vietnamese populations — on whether Vietnam had made the right strategic choices.[63] Many of the writings portrayed a debate in which some wondered whether a diluted version of socialism leavened by unalloyed market capitalism, the Chinese course to development, or a softened socialized socialism would meet Vietnam's developmental needs, without causing dislocations entailed in pursuing "socialist orientation."[64] The articles rejected those alternatives and urged a return to core Marxist-Leninist values, along with a concerted attempt to reclaim the vision that drove Ho Chi Minh to dedicate his life to preserving Vietnam's independence and sovereignty.[65]

Nevertheless, the articles showed that a debate over fundamental issues of direction and core policy decisions simmered through the end of the year's first quarter, up to the convening of the provincial congresses. The debate, characterized as profound in some of the writings, challenged the party on the issue of quality of members and ranking personnel, on the approach to and the effectiveness of party reform, and on the practical aspects of planning for modernization and industrialization (such as providing for the integration of export development into socialist economic development plans). The party came down strongly in support of preserving a preeminent role for the state sector of the economy, but the tone of the opinions on this suggested that the role of the state enterprises remained an issue. At least one article noted that questions concerning the rate of industrialization and modernization, the speed of urbanization of rural areas, and the rate of sectoral transition (that is, the changing ratio between agriculture, industry, and services that characterized Vietnam's economy) also remained at the center of debate.[66]

Some unidentified elements in the party appear to have challenged the direction and content of foreign policy discussions, according to late April articles in the military's daily newspaper. They argued that, in the aftermath of the dissolution of the Soviet Union, Hanoi should have focused on a less selective broadening of relations and expended more energy to define a course of foreign policy that owed less to principles and was governed more by an imperative to survive by entering into alliances. That seemed to be a veiled way of suggesting that relations with China had developed entirely too slowly for Vietnam's own good. The question of Vietnam's relationship with China was raised during the Third Military Region's Party Congress in late March. Delegates attending that meeting argued that geographic proximity posed a complication to an open door policy, which itself—alongside a market approach to economic development—made Vietnam vulnerable to the blandishments of forces favoring peaceful evolution. Nevertheless, the shared border, China's commercial ports, and its disposable capital made Beijing a very real, critical variable in Vietnam's economic strategy.[67]

Most importantly, the party was not prepared to characterize internal party organization reforms as stable, even as late in the preparatory process as April. In many instances party organizations through the municipal level were simply not up to fulfilling basic responsibilities. Basic party organizations had been slow in developing a core of capable leaders, and the overall process of managing chapters remained far from uniform at many levels within the VNCP. The party also seemed to have been embroiled in a debate over the utility of midterm conferences and over the length of the tenure for the Central Executive Committee and the district-level party committees, where some supported a three year term instead of a five year term of office. Many party organizations were clearly unsatisfied with the part of the draft political report on party building, and some congresses had heard recommendations that a separate report to the Central Committee on party building should be issued.[68]

3

From the Tenth Plenum to the National Congress

THE UNVEILING OF THE DRAFT POLITICAL REPORT

Hong Ha, then secretary of the Central Committee and director of the External Relations Department, announced the publication of the draft political report at a 9 April press conference in Hanoi, in accordance with the instructions of the Secretariat. Ha told assembled Vietnamese and foreign media representatives that the draft report — which was published on 10 April — reaffirmed the commitment to reform, called for the close combination of economic and political renovation, and reiterated the need to pair economic reform and the establishment of a multisector commodity economy with the invigoration of the role of state management in accordance with socialist principles.

Ha told the assembled journalists that the report brought party building tasks into line with the requirements of the "new period" by developing the "intellectual level" of the party, recruiting professionally qualified members, and improving leadership methods to ensure the party's vanguard role. Responding to questions from the media, Ha stated that the draft report dealt with the issue of preserving the role of the private economic sector, though the revised party statutes prohibited members from engaging in private capitalist activities. Ha noted that the report endorsed privatization of the state business sector — which remained a very difficult task — and sought to address weak points in the state's approach to the management of the various economic sectors. Referring to his recent visit to mountainous region provinces, Ha stressed the party's recognition of the problems confronting the "former revolutionary bases" and the ethnic enclaves of these provinces, and the need to contend with economic disparities between provinces and regions.[1]

THE TENTH PLENUM

The Tenth Plenum met in Hanoi from 12 to 20 April. The text of the plenary communiqué, broadcast on 21 April, indicated that the Central Committee voted on the contents of the draft documents. The plenary appears to have urged that the process of "supplementing, amending, and perfecting" the documents reflect the views put forth during this voting process. It is possible, judging from previous votes taken during plenary meetings, that the participants were asked to express their support for the successful process of eliciting critical contributions to the core draft documents. They may have also been asked to judge whether the process should continue through the round of congresses that had not yet convened, including meetings of entities directly subordinate to the Central Committee, or whether the draft documents should be adopted as authoritative texts to be set before the Central Committee at the Eighth Congress in June.

The Tenth Plenum, however, did not reach closure on the question of submissions to the upcoming congress. The Twelfth Plenum held in May 1991 in advance of the Seventh National Congress had unanimously approved a large number of key reports and documents for presentation to the congress. In contrast, the Tenth Plenum's communiqué was conspicuously silent on whether or not the draft political report, revised statutes, and socioeconomic plan had even been placed before the Central Committee for a final vetting before the national meeting.

There are other noteworthy contrasts between the Twelfth Plenum of 1991 and the Tenth Plenum of 1996. The Twelfth Plenum characterized the viewpoints solicited during the months of preparation for the Seventh Congress. The Tenth Plenum merely acknowledged that the Central Committee had discussed and decided on the views expressed during the process of revising the draft documents by the basic party organization, provincial and municipal congresses, as well as the meetings of mass organizations, sectors, and the Fatherland Front. The Twelfth Plenum communiqué indicated that the Central Committee had decided on the dates for convening the Seventh National Congress. The Tenth Plenum did not announce a firm schedule for the congress. The Twelfth Plenum had agreed to a name for the Seventh congress — the Congress of Renovation, Democracy, Discipline, and Solidarity — a decision that had a christening effect on the whole process. The Tenth Plenum did not take such a symbolic step, but rather acknowledged that there was much work to be done in the little time that remained before the Eighth Congress. Finally, the Twelfth Plenum noted the completion of the "first round party organization congresses." The Tenth Plenum indicated that though many preparatory congresses had taken place, provincial and city congresses as well as congresses of party blocs subordinate to the Central Committee had not yet been convened.

Do Muoi's opening and closing statements reflected the extent to which the process was still a work in progress. In his opening remarks Muoi made the case that character and competence — in the form of specialized capabilities as well as good leadership skills — and respect for the organization should be the foremost measures of cadre qualifications, in terms that suggested he was making the case to a forum that had yet to delve into the personnel issues confronting party organizations. Indeed, Muoi specified that these criteria should be borne in mind in the remaining congresses, and acknowledged that the Personnel Subcommittee — possibly a subordinate committee of the Organization Department — would report on this issue during the course of the plenary session.

Muoi mentioned in a rather elliptical way that the Politburo would "report and seek the advice" of the Central Committee "on some other specific tasks," possibly a reference to concrete personnel decisions, and a clear indication that unfinished business worthy of mention by the general secretary was to be placed before the Central Committee. In his closing speech Muoi noted that there would be an Eleventh Plenum, prior to the June congress, which would clarify issues raised but not resolved at the Tenth Plenum, and would also take up unspecified issues regarding which there were still major differences within the Central Committee in mid-April. The party, Muoi concluded, had to simultaneously manage the remaining provincial and city party meetings, and work quickly to put the finishing touches in place so that the congress could convene.

Muoi's closing speech sharply articulated bottom-line criteria for personnel choices. Muoi urged consistent efforts to recruit and develop personnel from the three age brackets and to rejuvenate the system by attracting younger leaders. Special attention must be given to political integrity, ethics, lifestyle, sense of discipline, and the spirit of solidarity of potential party leaders. Muoi emphasized that "anyone who is a political opportunist, who is lacking in political acumen or courage, or who is involved in corruption and so forth will never be chosen for the Central Committee."

Muoi's remarks underscored the extent to which the Tenth Plenum was not in a position to authoritatively characterize the criticisms and opinions rendered by basic- and higher-level party congresses regarding the draft documents. Muoi told the plenary session that Central Committee members basically shared the Politburo's judgment that the political report was prepared meticulously, seriously, and convincingly. Muoi did not offer a similar positive view of the other draft documents—the socioeconomic report and the revised party statutes. He did note that the Ninth Plenum had aired many issues regarding the three drafts, and had resolved many issues, which left the Tenth Plenum free to focus "mainly on analyses, clarifications, and supplements with a view to shedding more light on major issues included in the draft documents to be presented to the upcoming Congress." The Twelfth Plenum in 1991 was considerably more willing to reflect enthusiastic support for the draft documents, "absolute" majority support for the critical views contributed by lower party organizations, and "a high identity of views" regarding the Central Committee's decision to approve the texts that were prepared for presentation to the Seventh Congress.[2]

Six days after the Tenth Plenary meeting, the Foreign Ministry confirmed that Politburo member Nguyen Ha Phan, Central Committee party secretary and vice chairman of the National Assembly, was "expelled recently from the party for having committed serious mistakes in his past activities." Initial information from Western observers, journalists, and senior Vietnamese diplomats suggested that Phan was punished for breaking ranks over the pace and scope of the economic reform package, and particularly the opening up of the economy. Another explanation of Phan's expulsion offered by some observers was that he had revealed the identity of a number of Vietnamese communist operatives during a brief period of incarceration in southern Vietnam during the early 1960s.[3] Others speculated that this well-known episode was being used by one faction to weaken the influence of the group of conservatives with which Phan was said to be associated.[4] None of these analyses explained Phan's continuous close association with party and government positions, his involvement in guiding provincial-level preparatory congresses, and his participation in high-visibility parish visits to explain midcourse corrections and current "orientations" to local party structures.

THE TEXT OF THE DRAFT POLITICAL REPORT

The first public mention of the draft political report in any detail came in a mid–January Voice of Vietnam "topical talk" broadcast that outlined the organization and substance of the document in detail. The January media review suggested that the report aimed at conveying a carefully balanced message about the course of reforms since 1986. The party, according to the aforementioned broadcast, had crafted a fundamentally correct policy that was marred by faulty implementation, jeopardizing efforts to keep the reforms true to the socialist path.[5] The draft document underscored the enduring relevance of socialism and the indispensable role of the state as custodian of the economy. The January media review stated that the draft clarified the steps that Vietnam must take in the final years of the twentieth century to move various components of the multisectoral economy in the direction of industrialization and modernization; to "harmonize" the market; to perfect state laws governing the economy; to renovate planning work and financial and monetary policies; and to upgrade the state's performance as an economic manager. The draft report called for more effective attempts to resolve nagging social problems and urged active measures to foil peaceful evolution schemes "and other rebellious and subversive activities."

The final section of the January version of the draft report on party renovation urged the organization to reclaim its roots by invigorating the working-class nature of the party and supported a strict application of principles and theories that had shaped the party: democratic centralism, collective leadership, criticism, unanimity, close relations with the people, and international solidarity. The section stressed the need for strict regulations to govern party officials assigned overseas and urged close-knit management of the organization's rank and file. Finally, the draft stated the need for attention on leadership issues and urged clarity in the division of labor between the state and the party, which must operate "within the framework of the constitution and law."

The draft political report presented to the Tenth Plenum meeting differed very little from the preview offered in the topical talk broadcast, suggesting that the key issues had been hammered into the form in which they would be presented to the National Congress by early January. The introduction to the draft political report that was publicized in advance of the Tenth Plenum sketched the first steps toward extricating Vietnam from its socioeconomic crisis in the late 1970s, when the country faced an embargo and was confronted with large national defense expenditures, staggering inflation, and stunted production. The partial reforms put in place by the Sixth Party Congress were no match for the economic challenges that Vietnam faced. The country endured three consecutive years of triple-digit inflation, sharp declines in living standards, famine, stagnation in the state-run enterprises and cooperatives, spiraling unemployment, and the collapse of credit funds through 1989, when the multisector commodity economy, coupled with a reliance on market mechanisms under state management, began to make a small difference in Vietnam's economic performance. Inflation slowed, exports of rice grew, consumer goods production levels increased and some recovery took place. The Seventh Party

Congress in 1991 made a more profound commitment to economic reform, but the collapse of the Soviet Union had a serious impact on Vietnam's ability to stay its course of socialist economic development, and the U.S. embargo and other external challenges complicated full recovery. The political report gave the system credit for achieving a respectable annual growth rate, attracting foreign investment, tamping down inflation to between 12 and 14 percent in the 1994-95 period, and setting the stage for positive social changes.

The draft political report noted the restoration of relations with China, the strengthening of "relations of special solidarity and friendship" with Laos, entry into the Association of Southeast Asian Nations and other international and regional organizations, the normalization of relations with the United States, the establishment of ties with the countries in the Confederation of Independent States, and the broadening of links with South Asia, the Middle East, Africa and Latin America. Cambodia was conspicuous by its absence from this recitation of foreign policy achievements, perhaps because relations had soured temporarily over border issues and lingering problems associated with the ethnic Vietnamese in Cambodia. In December 1995 the Cambodian government complained that a Vietnamese military unit had transgressed the border, and they raised serious questions about the management of violations of the joint communiqué signed by the prime ministers of the two countries in mid–January 1995.[6] Another problem that complicated the relationship was the activities of ethnic Vietnamese anti–Hanoi activists affiliated with an organization called Free Vietnam, who were alleged to have operated from Cambodian soil since late 1994. In early 1996 the Cambodian government deported three ethnic Vietnamese leaders of this organization to Vietnam.[7] Vietnam clearly remained concerned about the potential for future antigovernment actions emanating from Cambodian soil in the early months of 1996. These problems were obviously important enough to the Central Committee drafters — probably including Hong Ha[8] — to prompt them to reduce Cambodia's profile in the description of Hanoi's foreign policy priorities.[9]

The draft report stated that Vietnam had encountered considerable problems during its struggle to modernize, including ingrained habits of wastefulness and poor personal saving practices that reduced individual capacity for capital development investments; ineffective state policies that crippled the ability to mobilize capital resources; continued failure to prod state enterprises and cooperatives to improve their performance; matching failures to encourage the private economic sector to fulfill its potential; and serious lapses in efforts to "equitize" or privatize inefficient, unproductive state enterprises (page 8).[10] An unsatisfactory pace of repairing financial, banking, and monetary policies, irrational income distribution, the absence of a coherent body of economic laws, and serious corruption had a negative impact on land policy, taxation, import and export activities, investment cooperation, and capital construction. Social problems — in the areas of health, education, income distribution, and ethnic policies — remained nagging obstacles to real growth. Finally, party, state, and mass organizations had reorganized slowly, had not shed negative bureaucratic habits, and had failed to attract new, younger members (pages 8–9).

Part three of the draft report offered an overall assessment that authoritatively pronounced the end of the socioeconomic crisis, and the completion of "the initial phase of the transition period." The country had launched into a new period of industrialization and modernization. The core of this section was a scant four sentences that set aside the debate over the economic takeoff point that had cropped up in various forums during the early 1990s. For example, the argument aired at the January 1994 midterm party conference about whether Vietnam had sufficiently satisfied the preconditions for industrialization and modernization was summarily turned aside by the draft political report, as it had been at the interim conference.[11] Other challenges first raised at the January meeting, including the argument that Vietnam did not need to think of modernization since industrialization was the most meaningful goal, were dismissed in 1994 and were given no further consideration in the 1996 draft political report.[12] Questions concerning the wisdom of according agricultural development central importance in the scheme to industrialize and modernize, which were the source of some discussion at the interim conference, were conspicuous by their absence in the clipped, preemptive language of the draft report.[13]

The draft political report reaffirmed a familiar litany of political values: Reform is socialism by other means; pluralism is anathema to political progress and economic development in Vietnam; political renewal means untangling decrepit and confused bureaucracies and pursuing effective government organization; the state has a role in national economic management that is essential and in keeping with a commitment to a modern, industrial economy; and market mechanisms are a means to a socialist end, not a capitalist deviation.

The draft political report offered an analysis of the world situation and the current political environment that paralleled the assessment set out at the Third Plenum (June 1992). This 1992 plenum forecast that Asia would become the world's most important region by the twenty-first century owing to its untapped resources, its rate of economic development, and its recognized strategic importance. The draft political report argued that only the "strong impact of major powers" stood as a potentially destabilizing factor. The report also was less enamored of the region's growth potential, and placed more emphasis on the meaningfulness of trade liberalization and economic integration. The Third Plenary session discussed the health of socialism in the aftermath of the breakup of the Soviet Union, the conditions for regional stability and the meaning of Vietnam's integration into the Association of Southeast Asian Nations (ASEAN), and the fundamental policy assumptions behind the effort to broaden bilateral relations on a global basis. The draft political report was more blunt about the lingering impact of the collapse of the Soviet Union and Eastern Europe, which had driven socialism into a temporary regression. The report stressed the value of employing "class struggle" and "contradiction" as the key prisms through which increasingly acute world conflict should be viewed. The Third Plenum depicted several global trends toward independence; resistance to imperialism; improved regional links; and cooperation between different political and social systems, with the goal of creating a durable peace.[14] The draft political report added some darker forces to this dialectic, demonstrating basic agreement with the proposition that peace and stability were more and more recognized as the prerequisites for achieving economic growth and development, but referring to local wars, ethnic and religious conflict, arms races, and terrorism as critical variables in this process.

The third part of the draft report — on developing orientations in key fields — advanced various development goals in economic sectors; reviewed economic management reform, including land, housing, stock market, and monetary policies; outlined scientific and technological requirements, and educational and training needs; and treated issues relating to culture, social problems, foreign policy and national defense, state reform, and party building (pages 21–47). For the most part, there was little divergence between key statements of economic plans and goals that emanated from plenary meetings and National Assembly sessions during 1994 and 1995 and the draft political report, although this latter document did take pains to sharply emphasize the basic orthodoxies in descriptions of economic reforms that veered toward market forms and relied on departures from socialist norms. For example, the section on distribution emphasized the need to "recognize the long-lasting existence of different forms of hired labor while barring them from turning into relations between the ruler and the ruled, leading to the polarization of society into two opposing poles" (page 26). The draft document seized repeated opportunities to spell out the role of the state sector as a catalyst in achieving rapid economic growth and resolving lingering social problems (pages 26–27). It drew firmer lines on the equitization of state enterprises, supporting steps to make such companies more efficient producers but ruling out privatization while encouraging wider shareholding, and stipulating the need for cautious judgment in leasing, selling, or changing the ownership of state companies (page 27). The draft report was also comparatively more exacting in its depiction of the role of market mechanisms in Vietnamese economic development, stipulating that "commodity production" was not an exclusively capitalist evolution, and firmly stating the symbiotic relationship between planning and market mechanisms.

The section of the report on social issues was more sketchy than the documents produced by the February 1993 Fourth Plenum, which was dedicated in its entirety to social problems and policies. The draft political report embroidered on the plenary themes slightly, introducing a humanitarian thread to social policy in the form of a commitment to "eradicating poverty," the creation of a "compassion fund," further work to develop concepts of "social insurance," and "paying debts of gratitude." The draft report endorsed a more systematic attempt to support war invalids and families of soldiers who died in action, an issue that dominated the media during mid-1995, around the time of the anniversary of the founding of the first veterans' association.[15]

Section ten of the political report, on state reform, was slightly more prescriptive than plenary documents and party instructions issued during 1994 and 1995 on the subject of corruption. For example, the draft report repeated the need for party, state, and mass organization vigilance against moral lapses, and added the proposal that the system should "study, promulgate, and gradually enforce" a system according to which public servants would declare their incomes. The report also called for laws on property ownership by officials, with the aim of achieving "transparency" in this area (page 47). The draft report also endorsed the involvement of the mass media in the campaign against corruption, probably as a result of the credibility that divulging the details of the detection, prosecution and punishment of government lawbreakers had brought to the regime during the early and mid-1990s.

The nine pages of part four on party building credited the party with initiating and shaping the renovation process and described the weaknesses of the party and the major problems that had emerged in recent years. Many in the ranks had lost their bearings and motivation and had become "politically degenerated" and corrupt. Basic-level organizations had weakened and become paralyzed, while bureaucratic ways suffocated the organization. The report drew sharper requirements regarding the probity of party officials, calling for clarity in regulations restricting the participation of public officials in businesses, especially joint ventures with foreigners; the issuance of regulations governing gift taking; and the establishment of mechanisms requiring regular reporting of incomes, financial resources, land, and homes of party and government officials.

The political report in its draft form was a cross between a guide to repairs required to fix and sustain the organization and an inventory of first principles intended to resurrect guideposts that had served the system well in the past and needed to be restored and reinvigorated as the fuel for the party in the period of reform and transition. Past political reports had involved both programmatic recommendations and more lofty efforts to set trajectories and long-term goals in accordance with ideological tenets. While the 1996 draft report included some of this, a lot more of the text simply redefined basic goals and specified minimal requirements for policies such as health care, education, and industrialization. There seemed to be more truisms and platitudes, broad goals and minimum requirements without the detailed prescriptions that dominated past documents. The goal may have been to demonstrate a willingness to keep the party out of the nuts and bolts business of daily governance and economic micromanagement, but the draft report remained a distant, somewhat abstract and superficial treatment of such internal party issues as recruitment, internal control procedures, leadership selection, and educational and training requirements.

This report did not provide anything more than a shallow pass at the ten years of reformist activity that, beginning in late 1995, was clearly intended to be the core goal of the congress. It is entirely possible that an in-depth study was undertaken — and revealed in controlled party documents — but the endorsement that the reform process received — and the brief review of the lineage and ancestry of reformist initiatives — could not have been satisfying to the young, enthusiastic, and candid officials who in the last months of 1995 looked forward to the Eighth Congress as the process that would vindicate their views that Vietnam would weaken and falter without sustained change.[16]

REFOCUSING POLITICAL DISCOURSE, CONTINUED DEBATE OVER THE DRAFTS

At about the time of the Tenth Plenum, the party and military newspapers began a daily series of commentaries on the draft political report and the fundamental issues that would confront the party at the Eighth Congress. The articles, which ran as features from early April to the convening of the congress in late June, restored industrialization and modernization as the organizing ideas for the congress, spent decidedly less time focusing on peaceful evolution, without minimizing security issues and defense requirements, and devoted less energy to the notion of the state enterprises as the mainstay of the multicomponent economy, without rejecting the leading role that the state sector would play in the marketized economy.[17] The articles reclaimed the middle ground as the starting point for the concepts and plans that would be placed before the Central Committee at the congress. They signaled what some Vietnamese officials viewed as a clear effort by General Secretary Muoi to guide the debate from the more extreme sides of the spectrum toward a more reasonable course, and away from the religious and ideological flavor that had begun to creep into discussions, especially as they concerned public security and political stability.

Beginning in January, Muoi's speeches sought to shift the focus from the past to the future and to underscore that science and technology would be a decisive factor in Vietnam's efforts to continue economic reform. Much of the backdrop to earlier speeches on the subject of cultural pollution and social evils, and the threat posed by peaceful evolution, dropped out as core themes, without being totally expunged from Muoi's public statements. The general secretary sought to spread his views by meeting with intellectuals and business interests, an indication that he wanted to reach a wider audience than party cadre. The fact that the draft political report and the draft revisions of the statutes stressed that the VNCP should not be above the law was a critical breakthrough in the minds of younger government officials, a message that gave them confidence in the system's capacity to renew itself. However, it was not until the Tenth Plenum — when the reform-minded elements of the party were able to sideline two authoritative conservatives (Nguyen Ha Phan and Dao Duy Tung, who was hospitalized in April with an ailment described as serious by middle-level Foreign Ministry officials) — that Muoi was able to assert these more reasonable messages. Until then, Muoi and other senior leaders were not able to win much support for a concept of industrialization and modernization that stressed the rural dimension of development, socioeconomic progress, and advances in state administration. Through late January the concept of industrialization and modernization had not been absorbed into the political mainstream in a meaningful way. Some provincial subordinates were denounced for treating industrialization and modernization as little more than a slogan. By mid-April, however, Muoi was able to take firmer control of these organizing concepts in a manner that had a dramatic impact on young, dedicated civil servants looking for the right message to support.[18]

The articles in *Nhan Dan* and *Quan Doi Nhan Dan* ranged in subject from the foundations for an advanced culture, to the simultaneous reform of party leadership and the development of state administration, and then to the party's creativeness in protecting sovereignty and stability. The essays were restrained, rational restatements of central issues. Some were cast in classical Marxist vocabulary; others harked back to critical moments in European revolutionary history or benchmarks in Vietnam's own struggle. Some of the writings were thoughtful, careful expositions of the origins of the current economic reforms or serious historic treatments of the evolution of key viewpoints regarding culture, foreign policy, party leadership, and economic policies.[19]

The commentaries that appeared in the military's newspaper tended to be more bluntly worded reminders of historic lessons, ideological basics, and conservative values, but also focused on stiffening the party's resolve to modernize and industrialize on the basis of sound Marxist-Leninist perspectives, trusted Ho Chi Minh thought, and recognition of the unique realities of the current period. The *Quan Doi Nhan Dan* articles placed special emphasis on returning industrialization and modernization to the center of all dialogue on development, reaffirmed the national goals of eliminating poverty and backwardness by the turn of the century, and were more explicit about the direct relationship between success in the economic realm and the effective fulfillment of minimum defense responsibilities.[20]

Many of the feature articles highlighted the importance of specialized training and general education as the resource necessary to energize industrialization and modernization by supplying a steady stream of competent people to run the economy, the reorganized state administration, the renewed party organizations, and the modern defense establishment.[21] The articles also focused on party weaknesses and lapses in the process of preparing for the national congress, noting that much of the debate over issues of importance to the people — presumably standard of living issues — lacked depth. The party, one commentary noted, could benefit from a more public system, from "transparency," and required a more sophisticated sense of the delicate balance necessary to sustain democratic forms without jeopardizing collective leadership.[22] Other feature articles observed that there was no clear definition of leadership roles for the party in the new environment, that cadre skills remained at an unacceptably low level, and corruption, smuggling, and other violations of discipline and internal laws threatened the credibility of the party.[23] Finally, they touched on cultural and social themes, asserting the inextricable link between development and an advanced society of equality, the positive impact exerted by social equality on production, the importance of resolving social problems, and the strong cultural foundation necessary for proceeding with industrialization and modernization.[24]

The articles sought to shape a political idiom that was not completely weighted to the conservative side and not entirely without strong roots in classic Marxist values to balance the nod toward practical market economic realities. The commentaries were enough of a mixed bag to suggest that the party was not able to devise a formula that melded all these views into a basket of ideals that could easily find consensual acceptance. Periodically, the articles veered back to a conservative extreme, perhaps to counterbalance the emphasis on industrialization and modernization as the buzzwords for the reformers. Occasionally, a keynote article heavily weighted down with conservative arguments was given prominence in the party's theoretical journal, reminding the party's readership of the risks of unalloyed change and the importance of staying in touch with founding ideals and precepts dating to the war for independence.[25]

From the point at which the draft report was made public

through midyear, the social and economic plans given attention in the draft political report remained at the center of a debate within the party. In mid–April a two part essay carried in *Nhan Dan* acknowledged that while many in the party agreed that the VNCP had basically pulled the nation out of the socioeconomic crisis, others argued that the party had only averted an economic crisis; it had not confronted the tenacious social difficulties such as corruption and inequality that pestered reforming Vietnam.[26] According to the article, some in the party took the view that measured objectively, Vietnam had solved its socioeconomic problems. Others made the case that residual problems were at least in part a result of deficiencies in party organization and government leadership, as well as a consequence of new difficulties engendered by the introduction of market forms and other experiments. Resolving these problems, the article argued, would be a long-term process.

Some party members argued that there was less clarity to the direction Vietnam was following so near to the turn of the century, and that attempts to seek clarity often created suspicions and anxieties. In years past Marxism and Leninism provided a rich guide for internal purposes, but in the 1970s the party had to define concepts for navigating Vietnam's next steps in socialist industrialization. The article implied that there was still a politically relevant debate over whether the reforms in the former Soviet Union, Europe, and China exerted influence on Vietnam's efforts to renovate its economy, or whether Vietnam's reforms sprung from internal sources and motivations (*Doi moi O Viet Nam bat nguong tu thuc tien Viet Nam*).

In mid–May commentators continued to mull over the practical aspects of commitment to a sustained role for state enterprises, raising questions concerning the pace and scope of divestiture and the draft report's commitment to ensuring that state enterprises accounted for at least 60 percent of the gross domestic product. One *Nhan Dan* article argued that the draft political report should introduce greater clarity on the subject of managing the breakup of state enterprises and on specific national health needs, such as the minimum number of doctors, clinics, and medical personnel necessary to meet the draft political report's commitment to achieving a high level of health service efficiency. Party members were critical of the draft report's shortcomings in operationalizing plans to modernize minority areas and mountainous zones, and asked for more concrete and practical prescriptions concerning the implementation of industrialization plans.[27]

In early June a media summary of the criticisms leveled at the draft document suggested a division of popular perceptions regarding major threats to the success of reform, with only 66 percent of the correspondence to the party's newspaper identifying corruption and smuggling as the greatest risk to the regime, and a large but unspecified number of letter writers arguing that corruption worked to make the system more vulnerable to attacks from antiregime organizations.

There was apparently less than unanimous agreement regarding the goal of building a "selective number of heavy industrial complexes in major sectors," and some significant concerns — represented by well-known commentators — regarding the system's commitment to the protection of the environment and the preservation of Vietnam's national heritage.[28]

From mid– to late June, just before the congress, the draft political report was pummeled in the press as often as it was praised for astutely pursuing the correct course, sometimes for odd and esoteric reasons. It was criticized for insufficient treatment of the development of laws, for underemphasizing control work, and for appropriating Western economic terminologies when perfectly effective Vietnamese alternatives existed. One precongress newspaper article recommended that the discussion of measures against bureaucratization in the draft political report be strengthened by clarifying party responsibilities for opposing "mandarinism" and eliminating corruption, and by adding an eighth "key issue" to the section on party building, thereby elevating the importance of programs opposing the proliferation of bureaucracies. Another in the long-running series of signed *Nhan Dan* commentaries made the point that the debate over the draft report's contents should have interjected more about global economic trends and their impact of Vietnam's industrialization.[29]

THE PROVINCIAL PARTY CONGRESSES, APRIL–MAY 1996

The provincial party committees convened their congresses between late April and the end of May. Media coverage of the provincial meetings was formulaic and generally unrevealing.[30] However, news reporting on some provincial meetings noted the proliferation of views expressed by participants on the key draft documents. Prominent attention was paid to local issues, such as the slow rate of development of economic structures (Khanh Hoa and Lang Son); the unevenness of standards of living from area to area within provincial borders (Khanh Hoa); the marginal level of investments in border areas and ethnic enclaves (Lang Son, Quang Nam-Da Nang, Lai Chau, and Yen Bai); the contrasting efficiency of investment from central government and foreign sources (Minh Thuan); the practical steps necessary to increase local standards of living (Bac Thai, Tuyen Quang, and Quang Tri); the role of cooperatives, the means of recruiting younger party members and representatives of minority groups (Tuyen Quang); methods of increasing cultivable land (Ha Giang); and the commitments necessary to control corruption (Thanh Hoa and Quang Ninh). The Quang Nam-Da Nang Party Committee raised the issue of transportation and communications assets, and health and education services in mountainous areas.[31] The Kien Giang Committee discussed port development, construction and maintenance of irrigation systems, and environmental protection. Ninh Thuan was preoccupied with real poverty among the 40 percent of its population that were ethnic minorities.[32] Tra Vinh raised development issues regarding its large Khmer population. The Yen Bai committee discussed commodity circulation to minority areas. The Ba Ria–Vung Tau congress focused on socioeconomic problems and infrastructure issues encountered by newly created congresses in new provinces. Hoa Binh's congress debated land issues, and Can Tho fixed on the matter of integrating with neighboring provinces to form a Mekong Delta economic center. Though several provincial party organizations called for more energetic efforts to attract foreign investment (Ha Bac, Khanh Hoa, and Tra Vinh, for example), media accounts did not indicate that other foreign policy issues had been raised at the meetings, though a handful of provinces oddly yet enthusiastically pointed to their campaigns to raise millions of dong to help the Cuban people (Tuyen Quang, Vinh Phu, and Son La).[33]

While the media accounts of the discussions at the 1991 provincial congresses described lively debate and pointed exchanges over the draft documents prepared for the Seventh Congress, the 1996 press summaries carried in the party's daily generally refrained from depicting the provincial meetings in such terms. The 1991 media accounts provided a good deal more background and specificity about positions taken by delegates on controversial issues such as the right to transfer land ownership, inheritance rights, the status of labor in a multisectoral commodity economy, the right of party members to engage in trade, and subsidies for state enterprises, as well as social welfare issues and highland province development problems. Indeed, in some instances media accounts in 1991 quantified the level of support that various sides of different arguments received from provincial delegates. The 1996 accounts were short, revealing little about the process and nothing about the means by which the party resolved differences over fundamental issues or defined consensus positions. While some of the 1991 provincial and municipal party congresses generated surprisingly trenchant commentaries on the manner in which the draft documents handled specific issues, the 1996 media references to the draft documents in the accounts of provincial proceedings were bland and unrevealing. In the main, the newspaper summaries of the 1996 provincial sessions paid scant attention to the draft political report and socioeconomic plan. One reason may have been continued differences over the text within the party center itself, which led to some speculation in April and May that the draft report would be gutted, reduced in size by half, and made into a more development-oriented document.

One of the consistent themes throughout the provincial congresses was the need to renew leadership. Of the 53 provincial party chairmen elected during the congresses in 1996, 34 were brand new to the job. Ten had served in the Central Committee elected by the Sixth National Congress, and nine were elected to the Central Committee for the first time at the Seventh Congress in 1991. In 1996, 20 southerners and 9 northerners who had not served in either the Sixth or the Seventh Central Committee were elected provincial party chiefs. Thirteen northerners who had served in the Seventh Central Committee were named provincial party chairmen in 1996, while four southern veterans of the Seventh Central Committee, and two central highlanders, were elected to the top provincial party posts in 1996. Of the eight minorities elected to the chairmanship of provincial party committees, three had served in the Seventh Central Committee and five were new: two from the north, two from the south, and one from the highlands. Of the eight party chiefs elected in 1996 to head Mekong Delta provincial committees, seven were new and one had been elected to the Central Committee in 1991. Three of the party chiefs elected in 1996 from Red River Delta provinces had served in the Seventh Central Committee, and four were new. One from the central highlands had served in the Central Committee elected at the Seventh Congress, and three were newcomers.

From The Eleventh Plenary Session to the Eve of the Party Congress

The Eleventh Plenary met from 3 to 9 June, and was addressed by General Secretary Do Muoi, though the party's daily newspaper did not publish any of the speeches or details concerning the proceedings. An 11 June notice of the proceedings, carried in *Nhan Dan*, stated that the Central Executive Committee continued to receive views from all provinces, cities, and party organizations subordinate to the center on the substance of the draft political report, the draft socioeconomic plan, and the revised party statutes. The plenary session also continued to work on personnel matters, debating and adopting draft regulations on organizational work, electoral statutes, and the programs of the local party congresses. The plenary discussed and decided on a convening and closing date for the congress (28 June to 1 July).[34]

Throughout June the feature commentaries on the draft report that were carried in *Quan Doi Nhan Dan* fixed their attention more directly on the modernization of defense industries, on rationalizing state administration of defense and security, and on turning out cadre with correct military rectitude.[35] In the three weeks before the congress opened, commentaries in the party's daily newspaper reinforced the VNCP's commitment to improving the country's health and education services and addressed cultural and minority affairs, corruption, and rural development.[36] Articles carried inside the party daily commented on specific sections of the draft report, laying out the details of state administrative reform, explaining approaches to cadre development, defending foreign policy, and restating the fundamentals of economic development policy and reforms.[37] Signed articles explained how the guidance articulated in the draft political report was acted upon in practical ways at the level of local party entities, translating principles and ideals into rules governing membership behavior, measures of organizational effectiveness, criteria for recruitment, goals for enlisting specialized personnel and intellectuals, and performance requirements for leadership cadre.[38]

4

The Eighth Party Congress

THE OPENING ACT

The Seventh Central Committee convened its twelfth and final plenary session on or around 23 June. The meeting ended on 26 June, two days prior to the first public session of the Eighth Congress. The Twelfth Plenary took the final steps toward defining Politburo composition and Central Committee membership, and presumably made the final adjustments in the text of the political report and the revisions to the party statutes that would be adopted by the Eighth Central Committee. The meeting was conducted in secrecy. The Western press speculated that the inability to agree on new leadership led to the compromise decision finalized at the Twelfth Plenary to retain the three top officials — Do Muoi, Le Duc Anh, and Vo Van Kiet — in their positions until the midterm party conference, which would, by statute, take place in 1998.[1]

In a 27 June news conference prior to the opening of the congress, Hong Ha, head of the Central Committee External Relations Department, and a member of the Eighth Congress Organizing Committee, stated that the congress would review the work of the Seventh national party meeting and the process of reforms conducted since the 1986 congress. Ha told assembled journalists that the congress would be open to the press. Journalists were invited to "monitor, report and comment" on the proceedings — a statement meant to demonstrate the meaning of Do Muoi's earlier announcement that the party would seek a new level of transparency, releasing documents for comment earlier in the process and conducting more of its business in public.

Ha stated that the congressional documents emphatically committed the party to continuing renovation along the socialist path, and that the core documents contained portions relevant to each of the social groups and other interests that composed Vietnamese society, aiming at building national unity. In answer to reporters' questions, Ha said that the political report rejected pluralism but embraced democratization; that the revised statutes forbade party members to engage in private capitalist enterprise; and that the final political report incorporated many of the comments and criticisms offered by the Vietnamese people. For example, the report added a section that sought to clarify the wider role accorded to overseas Vietnamese, in part as the result of critical comments from Viet Kieu representatives during the review of the draft report. Finally, Ha depicted the goal of developing a poverty-free country as one of the central tasks that would be addressed during the course of the congress.[2]

Up to the opening of the public sessions of the national party congress, young, middle-level diplomats and department-level officials thought that the meeting would represent a major clarifying moment for the country's economic reform goals. Such officials looked to the congress to clear the way for unfettered reform; loosen some of the limits that had been imposed on the market mechanism, private capitalism, and foreign economic activities; and cut through the ideological trappings that cluttered and complicated Vietnam's trajectory toward modernization.

The Congress

The Eighth Congress, "For the Continuation of the Renovation Along the Socialist Path," opened on 28 July with the participation of 1,198 delegates and an audience of foreign dignitaries and communist party representatives. That list unexpectedly included Chinese Prime Minister Li Peng, who on the first day of the congress was pictured on the front page of the party's daily newspaper shaking hands with Do Muoi in an article on the gathering of all international delegates that had been placed under the fold, in a manner that probably understated the importance of the moment in Sino-Vietnamese relations.³

President Le Duc Anh offered the opening remarks, a role fulfilled by the chairman of the Council of State Vo Chi Cong at the Seventh Congress. General Secretary Muoi read the political report directly after Anh's remarks, in the same way that his predecessor, Nguyen Van Linh, did at the 1991 meeting. The afternoon session on 28 July featured speeches by various delegations and statements by visiting foreign dignitaries, which continued through to the following day. On 30 June Defense Minister Doan Khue introduced Linh, who spoke in his capacity as an adviser to the Central Committee. He was followed by delegates from the provinces, cities, and blocs, whose speeches represented a cacophony of special interests and local, particularized views. The delegates expounded on themes in the political report, without departing from the broad thrust of the center's basic message. For example, Le Xuan Tung, secretary of the Hanoi Party Committee, asserted that the political report should focus more on urban issues. Haiphong Party Committee Chairman Le Danh Xuong stressed the importance of major infrastructure projects — such as harbor and port redevelopment — in major cities. Do Quoc Sam, a delegate from Lao Cai, vice chairman of the State Planning Committee at the time of his reelection to the Seventh Central Committee, emphasized the mobilization of savings as the key to sustaining investment levels, one of several factors in the formula for attracting investment defined by the political report. Bui Huu Hai, a delegate from Vinh Phu, addressed the customary concerns of mountainous area provinces, repeating the litany of social and economic problems of developing remote, multiethnic zones.⁴

The Seventh Central Committee elected a Politburo that consisted of 13 members. The Eighth Committee added six new slots to the party's highest body, which in turn elected a five-person Standing Committee that replaced the Secretariat, and was composed of General Secretary Do Muoi, President Le Duc Anh, Prime Minister Vo Van Kiet, director of the General Political Department Senior Lieutenant General Le Kha Phieu, and Deputy Minister of Interior Nguyen Tan Dung. The Eighth Central Committee named a seven-member Control Commission, two positions smaller than the commission chosen in 1991. In his closing remarks Do Muoi noted that the Central Committee's first plenary session had recommended that Nguyen Van Linh, Pham Van Dong, and Vo Chi Cong continue to serve as advisers. The Eighth Congress returned to the practice whereby the Central Committee elected the general secretary in what was considered the first plenary session for the new committee. In 1991 the Politburo elected the party's leader.

On the closing day, 1 July, the Eighth Congress issued a resolution which approved the political report and the socioeconomic plan and charged the Central Committee with the responsibility of perfecting and promulgating both documents. The resolution noted approval of the revised statutes and turned the task of implementing the provisions of all three documents over to the Eighth Congress.[5]

General Secretary Muoi's Opening Speech

Do Muoi opened the congress on 28 June with a presentation of the main contents of the political report. He crystallized the lessons learned during the ten years of reform from 1986 to 1996, repeating the formulation that emerged in the draft report: stick to the core goals of independence and socialism; adhere to Marxism-Leninism and Ho Chi Minh thought; combine economic and political renovation, cleverly and gradually; use market mechanisms to socialism's advantage; link social progress to economic growth; reach out to all corners of Vietnam to unite all interests; keep to a foreign policy that makes many friends and enlists willing assistance from many sources; and stay to a course of thoroughgoing party reform.

Muoi stressed the objectives of industrialization and modernization in the "new development period," and described the leading role that the state and cooperative economic sector should play. He spelled out a role for private capitalism in the new period and restated the need to preserve the socialist character of the renovated economy. Muoi asserted that the way to make this work was to eliminate much of Vietnam's hefty bureaucracy, halt subsidies for ailing state-operated firms, formulate laws and organize financial institutions, clarify monetary policies, and establish the conditions for effective state management of the market. He emphasized that lingering problems — poverty, illiteracy, injustice, and the lopsided and unequal distribution of advantages — must be solved in conjunction with economic development.

The general secretary also outlined the economic objectives for the five years from 1996 to 2000, and summarized the 11 program areas of the five-year plan, covering targets for agriculture, industry, construction, service sectors, foreign trade, technology transfer, and labor force development. He reviewed the national defense goals and foreign policy aims declared in the political report, giving prominence to the "open, multilateral, and diversified" external relations that Vietnam needed to protect its interests. The general secretary's speech replicated the sections of the political report on national unity, as well as the final section on party building. He emphasized the indispensability of the party, loyalty to Ho Chi Minh thought, and the need to reform the organization and repair grassroots party structures. Muoi committed to undertaking a review of the basic party structures associated with new economic forms, enterprises, and organizations, and concluded by reminding the party to invigorate control work at all levels.[6]

The Socioeconomic Plan

The socioeconomic plan for the years 1996 to 2000 was issued as part of the media's coverage of the proceedings of the Eighth Congress, on the third day of the party meeting, but curiously without any indication that the report had been read to the congress by a senior level official. This contrasted with the newspaper coverage of the Fifth Congress, during which the report was read by Pham Van Dong and the Sixth Congress, during which the report was read by Vo Van Kiet, and clearly acknowledged as such in the print media.[7] A special edition of the party's monthly journal issued in July 1996 included Do Muoi's presentation of the political report and the general secretary's closing remarks, the political report itself, Le Duc Anh's remarks, the revised party statutes, and the resolution of the

Eighth Congress, but not the socioeconomic plan.⁸ The socioeconomic plan may have merely been distributed at the congress without the fanfare accorded to the political report.

According to the first section of the socioeconomic plan, Vietnam had reversed its serious economic slide toward crisis, controlled damaging inflation, put much of its financial house in order, and achieved some measurable recovery in investment levels and productivity in agriculture, energy, and services.⁹ In addition, the regime had made some headway in upgrading infrastructure and rescuing the national standard of living. The plan claimed that some basic progress toward developing specialized economic zones in agriculture, forestry, and commerce, among other branches of the economy, had been made. Foreign trade and the investment situation had improved significantly, in part as a result of the passage of the investment law and as a result of broadening external trade relations and positive steps in Vietnam's relationships with the international financial institutions. Some social programs had succeeded, including steps to eliminate illiteracy, improve national education and health services, and the institution of a population control policy. In spite of these advances, the socioeconomic plan asserted that many aspects of the country's productive forces, finances, credit, infrastructure, and social policies were in disarray. Unhealthy trends—unchecked population growth, unemployment, and corruption—had a corrosive impact on the government and the party's credibility.

The plan restated the importance of the 1996–2000 time frame in preparing the country for the first major step toward industrialization and modernization. The second section urged developing the multisectoral aspects of the commodity-based, marketized economy in accordance with socialist rules and orientations and highlighted infrastructure and service sector development goals through the year 2000. The plan also focused on the expansion of foreign trading and economic relations, including markets for Vietnamese-produced export goods and tourism opportunities in Vietnam. The document singled out social development goals for particular emphasis, stressing educational system improvements on a national scale, scientific research and training, and investments in cultural development, health services, information networks, nutrition, and family planning policy.

Section two of part two specified 11 programs and areas of development, adding detail and specificity to the goals and targets set out in the first part of the report, and part three of the plan defined methods and policies in critical areas, including finance, banking, and capital investment. The plan pronounced authoritative guidelines for the multisectoral economy, the operations of the market mechanism, foreign economic relations, and economic management and administration. Most of section two reflected the policy concerns expressed during the course of plenary sessions, especially the views aired during the Third Plenary on health and education, the reduction of poverty, and family planning. One interesting addition to the plan was a lengthy section on programs for developing all Vietnamese territories. This addressed development concerns regarding strategic islands, rural delta areas, coastal zones, and mountainous regions, as well as problems associated with sustaining economic growth and infrastructure building in the north, the center and the south. This issue — along with mountainous area problems — was a subtext in several plenary sessions that focused on economic problems, but it was not given concentrated attention until the congress, suggesting that delegates representing these geographic interests were able to garner support to bring their concerns to national-level attention.

THE POLITICAL REPORT

In early June a senior Vietnamese official stated that the political report in its draft version was an excessively lengthy document heavy on ideology and would be cut in half by the Central Committee at the congress. However, except for some extremely marginal cuts, the delegates did little trimming of the draft text. In fact, at various points the document in the version that was approved by the Central Committee was actually lengthened, and no real substantial changes were made to the draft text that was publicized in April.

Some of the alterations that were made in the final text of the report reflected interesting shifts in standpoints and suggested a tendency to scale back some of the overstated optimism of the draft version. This draft report was meticulously scrutinized and revised to reflect nuances and details that were raised at the various party meetings between April and late June. For example, in discussing the symptoms of the economic crisis of the mid–1980s, the final report did not include the draft version's reference to the high level of defense expenditure as one of the problems that fueled the economic emergency.

The draft spoke of outside forces that "stepped up their activities of peaceful evolution, attempting to make rebellion and subversion." The final report did not draw that distinction between external forces of subversion and internal threats to stability. Rather, it spoke of a number of hostile forces that persisted in threatening peace and fomenting rebellion, suggesting that a subtle consensus had emerged acknowledging that certain internal forces were as much a menace to the regime as outright enemies operating from foreign shores. While the draft noted that "subversive plots and seditious political activities have been stamped out," that reference did not appear in the final report to the congress.

The final report was not as inclined to acknowledge positive advances in preventive medicine, primary health care, and the eradication of epidemics as was present in the draft document. While the draft version pointed to the virtual end of the working class habit of "over-reliance and dependence on the state and collectives," that reference was eliminated from the final report's characterization of labor dynamism. In describing strides made in political reform, the draft report said that state agencies had made progress toward "enhanced democracy, strengthened discipline, and heightened effectiveness," but the party was not prepared to go that far, and sometime between April and late June that assertion was dropped from the political report.

Vietnam's relationship with Cambodia was not mentioned in the April draft report's recitation of foreign policy achievements, perhaps because relations had soured temporarily over border issues and lingering problems associated with ethnic Vietnamese in Cambodia. However, Cambodia was restored to the list of countries of focus in the final political report, though not as a relationship of "special solidarity" as Laos was described, but merely as a country with which Vietnam had "built better relations." The improvements in Hanoi–Phnom Penh relations referred to the 1996 joint agreement to promote bilateral cooperation in trade, transport, and communications, conduct a third round of talks on the status of Vietnamese residents in Cambodia, sign a consular agreement, and convene a session of the experts' working group on border issues.

While the draft report's section on Hanoi's efforts to consolidate ties with the remnants of the Soviet Union mentioned only Vietnam's links to the Confederation of Independent States and Eastern Europe, the final report highlighted Vietnam's gradual restoration of relations with the Russian federation. The report presented to the Eighth Party Congress placed the expansion of relations with international and regional organizations last in the inventory of foreign policy successes, whereas the draft publicized in April listed that accomplishment immediately after the positive reference to improving ties with industrialized countries, the United States, Southern Asia, the Middle East, Africa, and Latin America.

Section two of part one of the final version of the political report — on deficiencies and weaknesses — preserved in order of priority the concern regarding poverty and low levels of capital accumulation, but elevated social problems to second place in the list of concerns, whereas it occupied fourth place in the draft document.[10] In the report presented to the congress, the party's third concern was the system's failure to establish an environment in which state businesses could improve their economic performance, the cooperative economy could become revitalized, the private sector could live up to its potential, and joint ventures with foreign interests might be managed more effectively. Those issues were the second most pressing matter in the draft version of the report. The party's fourth most pressing problem as articulated in the final political report was the weakly developed role of the state in the management of socioeconomic development, which had been third on the list of weaknesses in the draft report. Both this initial document and the final version listed weaknesses in the political system as the fifth and final shortcoming. These changes in presentation from the April draft to the final version suggest basic satisfaction among the delegates to the Eighth Congress with the pace of administrative reform and government revitalization, and a shared sense that of all the issues confronting Vietnam, poverty and the failure to inculcate good economic habits represented the most serious challenges. Moreover, the elevation of social problems to the second spot on the five-item list indicated considerably wider support for more investment in the area of social policies than the party was prepared to recognize in April. Underscoring this problem, the final document emphasized that funding from the state budget to support public utility projects was very limited and ineffectively deployed to solve fundamental traffic problems, pollution, and environmental degradation.

Interestingly, while the draft report pointed to a contradiction between the advocacy of massive privatization of state enterprises and "neglect of the task of guiding the cooperatives," the final report offered a more straightforward defense of equitization, state enterprise reform, and attempts to fix crumbling cooperatives. While the draft report mandated that the state economic sector should account for 60 percent of the gross domestic product, the final report dropped that stipulation, a change that supporters of reform regarded as a victory.

Part three of the draft version and the final political report offered an overall assessment that authoritatively pronounced the end of the socioeconomic crisis and the completion of the initial phase of the transition period. The draft report and the final version reiterated the four dangers pointed out by the interim party conference: the danger of the economy lagging further behind other countries, peaceful evolution, the contest for influence in Asia, and deviation from socialism. The draft document alone referenced the regional arms race as a palpable danger to the Asia-Pacific community.

For the most part, there was little divergence between statements concerning economic plans and goals in the two versions of the political report. The fourth and final sections of both reports credited the party with initiating and shaping the renovation process, and with mapping out the party's ideological and political orientations on the basis of Marxism-Leninism and Ho Chi Minh's thoughts. In both the draft and the final version the party urged the effort to maintain and enhance the working-class nature of the party and drew sharper requirements regarding the probity of party officials. However, in part three, section one, on industrialization and modernization, the draft version specified where the economy should be in terms of food production, animal husbandry, secondary crops, and other specific activities by the year 2000. The final report did not contain any specific production goals, though it did strongly endorse a course of agricultural development that would lead to such increases. The draft report's reference to the need to make adjustments in capital allocation and to raise funds to increase the state's investment capital and credit (with the goal of developing the rural economy) along with the support for adopting tax and price policies that would assist agriculture did not appear in the final document in the same detail as the draft version. The final report alluded broadly to the importance of mobilizing capital resources for rural development. The draft report's reference to raising funds from foreign and domestic sources to finance selective development of heavy industry was dropped from the final text. This final document spoke of the need to encourage logical urban development rather than changes that could lead to megacities, an issue that was not mentioned in the draft text.

The draft report warned that the relationship between domestic and external capital must be handled with flexibility, a message that did not appear in the final report. The final text urged that priority be accorded to importing goods that abetted the production of exportable items and that reasonable policies to protect domestic production be put in place, two points not articulated in the draft document.

Both the draft and the final version were clear about the leading role that the state sector should play in the economy, together with cooperative sectors, but the final version emphasized that all businesses and individuals should be "equal in rights and responsibilities before the law." Where the draft plan asserted a commitment to steadily carry out the equitization of state enterprises, the final report reflected a commitment to "review the development of a steady plan for equitization." The final report, more than the draft, addressed the importance of enforcing the law on cooperatives and stressed the state's role in mobilizing capital, technology, and management skills.

The report adopted by the congress was more specific than the draft about controlling illegal trade activities. Both the draft and the final versions of the report stressed financial reform and reform of tax programs, but the final report called for the organization of a system of people's credit funds, close supervision of commercial and foreign banks, active measures to reduce interest rates, the consolidation of national reserves, and the reform of reserve mechanisms and price stabilization funds. The final report was also more explicit about the legal exercise of state management prerogatives, especially concerning publicly owned state assets, and the prohibition on ministerial and administrative interference in business management.

The final version of the report added more to section nine — on achieving national unity — and on the subject of women, including a set of special pledges to provide vocational training, enhanced health care, and increased positions in party and state agencies for women. The final report also contained a reiteration of religious freedoms as guaranteed by state law, and reference to the overseas Vietnamese as "an integral part of the Vietnamese nation," items that were absent from the draft document. While the draft report was not at all explicit on the subject, the final version unequivocally forbade party members to conduct private capitalist economic activities "either personally or through their relatives." That is interesting because the first article of chapter one of the revised statutes — on party members — repeated the admonition that members must refrain from exploitative activities, an all-inclusive umbrella of sins that might have been intended to accommodate the requirement that party members refrain from becoming involved in private enterprise, but did not do so in explicit terms. That provision, and rumors suggesting that a much more explicit enunciation of the limits on party members regarding market activities would make its way into the revised statutes, had apparently attracted a good deal of criticism during the congress, so much so that the general secretary was said to have signaled his support for an arrangement under which the families of party members would be allowed to participate in the economy as private entrepreneurs, while party members themselves could not engage in private enterprise.[11] Lastly, the final political report went beyond the draft report's emphasis on cultivating a body of qualified inspection officials and asserted that "special attention should be paid to the task of internal political protection within the party," perhaps a reference to the work of the Central Internal Political Protection Committee (Ban Bao Ve Chinh Tri Noi Bo Trung Uong), charged with conducting investigative work pertaining to senior party officials.

The final version of the draft report did not deviate much from the text publicized in April, suggesting that, except for the nuances of economic priorities, social issues, the esoteria of party, and government reform, the central problems with the party's vision of its mandate had been smoothed over between May and late June. The political report did not, however, explain the thinking behind the elimination of the Secretariat, even though it did address superficially questions concerning central party organization. Nor did the report dwell on any of the issues pertaining to provincial party leadership and organization, matters that must have struck party officials as areas ripe for review, especially in the light of the early lapses of the provincial and basic party organizations in the context of preparatory meetings and congresses.

The Revised Party Statutes

The final version of the revised laws of the party that were presented to the Eighth Congress had the effect of concentrating authority in the hands of the Politburo, relieving the Central Committee of some of the responsibility reserved for that body by the 1991 statutes and defining a deciding role for the Politburo. This role was to include the determination to establish new party organizations, and matters of membership standards, the management of party finances, and the administration of intra-party disciplinary measures, among others.

The following are examples of these revised laws:

> 1. Whereas article 3, chapter 1, of the 1991 statute accorded party members the right to elect members, run for or be appointed to leading party organizations at various levels "in accordance with the regulations of the Central Committee," the 1996 statute conferred this right on the basis of Politburo regulations (article 3, section 2, 1996 statute).

> 2. Article 4, chapter 1, of the 1996 statute stipulated that problems regarding the political background (*lich su chinh tri*) of applicants for party membership would be resolved in accordance with the regulations (*qui dinh*) of the Politburo. The 1991 statute provided that such matters would be handled in accordance with rules established by the Central Committee.

> 3. Both the 1991 and the 1996 statutes described the chapter and committee processes of adjudicating applications for membership in virtually the same terms, except that the 1996 text specified that special cases would be resolved by the Politburo (article 4, section 3, chapter 1, 1996 statute).

> 4. Article 6 of the 1996 statute conferred responsibilities regarding the issuance of party membership cards, the supervision of membership records, and procedures governing transfers to the Politburo, whereas the 1991 version of article 6 delegated these responsibilities to the Central Committee.

> 5. Article 10, chapter 2, in the 1996 revision directed the Politburo to assume responsibility for setting up party organizations "in places with unique characteristics" (*o nhung noi co dac diem rieng*), a task reserved for the Central Committee in the 1991 statute.

4. The Eighth Party Congress

6. In Chapter 2, article 2, of the 1996 statute the Politburo was given a role in articulating the regulations governing the nomination of delegates by party organizations "operating under special conditions," responsibilities that had been assigned to the Central Committee in the 1991 statute.

7. In the 1991 statute, the Central Committee's guidance was the critical variable in determining the size of party committees and the number of Central Committee seats and Control Committee positions, while the 1996 statute (articles 12 and 20) transferred that role to the Politburo.

Thus, the 1996 statute relocated the center of decisionmaking authority upward, conferring a larger role on the Politburo, and trimming the areas where the Central Committee played a significant role in accordance with the 1991 party laws. In fact, the 1996 statute's article 16 on the duties of the Central Committee had less to say about that body's power and responsibilities than the 1991 statute (article 18).

The 1996 law eliminated the requirement that the Central Committee manage relations with foreign communist parties and national liberation movements, dropped the 1991 statute's words assigning responsibility for defining cadre standards to the Central Committee, removed the task of running party finances from the Central Committee's list of duties, and eliminated the portion of article 18 that required the Central Committee to forward a biannual situation assessment to lower committees. Article 46, chapter 11, on party finances reserved for the Politburo the right to "stipulate unified principles and systems for the management of the party's finances, assets and dues paid by party members," a function that the 1991 statute had assigned to the Central Committee (article 45, chapter 11, 1991 revision).

The 1996 revisions codified the purview of the newly created Standing Committee in a manner that pressed the locus of decisionmaking upward, closer to the Politburo. Section 1 of article 17 tersely assigned the duty of appointing a Standing Committee to the Politburo, and section 3 elaborated on the committee's duties. The Standing Committee assumed the Secretariat's responsibility for managing the party's routine and daily business and for staffing the issues requiring consideration by the Politburo, but the Standing Committee was assigned a much broader mandate relating to defense and security, economic development, foreign policy, and party building.

While the Secretariat was empowered to run party organizations and oversee membership policies, as well as being charged with the authority to issue resolutions and directives to accomplish those goals, the Standing Committee was not granted the ability to speak authoritatively to lower-level party organizations through resolutions and directives. So, while the Central Committee determined policies and the Politburo was the ultimate decisionmaking group, the Standing Committee functioned through its authority to review policy implementation, to organize the process of Politburo-level deliberations, and to direct the implementation of Politburo decisions concerning economics, defense, security, and party organization matters.

Importantly, article 28 of chapter 6 of the 1996 statutes on the party organizations in the army and the People's Security Force established for the first time a Party Central Committee Public Security Committee, duplicating the structure and function of the Military Committee. The 1991 statute did not go beyond stating that party organizations in the Public Security Force were determined by the Central Committee (article 31). The 1996 statute placed the power to appoint members to both the Military Committee and the Public Security Committee in the hands of the Politburo (articles 26 and 28). The 1991 party laws granted the Central Committee appointment powers regarding the Military Party Committee (article 29).

Other changes in the party's laws simplified reporting requirements[12]; clarified the authority of party committees to conduct congresses and interim meetings[13]; more stringently defined the discretion of the party chapters over issues such as the formation of cells and party membership recruitment[14]; and offered more exacting rules governing disciplinary measures that could be applied to party members and organizations.[15]

The Politburo

The 19-member Politburo consisted of nine newly elected officials and ten incumbents, two of whom were elevated to Politburo membership at the January 1994 midterm conference. Five of those elected to the Politburo at the Seventh Congress did not reclaim their seats at the July 1996 Congress. Dao Duy Tung was retired because of a serious infirmity. Nguyen Ha Phan who was added to the mid-term party conference in January 1994, was dropped from the Politburo in April, during the Tenth Plenum. Vo Tran Chi stepped down from his post as Ho Chi Minh City party secretary and relinquished his Politburo seat and Central Committee status in July. Le Phuoc Tho and Vu Oanh were also not reelected to the Politburo. Though Pham The Duyet retired as Hanoi party secretary in mid–May 1996, he retained his position on the Politburo and his Central Committee status. Nguyen Dinh Tu died on 28 June, shortly after being elected to the Politburo. The party preserved his place in the roster of elected officials that was publicized on the last day of the congress. Two Central Committee department deputies, the party secretaries from Ho Chi Minh City and Hanoi, two deputy interior ministers, a deputy minister of defense, and a deputy prime minister, along with former Hanoi Party Committee secretary Pham The Duyet and Nguyen Dinh Tu, filled out the lower 10 positions in the 19-member Politburo (see table 1).

Two deputy ministers from the Interior Ministry, Le Minh Huong (number 16) and Nguyen Tan Dung (number 19), were elected to the Politburo at the Eighth Congress. In contrast, the Seventh Central Committee included only one deputy interior minister, Bui Thien Ngo, who was subsequently elevated to ministerial rank. Phieu, who occupied the fifth seat on the Politburo, outranked Minister of Defense General Doan Khue, who was sixth in the lineup.

The military took three Politburo seats, two more than in 1991. Khue and Phieu were joined by Lieutenant General Pham Van Tra, deputy defense minister and director of the General Staff Department, who was ranked eleventh. In effect, the military's share of influence as a percentage of total Politburo seats went from 8 per-

Table 1. The Politburo Lineup: From the Sixth to the Eighth Congress

6th Politburo	7th Politburo	8th Politburo
Nguyen Van Linh	Do Muoi	Do Muoi
Pham Hung	Le Duc Anh	Le Duc Anh
Vo Chi Cong	Vo Van Kiet	Vo Van Kiet
Do Muoi	Dao Duy Tung	Nong Duc Manh
Vo Van Kiet	Doan Khue	Le Kha Phieu
Le Duc Anh	Vu Oanh	Doan Khue
Nguyen Duc Tam	Le Phuoc Tho	Phan Van Khai
Nguyen Co Thach	Phan Van Khai	Nguyen Manh Cam
Dong Sy Nguyen	Bui Thien Ngo	Nguyen Duc Binh
Tran Xuan Bach	Nong Duc Manh	Nguyen Van An
Nguyen Thanh Binh	Pham The Duyet	Pham Van Tra
Doan Khue	Nguyen Duc Binh	Tran Duc Luong
Mai Chi Tho	Vo Tran Chi	Nguyen Thi Xuan My
Dao Duy Tung		Truong Tan Sang
		Le Xuan Tung
		Le Minh Huong
		Nguyen Dinh Tu
		Pham The Duyet
		Nguyen Tan Dung

Note: The plenary communiqué preceding the January 1994 mid-term party conference announced the election of four additional Politburo members: Le Kha Phieu; Nguyen Manh Cam, Do Quang Thang, and Nguyen Ha Phan.

---

cent in 1991, to 12 percent in 1994, and then to 16 percent in 1996. Nong Duc Manh, the chairman of the National Assembly, ranked fourth in the lineup, rising from the tenth place that he held in the Seventh Central Committee, displacing Dao Duy Tung, the fourth-ranking member of the Politburo elected at the Seventh Congress. Deputy Prime Minister Phan Van Khai rose one step above his 1991 status, to seventh place in the lineup, and newly elected Deputy Prime Minister Tran Duc Luong was seated in twelfth place on the Politburo that emerged from the Eighth Congress proceedings. Foreign Minister Nguyen Manh Cam, elected to the Politburo at the 1994 interim conference, was reelected in 1996. He moved into the eighth slot, one rank above incumbent Nguyen Duc Binh, director of the Ho Chi Minh National Political Institute, formerly the Nguyen Ai Quoc Academy.

THE CONTROL COMMITTEE

The Control Committee was reduced by two seats, to seven members, of whom four were holdovers from the Seventh Central Committee's Control Committee. Five members of the Control Committee selected at the Seventh Congress (Do Quang Thang, Le Van Kien, Nguyen Duc Thieu, Tran Huu Dac, and Ha Tuan Trung) were dropped from the committee at the Eighth Congress. Three newcomers (Nguyen Van Tham, Hoang Kim Son, and Nguyen Minh Nien), none of whom were elected to the Central Committee, joined the Control Committee at the Eighth Congress. Three of the four holdovers (Nguyen Thi Xuan My, Truong Vinh Trong, and Vu Quoc Hung) were elected to the Eighth Central Committee, and Nguyen Thi Xuan My became a Politburo member, the first women elected to that body in VNCP history. The Control Committee elected at the Seventh Congress did not include a Politburo member. My's designation as the Control Committee chair signaled the Politburo's renewed attentiveness to enforcing discipline and laws governing party activities and membership behavior (see table 2).

Table 2. The Control Committee: From the Seventh to the Eighth Congress

7th Congress	8th Congress
Do Quang Thang	Nguyen Thi Xuan My
Le Van Kien	Truong Vinh Trong
Truong Vinh Trong	Vu Quoc Hung
Nguyen Thi Xuan My	Nguyen Van Tham
Nguyen Duc Thieu	Nguyen Anh Lien
Vu Quoc Hung	Hoang Kim Son
Tran Huu Dac	Nguyen Minh Nien
Nguyen Anh Lien	
Ha Tuan Trung	

The Standing Committee

There was much speculation on the motivation for reconfiguring the Politburo and eliminating the Secretariat. It was not immediately apparent that the new setup would help nudge the party toward generational change in the ranks of the leadership, making room for younger, more specialized officials with practical policy experience and technical competence. Given the council of elders' flavor to the composition of the Standing Committee, there was some basis for the argument that the Politburo would reconcentrate authority in the hands of the revolutionary veterans, leaving less opportunity for extra-party influences to make their views felt at the VNCP's highest levels, and little chance that the topmost party leadership could provide for mobility in the way that the Secretariat did, by seating Central Committee members and experts alongside Politburo leaders.

The elimination of the Secretariat may have been a reaction to the concentration of power in the hands of the party's workhorse, though it struck some delegates, including Tran Trong Tan, that the Standing Committee ran counter to the practice of democratic centralism, and itself represented a concentration of power that exceeded the authority vested in the Politburo.[16] Alternatively, the decision to replace the Secretariat with a standing committee could have been a reaction to the Secretariat's inability to provide the kind of management the Politburo felt it needed. It could have been a response to the imbalance in rank between the body charged with acting on behalf of the Politburo and the Politburo membership itself, or perhaps the collapse of a decade of efforts to equip cadre to perform secretarial functions, indicated by many years of criticism of the failure of specialized training efforts to form a reservoir of cadre capable of undertaking the daily management of the party policy process.

The party did not shed much light on the reason the Secretariat was abolished and a standing committee established in its place. Prior to the National Congress, Do Phuong, the head of the Vietnamese News Agency, told Western reporters that too rapid a change in the leadership could be unsettling for the Vietnamese people.

That explanation of why the leadership shifts would be modest suggested that the party placed a primacy on achieving stability and continuity in the leadership equation at the same time it was injecting new blood into the system. Creating the Standing Committee may have been thought of as a means of signaling that the changes in the texture of the party's leadership would not be dramatic, startling, or destabilizing.

One hint at how the party was thinking of this institutional change came in the form of mid–May comments by Le Xuan Tung, the newly elected secretary of the Hanoi party committee, to a correspondent from *Hanoi Moi* on the city's executive committee and the standing committee. Tung told his interviewers that the city's executive committee represented "quality and competence," characterized as they were by a higher level of education, diversity, and experience, indicated by the reelection of the eleventh party committee incumbents. The new committee, Tung stated, drew together representatives from "various departments, sectors, mass organizations, districts, and grassroots establishments," lending a "comprehensive character" to the new Hanoi executive committee.

In contrast, the 15-member Hanoi Party Committee Standing Committee elected by the new executive committee represented a larger body than previous standing committees and contained a more even mix of old, middle-aged, and young officials "to ensure different age groups in party committee echelons and guarantee succession and continuity to avoid a cadre gap in the future."[17] It did not seek ethnic, regional, and sexual diversity in its composition, or try to guarantee a concentration of educated and specialized talent with college training and university degrees. Rather, the Hanoi Party's Standing Committee was aimed at balancing generations and taking active measures to guarantee succession.

It is possible to look at the Politburo's Standing Committee as an attempt to bring together two or three generations of senior leaders who would act on behalf of the whole Politburo between formal sessions. That committee would function more as a body intent on grooming top-level leadership for the highest post by coupling the youngest senior leader (Nguyen Tan Dung) and the middle generation that came of age during the war for independence (Le Kha

Phieu) with the founding fathers (Do Muoi, Vo Van Kiet, and Le Duc Anh), and charging those five with handling the everyday affairs and policy decisions for the entire Politburo, which would then be free to become immersed in fundamental policy, strategy, and long-term planning, rather than merely vetting secretarial decisions.

The Secretariat had grown larger over the years, and perhaps had become unwieldy, generating a need for larger staffs, specialized personnel resources of its own, and encouraging a trend toward increasingly bureaucratic interactions with Central Committee departments and government ministries. Some of this is suggested in the way the responsibilities of the Secretariat evolved over time. In the 1968 party statutes the Secretariat was granted oversight responsibilities for the everyday work of the party and control over the work of implementing party resolutions under the leadership of the Central Committee and the Politburo.[18] In the 1977 statutes, the Secretariat was referred to as the body charged with handling the party's daily work, directing the work of party organizations, and coordinating among organizations to ensure the implementation of resolutions issued by the Central Committee and the Politburo.[19] In the 1987 revisions of the statutes the Secretariat's role were expressed in language that suggested a more activist, authoritative role in the bureaucratic world. The Secretariat was responsible for leading, not just handling, the party's daily work. Its special role in cadre work and party member work was highlighted in chapter 3, article 23 (1987). The Secretariat controlled the implementation of party resolutions, a more direct authority than the responsibility for coordinating among agencies with the goal of implementing and controlling resolutions.[20] Finally, the 1991 revisions widened the Secretariat's mandate to include responsibility for party development, cadre work, and mass mobilization, as well as the preparation of issues for presentation to the Politburo.[21] Media commentary in late January 1996 on the draft revisions of the party statutes noted that early in the process of preparing draft revisions for presentation to the preparatory party congresses, the party center wanted to divide the Secretariat's functions between the Politburo—which would have been granted a hand in cadre organization and preparations for plenary sessions, reporting to the Central Committee during plenary meetings — and the Standing Committee of the Politburo — which would have assumed the job of the Secretariat. This media commentary defined the Standing Committee's responsibilities as supervising and controlling the implementation of resolutions, undertaking actions related to party- and cadre-related tasks, and the additional responsibility of the guiding implementation of policy in the realm of socioeconomic issues, national defense, and foreign affairs.[22]

Section 3, article 17, of the 1996 revised party statutes indicated that the Standing Committee had assumed the Secretariat's responsibility for managing the party's routine and daily business and for staffing the issues requiring consideration by the Politburo. However, while the Secretariat was empowered to run party organizations and oversee membership policies — as well as charged with the authority to issue resolutions and directives to accomplish those goals — the Standing Committee was not granted the ability to speak authoritatively to lower-level party organizations through resolutions and directives. This may have been an indication of the extent to which elements in the party were ill at ease with the decision to concentrate the equivalent of the Secretariat's authority under the 1991 statutes in a subset of the Politburo itself. Alternatively, opponents of the concept of a standing committee may have merely taken exception to the manner in which the revision of the statutes and the consequent elimination of the Secretariat were managed in the period prior to the National Congress. According to middle-level Vietnamese officials, on the last day of the congress the head of the Central Committee's Ideology and Culture Department, Tran Trong Tan, objected that the authority invested in the Standing Committee was excessive. His recommendation to the delegates that the new body not be granted decisionmaking authority distinct from the whole Politburo was accepted by the Eighth Congress. The purview of the Standing Committee was limited in a manner that defused the argument over its being a "Super Politburo." The final version of the Standing Committee left it without the power to decide critical policy issues on its own. The harder issues would be referred to the whole Politburo for a decision. The Standing Committee remained the manager of the Politburo's daily business, running the bureaucratic life of the Politburo between sessions. Middle-level officials suggested that the decision to eliminate the Secretariat was a result of the party's diminishing comfort level with a body that, over the years, had aggregated a good deal of power and moved beyond merely running the administrative side of things on a daily basis to making decisions. The head of the External Relations Department of the Central Committee, Hong Ha, and Le Kha Phieu had risen beyond the role envisioned for individuals in their positions.[23]

THE CENTRAL COMMITTEE

The Eighth Congress elected a Central Committee consisting of 170 members: 68 government officials (ministers, deputy ministers, general department directors, and state corporation heads); 7 university chancellors and research institute and college officials; 48 party officials (Central Committee department directors and deputies, provincial and municipal party secretaries, Central Committee office directors, and chiefs of party institutes); 31 officials "dual hatted" as both provincial party committee secretaries and people's committee chairs; plus 16 military officers (military region commanders, general department heads, and service representatives).

Ninety-seven of the 170 members were newly elected and 73 were incumbents. In 1991 incumbents from the ranks of government, central party officials, and provincial secretaries outnumbered new members, and military incumbents were roughly equal in number to newly elected military professionals. In 1996 there were almost twice as many new Central Committee members from the ranks of provincial party secretaries as there were incumbents. Military officers who were newcomers to the Eighth Central Committee outnumbered incumbents by 4:1. However, incumbents whose primary jobs were in the government bureaucracy held eight more Central Committee seats than did new members from the ranks of the state bureaucracy. An equal number of newcomers and incumbents from the ranks of central party officials were elected to the Eighth Central Committee. Real growth in institutional influence and generational leadership change was taking place first in the ranks of the military, where new Central Committee members had grown the fastest, and then among the provincial party secretaries, where new members had increased more modestly from the 1991 Congress (see table 3).

Table 3. Composition of Seventh and Eighth Central Committees

	1991		1996	
	New	Incumbent	New	Incumbent
GOVT	14 (9.6%)	46 (31.5%)	30 (17.6%)	38 (22.4%)
PARTY	6 (4.1%)	13 (8.9%)	9 (5.3%)	9 (5.3%)
PROV	12 (8.2%)	27 (18.4%)	19 (11.2%)	11 (6.5%)
DUAL	7 (4.8%)	6 (4.1%)	20 (11.8%)	11 (6.5%)
MILITARY	6 (4.1%)	5 (3.4%)	13 (7.6%)	3 (1.8%)
ACADEMIC	1 (.7%)	3 (2.1%)	6 (3.5%)	1 (.6%)

Approximately 40 percent of the Central Committee elected in 1991 were party officials. In contrast, about 47 percent of the 1996 Central Committee were party officials, including provincial party secretaries (18 percent), Central Committee members who were "dual hatted" as party secretaries and people's committee chairs, and Central Committee department officials, party media representatives, and Central Committee office managers (11 percent). Thirty percent of the Central Committee were party secretaries, 33 percent of whom were incumbents (10 percent of the total Central Committee), and 66 percent of whom were newly elected (20 percent of the total Central Committee). Oddly, two former party secretaries (Do Van An of the Son La Province Party Committee and Pham The Duyet of the Hanoi Party Committee) were elected to the Central Committee. The only deputy secretary elected to the Central Committee was from Gia Lai Province, and Ha Tinh Province did not place anyone on the committee. Seven deputy provincial party committee secretaries were elected to the Central Committee at the Eighth Congress, amounting to 4 percent of the total Central Committee membership. Twelve deputies were elected to the Central Committee in 1991, representing 8 percent of the membership. While incumbent deputy party secretaries outnumbered new members in 1991, the reverse was true in 1996. Incumbent deputy secretaries declined as a percentage of the Central Committee between 1991 (5 percent) and 1996 (1 percent). Newcomers from the ranks of deputy provincial party committee secretaries also declined as a percentage of the Central Committee between 1991 (4 percent) and 1996 (3 percent), but less steeply than was the case for incumbents. The party's conscious effort to infuse new blood into the Central Committee was not to be accomplished by promoting second stringers from within the party's provincial organizations (see table 4).

Table 4. Provincial Party Deputy Secretaries — Incumbents and Newcomers — Elected to the Seventh and the Eighth Central Committees

	Newcomers	Incumbents
Seventh Congress	5 (3.4%)	7 (4.8%)
Eighth Congress	5 (2.9%)	2 (1.2%)

Provincial secretaries — minus the number who were dual hatted — declined as a percentage of the Central Committee from the Seventh to the Eighth Congress, from 27 percent in 1991 to 18 percent in 1996. Central party bureaucrats decreased from 14 percent of the Seventh Congress membership to 11 percent of the Eighth Congress membership. Dual hatted officials, with one foot in the realm of the provincial party bureaucracy and the other in the world of provincial governance, rose from about 9 percent of the Central Committee's membership in 1991 to about 18 percent in 1996.

The percentage of military professionals in the Central Committee rose only slightly and insignificantly from about 8 percent in 1991 to 9 percent in 1996. Of the 11 military officials elected to the

Central Committee in 1991, 6 were newcomers and 5 were Sixth Central Committee incumbents. Of the 16 military officials elected to the Central Committee at the Eighth Congress, 13 were new members and 3 were incumbents. While incumbents from the ranks of military professionals fell from just above 3 percent of the Seventh Central Committee to less than 2 percent of the Eighth Central committee, newcomers in uniform rose as a percentage of the Central Committee membership, from slightly above 4 percent in 1991 to almost 8 percent of the Eighth Central Committee (see table 5).

Table 5. Military Professionals in the Central Committee: From the Seventh to the Eighth Congress

	Seventh Congress	Eighth Congress
Incumbents	5 (3.4%)	3 (1.8%)
Newcomers	6 (4.1%)	13 (7.6%)

The makeup of the security ministries—the ministries of Defense, Interior, and Foreign Affairs—changed from the rough parity between the three ministries in 1991 to a situation in 1996 where the Foreign Ministry had more Central Committee members than Defense and Interior separately, and only one less member than the later two ministries together. This equation was the reverse of the Seventh Congress's makeup, where the Defense Ministry had one more member on the Central Committee than Interior and Foreign Affairs. Interestingly, the Foreign Ministry and Interior fielded a newer membership than Defense (see table 6).

Twelve ministers and 19 deputy ministers were elected to the Eighth Central Committee, a ratio that resulted in part from retirement or dismissal of senior ministers who were not replaced prior to the 1996 Congress. In 1996 deputy ministers accounted for 4 percent more of the Central Committee membership than did ministers. Key ministries such as Interior, Commerce, and Finance were not represented on the Central Committee.

Among the economic ministries, only two of the six ministers

Table 6. The Security Ministries from the Seventh to the Eighth Congress

	Seventh Congress			Eighth Congress		
	New	Inc	Total	New	Inc	Total
Foreign Ministry	1	2	3	1	3	4
Interior Ministry	1	2	3	1	2	3
Defense Ministry	1	3	4	0	2	2

elected to the Eighth Central Committee were joined on that body by their deputies: Agriculture and Rural Development, and Marine Products placed both the number one and number two ministerial officials on the committee. The ministers of Building; Communications and Transportation; Industry; and Science, Technology, and Environment were elected to the Central Committee, but none of their deputies made the grade. In contrast, four ministries — Commerce, Finance, Trade, and Planning — placed only deputy ministers on the Central Committee. In the case of the Planning Ministry, four deputies were elected in 1996. Ministerial-level representation for the economic ministries dropped slightly in 1996, but the number of deputy ministers elected to the Central Committee rose threefold. The number of ministers elected to the Central Committee from the social ministries — Public Health; Culture and Information; Labor, War Invalids, and Social Welfare; Education and Training; and Youth and Sports — remained unchanged from 1991 to 1996, and the number of deputies placed on the Central Committee in 1996 increased by only one over the 1991 number (see table 7).

The National Assembly made some gains in influence, placing three new members on the Central Committee alongside of the three incumbents who were elected at the Seventh Congress. Seven academic and research administrators were elected to the Central Committee in 1996. The only incumbent in the group was Nguyen Duy

Table 7. Ministerial-level Representation on the Central Committee: From the Economic, Social, and Security Ministries, 1991–96

Ministries	Ministers		Deputy Ministers	
	7th	8th	7th	8th
Economic	8	6	3	9
Social	4	4	2	3
Security	2	2	9	7

Quy, director of the National Center of Social Sciences and Humanities (who was elected to the Seventh Central Committee with the position of deputy director of the party's Commission for Science and Education). The deputy chancellors of Hanoi National University, the Ho Chi Minh National Institute of Politics, and the Ho Chi Minh City University, as well as the directors of the Institute of Economics of the National Center of Social Sciences and Humanities, Hanoi Polytechnic College, and Hanoi Commercial College, were named to the Central Committee for the first time. In 1991 three incumbent representatives of academic institutions (the directors of the Institute of Sciences, the Marxist-Leninist Institute, and the Nguyen Ai Quoc Institute) and one newcomer (deputy director of the Institute of Sciences) were named to the Central Committee. Five new members from national-level mass organizations joined three incumbents first elected to the Central Committee at the Sixth Congress and one holdover from the Seventh Congress on the Eighth Central Committee.

Conclusions

The Central Committee elected by the 1996 Eighth Party Congress was characterized by a number of eccentricities in composition, as well as some deliberate attempts to reflect priority requirements for qualified specialists, to inject younger blood into the Central Committee mainstream, and to select cohorts of leaders focused on critical social and developmental issues. The Eighth Congress elected two former provincial party secretaries to the Central Committee and one representative of an ethnic organization (Lam Phu, deputy chief of the Nam Bo Khmer People's Representation), but failed to elect any ambassador or friendship group association officials, another minor but noticeable departure from prior patterns. In 1991 then ambassador to the Soviet Union, Nguyen Manh Cam, earned his Central Committee seat. A small group of prominent friendship association representatives were elected to the Fifth and Sixth congresses.

In view of the regime's concerted effort to establish a body of law to govern Vietnam in the midst of its economic reforms and the party's attempt to emphasize statutes and other legal guidelines as the starting point for institutional behavior, legal specialists were curiously underrepresented on the Eighth Central Committee. Pham Hung, president of the People's Supreme Court, elected to the Central Committee for the first time at the Sixth Congress in 1986, was the only representative of the judicial apparatus elected to the Seventh Central Committee in 1991. In 1996 only Ha Minh Tri, who was elected to the Central Committee at the January 1994 interim party conference, and Nguyen Van Yeu represented the regime's legal institutions on the Central Committee in their capacities as director and deputy director of the National Assembly Legislative Committee, respectively. Nguyen Ngoc Hien, Minister of Justice, who assumed that portfolio in 1992, was not named to the Central Committee at either the interim conference in 1994 or the 1996 National Congress.

In 1996 only one provincial party committee standing committee member — Pham Thi Son, a member of the Ba Ria–Vung Tau Standing Committee and the chair of the provincial party organization's Mass Mobilization Committee — was elected to the Eighth Central Committee. No district party secretaries or people's committee chairs were elevated to Central Committee status at the 1996 party meeting. In contrast, in 1991 three district party committee secretaries and one lone people's committee chair from Hoang Lien

Son Province were elected to the Central Committee, an imbalance that was curious in light of the party's commitment to lowering the average age of Central Committee members and introducing younger members. The party center may have turned away from that layer of bureaucrats because of the deficiencies some revealed by the provincial committees in the course of conducting preparatory congresses.

Three election trends telegraphed the party's serious commitment to social issues, education, and the status of the state enterprises.

Two officials with primary responsibility for social issues were elected to the Eighth Central Committee: Hoang Duc Nghi, an incumbent first elected at the Sixth Congress, who was chairman of the Nationalities and Mountain Region Committee of the National Assembly, and Nguyen Thi Hoai Thu, deputy chairman of the National Assembly for Social Issues. The minister and deputy minister for Labor, War Invalids, and Social Welfare; the deputy minister for Public Health; the minister for Youth and Sports; and the minister-director of the Committee for the Protection and Care of Children filled out the ranks of Eighth Central Committee personnel focused on social issues, exceeding the number of members elected to the Seventh Central Committee who focused on social policy.

Apart from university and research institute directors, the 1996 Central Committee included a group of government officials responsible for education, science, and technology policy. This group reflected the party's awareness of the need to cultivate technically specialized personnel, the importance of encouraging postgraduate studies, and the need to invigorate training programs and basic educational institutions. Seven Central Committee members — one newcomer and six incumbents — from the ranks of ministers and National Assembly committees joined the eight representatives of educational and research facilities, together amounting to about nine percent of the Central Committee membership.

In 1991 the Sixth Party Congress alternate Central Committee member, Tran Thi Duong, deputy director general of the Union of Textile Enterprises, was the only representative of an enterprise elected to the Central Committee. In January 1994, at the interim party conference, Vo Van Cuong, a Hanoi Party Committee Standing Committee member and head of the Hanoi Electronics Company, was elected to the Central Committee. In 1996 the Congress elected five directors of general corporations or enterprise unions — largely and perhaps symbolically from critical sectors with an impact on national security interests: steel, coal, railway transport, power, and food — as a means of reinforcing the party's continued devotion to state-owned enterprises, and emphasizing the continuing importance the state sector would wield in the economic realm, even as market experiments and other economic reforms proceeded.

The Eighth Congress did not represent a path breaking act of leadership renewal, but it was the first major step in introducing a younger cadre into the ranks of the senior leadership. Significant numbers of incumbents kept their Central Committee seats, though newcomers to the Eighth Congress exceeded the number of first-term members elected to the Central Committee in 1991. The average age of the Eighth Central Committee was about 55 years, 10 years younger than the average Seventh Central Committee member. However, that average age did not ensure that a majority of the Central Committee would be able to serve two terms without exceeding the 55-year age cap decreed for Central Committee members at the Eighth Congress.

The 1996 National Party Congress did not result in a massive turnover of central party officials, provincial party secretaries, government bureaucrats or dual hatted officials on the Central Committee. While turnover rates were appreciable, there was no overwhelming bias against incumbents. The least amount of renewal took place in the ranks of party bureaucrats who served the central mechanisms of the VNCP. The Eighth Central Committee seated fewer secondary-level party functionaries and state bureaucrats than the Seventh Congress. The Eighth Congress seated a higher number officials who held collateral appointments in the provincial party apparatus and the provincial governing bureaucracy, suggesting the increasing relevance of officials straddling both realms.

To at least some reform-minded government officials, both Do Muoi's speech and the political report seemed to have fallen short of the expectation that the congress would enshrine renovation in a dramatic, unequivocal manner. These officials, who tended to be young, cosmopolitan, well-educated, and long-time civil servants, thought that the congress would support a course that would make Vietnam a country of laws and not concentrated power or random authority, enlarge the leeway for market forces, and reaffirm the legal status of private and mixed economic enterprises. However, the congress took a more conservative approach and placed its faith in a system that remained essentially state-controlled, even as it granted the market some operating room. The congress called for the passage of new laws governing aspects of the economy but forbade party members to engage in market activities because commerce would stain and corrupt the party. Political reform was called for, still closely paired with economic renovation, but the system remained concerned with the possibility that such political reform would create countervailing powers or alternative means of organizing interests and galvanizing political views. The congress essentially restated the overwhelming authority of the party and its rightful status as the center of Vietnam's political universe.

Nevertheless, the key documents offered some consolation to leading-edge reformists, who in their reading of the documents and speeches glossed over the bureaucratic language and grasped at phrases that captured reformist values and goals. Many viewed the significant modifications made in the political report as a real victory, and a measure of the relative strength of rational, modernizing interests. Young, educated officials seemed attentive to the general secretary's characterization of continued weaknesses in state economic management and the disarray of production relations, especially in view of Muoi's repetition of the political report's evaluation of the effectiveness of the commodity-based multisectoral economy, performing under state management, and operating in accordance with socialist orientations.

It appears that Vietnamese government functionaries drew some satisfaction from the general secretary's generally favorable assessment of the implementation of the "renovation line." Such officials appeared similarly attentive to the portions of both the political report and the secretary's speech that noted serious shortcomings in the implementation of reform policies that threatened to weaken the party. They appeared to entertain some reservations regarding the reaffirmation of the leading role that the political report accorded to the state sector. The debate that took place during the course of the preparations for the congress (and among the delegates at the national meeting itself) did not dent the party's commitment to keeping the reforms firmly under the aegis of the state, and did not go nearly as far as some young government officials had hoped toward liberating the economy from the tyranny of state-operated enterprises. Though the party backed away from the draft report's position that state enterprises should account for 60 percent of the gross domestic product, and though reform-minded government functionaries viewed this as a rational step, there was a real sense that the congress did not go as far as it could have in an area where the state acted as more of an economic albatross than as a catalyst for growth and production. However, reform supporters were prepared to represent the party's decision to modify the language of the draft political report on the state enterprises as an example of the positive, proreform decisions the congress did make. Ultimately, reform supporters saw this as both a satisfying resolution to a troubling portion of the first draft document and an indication of the responsiveness of the system to their concerns.

Young officials who supported reform highlighted the general secretary's confirmation of the durability of the reforms as national policy, as well as the party's pledge to establish an environment in which enterprises and individuals could conduct business and extract dividends from such undertakings in accordance with laws applied equally to all economic sectors. Reform-minded bureaucrats viewed the general secretary's restatement of the need to curtail government intervention in the management of business enterprises as an acknowledgment that the party and the government should withdraw still further from any managerial role in the practical affairs of enterprises, allowing the market—and socialist ethics—to guide economic decisions.

5

Conclusion: The Congress and Change in the Vietnamese Political System

PREPARATORY MEETINGS

Local party committees of the Vietnamese Communist Party experienced disorderliness and confusion in the grassroots sessions and experimental congresses that prefaced the Eighth National Congress, replicating some of the disorganization that characterized the 1991 preparatory party sessions in advance of the Seventh Congress. In 1995, however, the party center was careful to limit the number or rounds of congresses that were convened by lower level organizations, to minimize the number of sessions conducted by superior echelons to review proceedings of local party committees, and to involve Central Committee members in providing guidance to local experimental congresses at an earlier stage and in a more public manner. In spite of earnest efforts to manage the process, local committee debates sprawled across issues in an unfocused manner, comments on the draft documents lacked the punch and specificity that was sought by the Central Committee, and drafts of local party reports did not meet Central Committee standards.

In 1995 and 1996 the preparatory congresses progressed in fits and starts, and local party organizations performed unevenly in organizing elections and orchestrating critical evaluations of the draft documents for the Eighth Congress. Basic level organizations and municipal committees interpreted Central Committee directives in a fashion far from uniform or consistent. At critical junctures the Secretariat and various Central Committee departments issued correcting instructions aimed at putting the conduct of basic congresses back on track. The involvement of Politburo-level officials in shaping the process, defining agenda items, and contributing guidance to outcomes appears to have had minimum or mixed impact on the process of conducting preparatory congresses as it unfolded from the basic to the provincial committee level.

THE CONGRESS

The Eighth National Party Congress restated the core values of Vietnamese communism and the wisdom of the reformist course, and reminded the party of the need to practice caution, preserve stability, and implement change prudently. The political report stressed the objectives of industrialization and modernization in the new development period and described the importance of efforts to eliminate much of Vietnam's hefty bureaucracy, eliminate subsidies for ailing state-operated firms, formulate laws and establish financial institutions, clarify monetary policies, establish the conditions for effective state management of the market, and implement correct social policy.

The congress emphasized the indispensability of the party, fealty to Ho Chi Minh thought, the need to reform the organization and repair grassroots party structures, and defended an open-door foreign policy.

The congress (1) affirmed the importance of adhering to independence and socialism as twin goals in the process of renewal, emphasizing that renovation was not changing socialism but adopting a more correct view of socialism; (2) defined the appropriate balance and relationship between political and economic reform, emphasizing the need for stability and categorically rejecting pluralism and a multiparty system for Vietnam; (3) reiterated the need to match a shift toward market mechanisms with a strengthened role for the state in economic management; (4) restated the party's commitment to sustaining a broad-based coalition of interests as the foundation of popular support for reform; (5) defended the open-door foreign policy; and (6) stressed the need to address structural and leadership lapses in the party, arrest trends that threatened stability and organizational integrity, and preserve the revolutionary heritage of the party.

LEADERSHIP CHANGES

The Eighth National Party Congress added six new slots to the Politburo, which in turn elected a five-person Standing Committee that replaced the Secretariat. The congress elected a Central Committee consisting of 170 members, 36 seats more than the committee elected in 1991. Ninety-seven of the 170 members were newly elected and 73 were incumbents. While 54 percent of the Central Committee elected at the Eighth Congress were new members, only 31.5 percent of the Seventh Central Committee elected in 1991 were newcomers to that body.

In 1991 incumbents from the ranks of government, central party officials and provincial secretaries outnumbered new members, and military incumbents were roughly equal in number to new Central Committee members who were military professionals. In 1996 there were almost twice as many new Central Committee members from the ranks of provincial party secretaries as there were incumbents. Military officers who were newcomers to the Central Committee outnumbered incumbents by a ratio of more than 4:1. However, incumbents whose primary jobs were in the government bureaucracy held eight more Central Committee seats than did new members from the ranks of the state bureaucracy, and an equal number of newcomers and incumbents from the ranks of central party officials were elected to the Eighth Central Committee (see table 3, page 93). Real growth in institutional influence and generational leadership change was taking place first in the ranks of the military, where new Central Committee members had grown the fastest, and then among the provincial party secretaries, where new members had increased more modestly from the 1991 Congress.

INSTITUTIONAL CHANGE

The Standing Committee

The Standing Committee replaced the Secretariat, which had come to be the Central Committee's engine, powering activities between plenary sessions, staffing issues, sustaining the formidable paperwork necessary to keep the system communicating with its various parts, and issuing the resolutions and other operating instructions on which all authority rested. However, the Secretariat's mandate had spread beyond the management tasks intended by the earliest statutory descriptions of that entity. The Secretariat had come to represent a significant concentration of power that invested a small number of officials with an influence over policy that was out of proportion with the original purpose the Secretariat was intended to serve. The Eighth Congress attempted to reshape that equation by establishing a standing committee that was smaller that the Secretariat and that drew on Politburo members exclusively, eliminating the outsiders who had come to exercise influence beyond the originally intended managerial function defined for the party center's secretaries. Additionally, the final version of the revised laws of the party that were presented to the Eighth Congress had the effect of concentrating authority in the hands of the Politburo, relieving the Central Committee of some of the responsibility arrogated to that body by the 1991 statutes, and defining a deciding role for the Politburo in areas including the determination to establish new party organizations, membership standards, the management of party finances, and the administration of intraparty disciplinary measures.

Central Committee Blocs

Beginning during the precongress preparations, Central Committee blocs appeared to emerge as a new focal point. Bloc preparatory party congresses received greater press attention in the weeks before the congress. Additionally, bloc delegates played a more public role on the floor of the congress. The number of bloc delegates whose speeches were singled out for media attention climbed steadily from 1982 to 1996. During the Sixth Congress, one bloc representative's speech was signaled out for publication in *Nhan Dan*. During the Seventh Congress, the speeches of three bloc representatives were included in *Nhan Dan*'s coverage of delegates' speeches. During the Eighth Congress, six speeches made it into the pages of *Nhan Dan*.

In contrast, the number of delegates from provincial party organizations whose words to the congress were featured in press accounts of the party meeting declined from 1982 to 1991, leveling off at this diminished number during the Seventh and Eighth congresses. The number of representatives of central party organizations whose speeches received press coverage remained essentially steady from the Sixth to the Eighth congress, after falling off significantly during the Fifth Congress. Finally, whereas the media coverage of the delegate speeches to the Fifth, Sixth and Seventh congresses featured the words of some unique delegates — retired cadre, general corporation representatives, and enterprise heads — the Eighth Congress followed a stricter protocol, affording the distinction of press coverage to the speeches of mainstream bloc, provincial, or central party delegates. This is admittedly partial evidence, but it seems to suggest that party bloc officials were positioned to emerge as a repository of influence hitherto concentrated in the hands of other delegates.

Party Statute Revisions

Changes in the party's laws passed during the Eighth Congress simplified reporting requirements for party committee organizations. Provisions in the 1996 statutes clarified authority regarding the composition and activities of party committees and eliminated the option of a midterm session for organizations below the level of the party center. The disorganized performance of some basic party organizations in the round of congresses during the last half of 1995 and the first months of 1996, and the uneven conduct of provincial meetings during mid–1996, probably prompted the more exacting guidelines in the 1996 law governing the frequency with which basic party organization congresses of delegates should convene. The 1996 statute more stringently defined the terms according to which chapters or cells could be established and the rules governing discipline for party members and organization. This statute also made it somewhat easier to dissolve a party organization on the basis of a recommendation from a senior-echelon party committee and a decision from the next higher level.

The final version of the revised laws had the effect of concentrating authority in the hands of the Politburo, relieving the Central Committee of some of the responsibility assigned to that body by the 1991 statutes.

The 1996 law eliminated the requirement that the Central Committee focus on managing relations with foreign communist parties and national liberation movements, dropped the 1991 statute's words assigning responsibility for defining cadre standards and overall policy regarding cadre organization to the Central Committee, removed the task of running party finances from the Central Committee's list of duties, and eliminated the reporting requirement that mandated the Central Committee to forward a biannual situation assessment to lower committees.

These 1996 revisions defined a deciding role for the Politburo in certain areas, including the determination to establish new party organizations, membership standards, the management of party finances, and the administration of intraparty disciplinary measures. The revised party laws also required that the Politburo, as opposed to the Central Committee, be the arbitrating authority in the event of a disagreement over the terms of discipline or judgments of party organization or member culpability. In the 1996 statute the resolution of the following problems was placed in the hands of the Politburo: regarding the political background of applicants for party membership, the adjudication of special cases of chapter and committee applications for membership, the issuance and management of party membership cards, the supervision of membership records, responsibility for setting up party organizations "in places with unique characteristics," decisions regarding the number and distribution of delegates, and determinations regarding the size of standing boards and control committees.

The Interim Party Conference

The January 1994 interim conference provided the party with an opportunity to take stock of accomplishments at the halfway point in its tenure and to make necessary adjustments with sufficient time before the next national meeting to test those changes. The interim meeting also allowed for a restocking of the Central Committee, whose aging leaders were succumbing with increasing frequency. Finally, the midterm session provided the party with a means of injecting new blood under circumstances that enabled it to make judgments about the performance of these newcomers before they stood for election at the next congress that would entitle them to a full term as Central Committee members.

The 1996 party statute that was presented to the Central Committee at the Eighth Congress was somewhat more specific than the 1991 revisions regarding the terms under which an extraordinary session of the congress could be convened. The 1991 laws noted that in unspecified special cases a congress could be called sooner or later, but not later than one year beyond the normal five-year term. According to the 1996 revisions of the party statutes, an extraordinary congress could be called on the basis of a Central Committee determination that such a convocation was required or when more than half the subordinate party committee echelons requested such a session. This additional specificity about the convening of interim party congresses suggested that the party had decided to make the interim meeting a part of the political landscape because of the additional flexibility it afforded the party center in making decisions on leadership succession and managing increasingly complex policies.

THE PARTY UNDER DO MUOI

Muoi placed a primacy on achieving and sustaining consensus. To the general secretary the single most important part of the process was developing basic agreement over goals and practical aspects of the party's work through patient, often plodding exercises in building such consensus. Muoi worked to develop coordinated positions and to secure support in the government for programs and policy approaches. For example, he presented a case for an experimental shareholding system in state enterprises to the Third Plenum (June 1992) and to the Sixth Plenum (December 1993) that replicated the argument in favor of the approach made before the National Assembly by Vo Van Kiet, suggesting that he was fully aware of the need to build a constituency favorable to this particular plan before establishing it as policy.

The general secretary introduced into the conduct of routine Central Committee business — such as plenary sessions — a process of small group work that drew on the recommendations of participating technical specialists, unidentified scientific groups, "intellectuals at home and abroad" (possibly a reference to overseas Vietnamese investors, businessmen, and economists), and veterans, as well as the conventional assortment of party cadre, members, and party committee representatives in preparing specific policy assessments. Preparatory work for party meetings placed a primacy on canvasing all levels of committees and soliciting views from groups and interests whose input was not customarily sought, including scientists, specialized cadre, and representatives of mass organizations. Muoi openly acknowledged that the subject matter confronting the party was complex enough to exceed the limits of elected members of the Central Committee, and that the party center must increasingly rely on specialists.

Do Muoi believed that long-term, evolutionary progression and political renovation had begun with the Sixth Party Congress in 1986 and was still unfolding on the eve of the Eighth Congress. He argued that efforts to carry out economic reform revealed glaring weaknesses on the political side of the equation, prompting focused efforts to renovate the political system. To Muoi, the renovation process required that the system focus on repairing its structures, laws, and governing practices, not altering the nature of the political system but reforming existing processes. Muoi reinforced these views in the course of preparations for the National Congress and in his statements at the national party meeting. Echoing the message in the political report, Muoi stated that parallel, continuous improvements in government administration, party leadership and organization,

5. Conclusion: The Congress and Change

and cadre selection and training were critical to the success of the economic reform program.

Muoi was distressed that the earliest efforts to coax basic party organizations to conduct congresses and write political reports reflecting local conditions had foundered because fundamental-level party organizations were generally ill-equipped to address some of the policy issues and social problems that confronted local organizations. In rescheduling the final dates for basic and district party committee congresses and pushing back the expected time of completion for the provincial meetings, Muoi sought to maximize the possibility that local forces would be able to fashion some agreement on how to resolve their own most pressing issues, and that constructive consensus on preferred methods for attacking poverty, social crises, weaknesses in economic performance, and leadership lapses could be reached with minimal central party intervention. Though clearly prepared to lend guidance to provincial and sub-provincial entities when they strayed or broke the rules, Muoi's preference was to allow local creativity the leeway to fix local problems.

The general secretary's leadership nudged the party in the direction of reasoned, more sure-footed organizational responses to serious changes in its environment, including global political transition and economic change, parallel regional shifts, and changing local socioeconomic realities. Under Muoi the party trimmed reporting requirements, eliminated some types of meetings, and was more exacting in its definition of party committee responsibilities, chains of command, and decisionmaking authority. His aim was a Central Committee capable of policy-oriented deliberations and sharpened, more technically inclined dialogue about lingering economic problems and social issues, as well as a decisionmaking process relieved of some bureaucratic burdens, and plenaries less encumbered by obligations to intervene in local committee processes.

The party under Muoi took some steps aimed at reinvigorating its leadership, cleansing and strengthening the various components of the organization, and acknowledging the leverage and staying power of some of the social forces and economic interests spawned by ten years of economic reform. The party toyed with openness and transparency, waging a few more of its debates in a public manner and using electoral devices to make leadership choices at basic positions. The party sought a level of responsiveness to dissenting and minority views made compellingly by party members, as in the instance of the last-minute debate at the congress over the shape of the Standing Committee. Under Muoi's stewardship the party kept a flock of advisers and technicians busily employed in deliberating about solutions to social crises and economic problems, injected a shot of new blood into the Central Committee, and preserved a role for nonparty interests in some aspects of the process.

The Future of Renovation

It was not clear, though, just how much of a difference the reconstituted Politburo, the new Standing Committee, the group of young, newly elected Central Committee members, a platform that vigorously endorsed reforms, new institutional structures, and changing bureaucratic practices would make in terms of granting the party a new lease on life as an organization. By the Eighth Congress corruption had reached epidemic proportions, permeating all levels of the party. It was increasingly difficult for this institution to lay claim to status, rights, and privileges on the basis of its historic role in bringing independence to Vietnam, while candidates for Central Committee slots and provincial leadership roles barely met the VNCP's own standards of rectitude. Attempts to check the growth of the labyrinthine bureaucracy made little headway against a system whose answer to crisis was to invent more layers of bureaucracy. The leadership had bred a successor generation characterized in large part by uncertain skills, stifling caution, indifference, and incompetence, without providing for more than the trappings of succession.

The party's capacity to remake itself was limited, and there was a shortage of the political will necessary to go beyond the values and organizing devices that had long been the stock-in-trade of the VNCP. But circumstances had left the party without very many options. The party needed some successes in order to recruit and retain younger, better educated personnel and in order to reclaim credibility and legitimacy in ruling. It required better trained, technical cadre and members in order to invent clever policy fixes to address the social, economic, security, and political issues confronting Vietnam. Feints in the direction of openness and the halting steps toward reform in the political realm were not quite enough to rescue the party from the drift toward irrelevance.

Dramatic changes in the terrain in which the party functioned left the organization without a reliable compass. For example, the one party–dominant systems in neighboring countries to which many in the ranks of the VNCP had looked as the next stage in institutional evolution for Vietnam had themselves begun to fray around the edges as vehicles for mobilizing capital, provoking increasing productivity, and preserving stability, aspects of which had long been admired in Hanoi.

Given the wherewithal of domestic groups that had profited from economic success, the party was increasingly less able to attract new constituencies, social groups, and economic interests into comrade-like association, much less subordination, without delivering guarantees that at least some part of the aims of such groups could be served by the party. In order to reinvent itself the party would have to accommodate the portion of the organization that had embraced radical market-oriented reforms, as well as the strong conservative element that clung to core Marxist-Leninist values and socialist ideology. The middle road — allowing the market some leeway, while reasserting the state's purview over a big part of the economy — stifled supply and demand forces that could have brought order to the market. That course enabled ineffectual state enterprises to have continued protection and reinforced state control over strategic industries, all of which combined to stave off the real economic reforms. By the mid–1990s the middle road had decidedly less to offer Vietnam.

Notes

The following abbreviations are used in the Notes and Bibliography:

DRV	Democratic Republic of Vietnam
FBIS	Foreign Broadcast Information Service
SRV	Socialist Republic of Vietnam
TP	Thanh Pho, city
TU	Trung Uong, Central Committee
VNCP	Vietnamese Communist Party

INTRODUCTION

1. Foreign Minister Nguyen Manh Cam, keynote speech to the U.S.–Vietnam Trade Forum Conference on economic normalization, Washington, D.C., October 1995.

2. "Xa Luan: Toan Dang Ta Tien Va Dai Hoi VIII," *Nhan Dan*, 4 December 1995, pp. 1, 2; and "Xa Luan: To Chuc That Tot Dai Hoi Dang Co So," *Nhan Dan*, 5 December 1995, pp. 1, 2. Also see Nguyen Trong Phuc, "Dang Ta, Dang Cua Tinh Than Doc Lap, Tu Chu va Sang Tao," *Nhan Dan*, 4 December 1995, p. 3; "Ve Dai Hoi Dang Bo Cac Cap," *Nhan Dan*, 11 December 1995, p. 3; and "Xa Luan: Tich Cuc Chuan Bi, Bao Dam Cho Dai Hoi VIII Cua Dang Thanh Cong Tot Dep," *Tap Chi Cong San*, 17 (December 1995): 7.

CHAPTER 1

1. The military version of this process of appraising party membership proceeded through late June at the corps and group level. See Hanoi Voice of Vietnam Network in Vietnamese, 2330 GMT, 29 June 1995, *FBIS-EAS* 95-128, 5 July 1995, p. 106.

2. "Nghi Quyet Hoi Nghi Lan Thu Ba Ban Chap Hanh Trung Uong Dang, Khoa 7 Ve Mot So Nhiem Vu Doi Moi Vu Chinh Don Dang," 3-NQ/HNTW, 29 June 1992, in Quan Doi Nhan Dan Viet Nam (Tong Cuc Chinh Tri), *Quan Triet Va Thuc Hien Nghi Quyet Hoi Nghi Trung Uong Lan Thu 3*, pp. 42–72.

3. "Hoat Dong Cua Lanh Dao Dang, Nha Nuoc: Cac Dong Chi Nguyen Duc Binh, Vu Oanh, Nguyen Ha Phan, Do Quang Thanh, Truong My Hoa Tham Va Lam Viec Voi Cac Dia Phuong," *Nhan Dan*, 15 May 1995, pp. 1, 2; "Thu Truong Vo Van Kiet Lam Viec Voi Tinh Kien Giang Va Du Hoi Nghi So Ket 'Chuong Trinh Bao Dam Nuoc Sach Va Sinh Moi Truong' Cua Tinh Soc Trang," *Nhan Dan*, 11 May 1995, pp. 1, 4; "Tong Bi Thu Do Muoi Lam Viec Voi Mot So Giam Doc Doanh Nghiep O Ha Noi," *Nhan Dan*, 12 May 1995, pp. 1, 4; Vu Oanh, "Cong Nghiep Hoa," *Nhan Dan*, 12 May 1995, p. 3; and "80% Dang Bo Cac Truong Dai Hoc, Cac Dang O Ha Noi Xay Dung Quy Che Cong Tac," *Nhan Dan*, 22 May 1995, p. 1.

4. Hanoi Voice of Vietnam Network in Vietnamese, 2300 GMT, 19 June 1995, *FBIS-EAS* 93-119, 21 June 1995, p. 74.

5. On Hai Hung Province's meeting to implement Directive 51, see P.V., "Hai Hung: Chuan Bi Dai Hoi Dang, Cap Huyen, Thi Va Co So," *Nhan Dan*, 17 June 1995, pp. 1, 4.

6. "Hoat Dong Cua Lanh Dao Dang Va Nha Nuoc," *Nhan Dan*, 14 June 1995, p. 1.

7. "Tong Bi Thu Do Muoi Lam Viec Boi Bon Tinh Tay Nguyen," *Nhan Dan*, 16 June 1995, pp. 1, 3.

8. Nguyen Duc Ha, "Nhung Dieu Rut Ra Qua Dai Hoi Diem O Cac Co So," *Nhan Dan*, 8 December 1995, pp. 1, 3.

9. "Trao Doi Kinh Nghiem Ve Than Tra, Xac Minh Trong Cong Tac Kiem Tra Cua Dang," *Nhan Dan*, 10 June 1995, pp. 1, 2. On precinct-level party congress preparations, see Nhom Phong Vien Chinh Tri, "Dang Bo Cac Quan 3, 10 Mo Hoi Nghi Chuyen De Phuc Vu Viec Xay Dung Van Kien Dai Hoi," *Saigon Giai Phong*, 20 June 1995, pp. 1, 5. On Resolution 8B see Hanoi Voice of Vietnam Network in Vietnamese, 1430 GMT, 7 June 1995, *FBIS-EAS* 93-111, 9 June 1995, pp. 52–53.

10. Hanoi Voice of Vietnam Network in Vietnamese, 2300 GMT, 6 July 1995, *FBIS-EAS* 93-132, 11 July 1995, p. 86.

11. Ibid., 1400 GMT, 17 July 1995, *FBIS-EAS* 93-139, 20 July 1995, p. 104; and ibid., 2330 GMT, 17 August 1995, *FBIS-EAS* 93-165, 25 August 1995, p. 55.

12. Hai Duong, "Truoc Dai Hoi Dang Bo Co So, Xuan Thuy Voi Cac Chuong Trinh Trong Diem," *Nhan Dan*, 19 July 1995, p. 3; Tan Thinh and Pham Van Khanh, "Tinh Uy Ba Ria-Vung Tau: Gan Viec Chuan Bi Dai Hoi

Dang Voi Thuc Hien Cac Nghi Quyet Cua Trung Uong," *Nhan Dan*, 18 July 1995, pp. 1 and 3; T.H., "Hoat Dong Cong Tac Dang," *Nhan Dan*, 21 July 1995, p. 3; and Pham Van Khanh, "Tinh Uy Ha Tay: Tong Ket Thuc Hien Doi Moi, Chinh Don Dang Va Cong Tac Dan Van," *Nhan Dan*, 23 July 1995, pp. 1, 4. Also see Vu Oanh, "Day Manh Cong Tac Dan Van O Co So," *Nhan Dan*, 5 August 1995, p. 3. This theme of developing the ranks of female cadre and improving the lot of women was aired at congresses of subprovincial party committees through late October. See Le Hoang, "Tinh Uy Lang Son Chuan Bi Dai Hoi Dang Cac Cap Gan Voi Tong Ket Cac Nghi Quyet Cua Trung Uong," *Nhan Dan*, 23 October 1995, p. 1.

13. T.B.L., "Ta Ca Cac Co So Dang Tien Hanh Dai Hoi Truoc Thang 12–1995," *Saigon Giai Phong*, 30 July 1995, pp. 1, 7.

14. Duc Luong and Mai Phong, "Xay Dung Dang: Nhung Dieu Rut Ra Qua Dai Hoi Diem Dang Bo Co So O Ninh Binh," *Nhan Dan*, 4 August 1995, p. 3.

15. P.V., "Tong Ket Doi Moi Chinh Don Dang Chuan Bi Dai Hoi Dang Bo Co So Cac Cap," *Nhan Dan*, 8 August 1995, p. 1; Hanoi Voice of Vietnam Network in Vietnamese, 1430 GMT, 6 September 1995, *FBIS-EAS* 95-154, 6 August 1995, p. 75; Hanoi Voice of Vietnam Network in Vietnamese, 0500 GMT, 30 August 1995, *FBIS-EAS* 95-172, 6 September 1995, p. 70; Hanoi Voice of Vietnam Network in Vietnamese, 2300 GMT, 29 August 1995, *FBIS-EAS* 95-172, 6 September 1995, p. 70; and Hanoi Voice of Vietnam Network in Vietnamese, 2390 GMT, 9 September 1995, *FBIS-EAS* 95-178, 13 September 1995, p. 54.

16. In addition to conducting the prescribed internal organization performance reviews and discussions of party documents, the primary party organizations elected new committee members including females, who represented 11 percent of the total number of newly elected committee members. The average age of the new committee members was 40. Approximately 70 percent of the incumbents were reelected. Hanoi Voice of Vietnam Network in Vietnamese, 1100 GMT, 7 September 1995, *FBIS-EAS* 95-177, 13 September 1995, p. 71; and Hanoi Voice of Vietnam Network in Vietnamese, 100 GMT, 24 September 1995, *FBIS-EAS* 95-186, 26 September 1995, p. 101.

17. Hanoi Voice of Vietnam Network in Vietnamese, 1430 GMT, 24 September 1995, *FBIS-EAS* 95-186, 26 September 1995, p. 101; and T.B.L., "Thanh Uy Chi Dao: Tiep Tuc Thi Diem, Rut Kinh Nghiem To Chuc Tot Dai Hoi Dang Bo Cac Cap," *Saigon Giai Phong*, 8 September 1995, pp. 1, 5.

18. "Ve Dai Hoi Dang Bo Cac Cap," *Nhan Dan*, 11 December 1995, p. 3. The Ho Chi Minh City party organization was to conduct its congress in April 1996. See T.B.L., "Thanh Uy Chi Dao: Tiep Tuc Thi Diem, Rut Kinh Nghiem To Chuc Tot Dai Hoi Dang Bo Cac Cap," *Saigon Giai Phong*, 8 September 1995, p. 1.

19. P.V., "Lop Nghien Cuu Duong Loi, Quan Diem Cua Dang Cho Can Bo Cac Cap," *Nhan Dan*, 12 September 1995, pp. 1, 3; P.V., "Dot Hai Lop Can Bo Cao Cap Nghien Cuu Dong Loi, Quan Diem Cua Dang," *Nhan Dan*, 3 October 1995, pp. 1, 2; and "Be Mac Lop Can Bo Cao Cap Nghien Cuu Duong Loi, Quan Diem Cua Dang (Dot Ba)," *Nhan Dan*, 10 November 1995, p. 4.

20. Pham Van Hoa, "To Chuc Tot Dai Hoi 3 Cap Dang Bo Thanh Pho Cho Chi Minh," *Saigon Giai Phong*, 16 October 1995, pp. 1, 5.

21. Le Van Ton, "Ha Tinh Cung Co Co So Dang," *Nhan Dan*, 1 November 1995, p. 3; Nguyen Nghia Vu, "Doi Moi Va Chinh Don Dang, Nhan To Quyet Dinh Qua Trinh Phat Trien O Lao Cai," *Nhan Dan*, 1 November 1995, p. 3; "Hanoi Tiep Tuc Doi Moi Cong Tac Van Dong Quan Chung," *Nhan Dan*, 25 November 1995, p. 1; P.V., "5 Nam Thuc Hien Nghi Quyet Trung Uong 8B O Yen Bai," *Nhan Dan*, 3 December 1995, pp. 1, 4; The Gia, "Tang Cuong Cong Tac Kiem Tra, Phuc Vu Dai Hoi Dang Cac Cap," *Nhan Dan*, 25 November 1995, pp. 1, 2.

22. "Hoi Nghi Can Bo Toan Quan Nghien Cuu Cac Dinh Huong Trong Cong Tac Tu Tuong Va Chuan Bi Dai Hoi Dang Cac Cap," *Nhan Dan*, 6 October 1995, pp.1, 4.

23. Hai Duong, "Dang Bo Quan Doi Chuan Bi Tien Hanh Dai Hoi Dang Bo Cac Cap," *Nhan Dan*, 9 October 1995, p. 1.

24. "Xa Luan: To Chuc Tot Dai Hoi Dang Cac Cap Trong Toan Quan, Tien Toi Dai Hoi Dai Bieu Toan Quoc Lan Thi VIII Cua Dang," *Tap Chi Quoc Phong Toan Dan*, October 1995, pp. 1–4.

25. Hanoi Voice of Vietnam Network in Vietnamese, 1100 GMT 8 November 1995, *FBIS-EAS* 95-222, 17 November 1995, pp. 74–75; and Duy Thuy, "Dang Bo Co Quan TCCT: Lam Tot Cong Tac Doi Moi Va Chinh Don Dang, Cong Tac Van Dong Quan Chung," *Quan Doi Nhan Dan*, 18 December 1995, pp. 1, 2.

26. "Dai Hoi Dang Bo Trung Doan 141 (Su Doan 312): Phat Huy Dan Chu, Dong Gop Nhieu Y Kien Vao Cac Van Kien Dai Hoi Dang VIII," *Quan Doi Nhan Dan*, 18 December 1995, p. 1.

27. Quoc Viet, "Tai Hoi Dang Bo Trung Doan 141 (Su Doan 312): Phat Huy Tri Tue Cua Dang Vien, Tap Trung Dong Gop Y Kien Vao Noi Dung Chu Yeu Du Thao Cac Van Kien Cua Dang," *Quan Doi Nhan Dan*, 25 December 1995, pp. 1, 4.

28. "Thong Bao Hoi Nghi Lan Thu Chin BCHTU (Khoa VII)," *Tap Chi Cong San* 17 (December 1995): 3.

29. Ibid.

30. Ibid., p. 4.

31. Ibid., p. 4. Also see Hanoi Voice of Vietnam Network in Vietnamese, 2300 GMT, 15 November 1995, *FBIS-EAS* 95-221, 16 November 1995,

pp. 84–85; and Hanoi Voice of Vietnam Network in Vietnamese, 2300 GMT, 15 November 1995, *FBIS-EAS* 95-222, 17 November 1995, p. 74.

32. Do Muoi, "Neu Cao Tinh Than Doc Lap Tu Chu Va Nang Luc Sang Tao, Phan Dau Hoan Thanh Xuat Sac Nhiem Vu Cua Dai Hoi VII Va Tich Cuc Chuan Bi Cho Dai Hoi VIII," *Tap Chi Cong San* 17; and "Du Thao," *Hanoi Moi*, 28 November 1995, pp. 1–4.

33. "Noi Dung Bai Phat Bieu Be Mac Hoi Nghi Lan Thu 9," p. 6; and "Du Thao: Bao Cao Chinh Tri Tai Dai Hoi Dai Bieu Dang Bo Thanh Pho Hanoi Lan Thu XII," *Hanoi Moi*, 28 November 1995, pp. 1–4.

34. "Xa Luan: To Chuc That Tot Dai Hoi Dang Co So," *Nhan Dan*, 5 December 1995, p. 3. The editorial also stressed the importance of conducting appropriate inspection activities before holding elections.

35. Thuan Huy, "Qua Mot So Dai Hoi Dang Bo Co Su O Cac Tinh Mien Trung: Can Co Thoi Gian, Chuan Bi Tot Hon Ve Noi Dung Va Nhan Du," *Nhan Dan*, 5 December 1995, pp. 1, 4.

36. Nguyen Duc Ha, "Nhung Dieu Rut Ra Qua Dai Hoi Diem O Cac Co So," *Nhan Dan*, 8 December 1995, pp. 1, 3.

37. "Ve Dai Hoi Dang Bo Cac Cap," *Nhan Dan*, 11 December 1995, p. 3.

38. Ibid.

39. Pham Van Khanh, "Ghi Nhan Tu Dai Hoi Diem Dang Bo Co So O Hai Hung," *Nhan Dan*, 7 December 1995, pp. 1, 4; "Xa Luan: Tich Cuc Chuan Bi, Bao Dam Cho Dai Hoi VIII Cua Dang Thanh Cong Tot Dep," *Tap Chi Cong San* 17 (December 1995): 7; and P.V., "TP Ho Chi Minh: Mot So Kinh Nghiem Qua Dai Hoi Cac Co So Dang Duoc Chon Thi Diem," *Nhan Dan*, 18 December 1995, pp. 1, 3.

40. "Ban Bi Thu T.U. Dang Chi Thi: Phat Dong Phong Trao Thi Du Lap Thanh Tich Chao Mung Dai Hoi Lan Thi VIII Cua Dang," *Nhan Dan*, 29 December 1995, pp. 1, 3.

41. Though Muoi conducted the inspection tour in late December, the 30 December speech was not carried in the party's daily newspaper until mid–January. See Do Muoi, "Cong Nghiep Hoa, Hien Dai Hoa Phai Duoc Quan Triet Trong Dai Hoi Dang Bo Cac Cap, Truoc Het Tu Co So," *Nhan Dan*, 11 January 1996, pp. 1, 4. Similarly, Muoi's working visit in the first days of January 1996 to Ho Chi Minh City and Can Tho, Dong Nai, Ba Ria-Vung Tau did not receive press coverage until mid–January. See "Tong Bi Thu Do Muoi Tham Va Lam Viec Tai TP Ho Chi Minh, Cac Tinh Can Tho, Dong Nai, Ba Ria-Vung Tau," *Nhan Dan*, 12 January 1996, pp. 1, 2.

42. Muoi, "Cong Nghiep Hoa, Hien Dai Hoa Phai Duoc Quan Triet Trong Dai Hoi Dang Bo Cac Cap, Truoc Het Tu Co So," *Nhan Dan*, 11 January 1996, pp. 1, 4.

Chapter 2

1. "Bo Chinh Tri Ban Hanh Nghi Quyet Ve Tiep Tuc Doi Moi To Chuc Va Hoat Dong Thuong Nghiep, Phat Trien Thi Truong Theo Dinh Huong Xa Hoi Chu Nghia," *Nhan Dan*, 19 January 1996, pp. 1, 3.
2. *Saigon Giai Phong*, 7 January 1996, p. 1.
3. "Tong Bi Thu Do Muoi Tham Va Lam Viec Tai TP Ho Chi Minh, Cac Tinh Can Tho, Dong Nai, Ba Ria-Vung Tau," *Nhan Dan*, 12 January 1996, pp. 1, 2.
4. Pham Van Dong, "Mot Su Kien Lon Va Dau An Cua No," *Nhan Dan*, 1 January 1996, pp. 1, 3; "Dien Dan: Tong Ket La De Vuon Len Tam Cao Moi," *Nhan Dan*, 2 January 1996, pp. 1, 3.
5. "Xa Luan: Dai Hoi Dang Bo Co So Can Ban Nhung Van De Cu The, Thiet Thuc," *Nhan Dan*, 27 December 1995, pp. 1, 4. The editorial pointed out that Muoi had paid special attention to industrial, multisectoral economic development policy, the consolidation of production relations, and social welfare issues. The general secretary advised that the local party organizations take their clues for conducting congresses from the results of inspections of grassroots-level congresses conducted by the party center and the guidance generated by that process.
6. Throughout late January the Central Committee anticipated that provincial congresses would begin after the New Year in mid–February, according to a senior Central Committee department–level official.
7. Hanoi Voice of Vietnam Network in Vietnamese, 1100 GMT, 21 January 1996, *FBIS-EAS* 96-019, 29 January 1996, p. 58.
8. Hanoi Voice of Vietnam in English, 1000 GMT, 19 January 1996, *FBIS-EAS* 96-018, 26 January 1996, pp. 87–88; and Hanoi Vietnamese News Agency in English, 0647 GMT, 27 January 1996, *FBIS-EAS* 96-022, 1 February 1996, p. 77.
9. Nguyen Kien Phuoc, "Dai Hoi Dang Bo Co So: Phai Tao Ra Su Chuyen Bien Manh Me Ve Chat," *Nhan Dan*, 15 January 1996, pp. 1, 3. Also see Duc Luong, "Tap Trung Chi Dao Dai Hoi Dang Bo Co So," *Nhan Dan*, 16 January 1996, p. 1.
10. Luong, "Tap Trung Chi Dao Dai Hoi Dang Bo Co So."
11. For example, according to a 22 January article in *Nhan Dan*, by the end of the month more than three-quarters of the basic organizations in Kon Tum had concluded the congresses, making Kon Tum one of the provinces to complete the basic level meetings early. See Duc Luong, "Tinh Uy Kon Tum Chuan Bi Dai Hoi Cap Tren Co So," *Nhan Dan*, 22 January 1996, pp. 1, 4.
12. Phan Huy, "Can Tho Phat Dong Thi Dua Huong Toi Dai Hoi VIII Cua Dang," *Nhan Dan*, 25 January 1996, pp. 1, 4.

13. "Dong Chi Dao Duy Tung Du Va Noi Chuyen Tai Dai Hoi Dang Bo Huyen Cam Binh," *Nhan Dan*, 29 January 1996, pp. 1, 4.

14. "Dong Chi Nguyen Manh Cam Lam Viec Voi Tinh Thanh Hoa," *Nhan Dan*, 30 January 1996, p. 1.

15. See, for example, Duc Luong, "Dai Hoi Dang Bo Cap Tren Co So O Tuyen Quang: Nhieu Dai Bieu Ung Cu Va Ban Chap Hanh Moi," *Nhan Dan*, 30 January 1996, pp. 1, 4; and "Cac Tinh: Thai Binh, Yen Bai, Quang Nam-Da Nang Co Tu 63 Den 87% Dang Bo Co So Dai Hoi Xong," *Quan Doi Nhan Dan*, 5 February 1996, p. 1.

16. P.V. and Do Ngoc Dang, "Ha Tay: Cu Them Can Bo Giup Chi Dao Dai Hoi Co So," *Nhan Dan*, 6 January 1996, pp. 1, 3; and "Cong Tac Tu Tuong Nam 1996 Tap Trung Tuyen Truyen, Co Dong Ve Dai Hoi VIII Cua Dang," *Nhan Dan*, 7 January 1996, pp. 1, 2.

17. Le Minh Tuan, "Qua II Co So Dang O Binh Dinh Tien Hanh Dai Hoi Diem," *Nhan Dan*, 12 January 1996, p. 3.

18. Vu Dieu, "Dai Hoi Dang Bo Thanh Pho Ha Long: Khai Thac Loi The, Tang Nhanh Nhip do phat trien," *Nhan Dan*, 11 February 1996, p. 1.

19. "Thu Thuong Vo Van Kiet Lam Viec Voi Tinh Lam Dong Ve Kinh Te-Xa Hoi Va Cong Tact Chuan Bi Dai Hoi Dang," *Quan Doi Nhan Nhan*, 16 February 1996, pp. 1, 4.

20. "Ban Bi Thu To Chuc Y Kien Nang Cao Chat Luong Dao Hoi Dang Bo Cac Tinh Dong Bang Song Cuu Long," *Quan Doi Nhan Dan*, 15 February 1996, pp. 1, 4; Hanoi Voice of Vietnam Network in Vietnamese, 2300 GMT, 12 February 1996, *FBIS-EAS* 96-031, 14 February 1996, p. 87; and Hanoi Voice of Vietnam Network in Vietnamese, 0500 GMT, 14 February 1996, *FBIS-EAS* 96-031, 14 February 1996, p. 87.

21. Thanh Phong, "Cac Dong Chi Nguyen Duc Binh, Nguyen Ha Phan, Le Kha Phieu Kiem Tra Dai Hoi Dang Bo Cac Cap O Ha Tinh, Nghe An," *Nhan Dan*, 12 February 1996, pp. 1, 4.

22. "Thu Tuong Vo Van Kiet Lam Viec Voi Ba Tinh Tay Nguyen Ve Kinh Te-Xa Hoi Va Cong Tac Chuan Bi Dai Hoi Dang," *Nhan Dan*, 15 February 1996, pp. 1, 3; "Thu Tuong Vo Van Kiet Lam Viec Voi Ba Tinh Tay Nguyen Ve Kinh Te-Xa Hoi Va Cong Tac Chuan Bi Dai Hoi Dang," *Quan Doi Nhan Dan*, 15 February 1996, pp. 1, 3; and "Ban Bi Thu To Chuc Dang Gop Y Kien Nang Cao Chat Luong Dai Hoi Dang Boi Cac Tinh Dong Bang, Song Cuu Long," *Nhan Dan*, 15 February 1996, pp. 1, 4.

23. Ngo Le Dan and TTXVN, "Chu Tich Le Duc Anh, Thu Tuong Vo Van Kiet Lam Viec Voi Mot So Tinh Phia Nam," *Nhan Dan*, 16 February 1996, pp. 1, 4.

24. "Cac Dong Chi Dao Duy Tung, Nong Duc Manh, Hong Ha Lam Viec Voi Cac Tinh Uy Hoa Binh, Son La va Lai Chau Ve Chuan Bi Dai Hoi

Dang Cac Cap," *Nhan Dan*, 17 February 1996, pp. 1, 4. New Year's visits by senior leaders provided opportunities to restate the party's focus on modernization and to urge all members to exert themselves at this stage of preparations for the congress. See, for example, P.V. and TTXVN, "Chu Tich Le Duc Anh Tham Va Chuc Tet Can Bo, Phong Vien Bao *Nhan Dan*, Can Bo, Cong Nhan Cong Ty In Tien Bo," *Nhan Dan*, 17 February 1996, pp. 1, 4; and Thanh Giang, "Cong Nghiep Hoa Dat Nuoc The Hien Tu Tuong Va Mo Uoc Cua Chung Ta," *Nhan Dan*, 21 February 1996, pp. 1, 3.

25. "Tong Bi Thu Do Muoi Lam Viec Vo 14 Tinh, Thanh Pho Ve Chuan Bi Cho Dai Hoi Dang Bo Cac Cap," *Nhan Dan*, 1 March 1996, p. 3. Muoi visited Thua Thien-Hue, Quang Ngai, Binh Dinh, Phu Yen, Khanh Hoa, Haiphong, Hai Hung, Quang Ninh, Thai Binh, Ninh Binh, Nam Ha, Ha Tay, Ha Bac, and Vinh Phu, mostly northern and central provinces. Muoi's choice of traveling companions — Vu Oanh, Do Quang Thang, and Nguyen Dinh Tu — reflected an attempt to balance the views of the party, the government, and mass organizations. Thang was the secretary of Quang Ngai's party committee in 1991 when he was relected to the Central Committee at the 1991 Congress. Tu was a state council member and director of the Atomic Energy Institute when he was reelected to the Central Committee, also in 1991. Tu died on 28 June 1996, shortly after being elected to the Politburo. Vu Oanh was in charge of mass mobilization for the Central Committee and an incumbent member of that committee at the time of his 1991 reelection.

26. "Tim Loi Giai Cho Buoc Di Cong Nghiep Hoa," *Nhan Dan*, 1 March 1996, pp. 1, 3.

27. "To Chuc Lay Y Kien Va Tong Hop Y Kien Nhan Dan Gop Vao Ban Du Thao Bao Cao Chinh Tri Trinh Dai Hoi VIII," *Quan Doi Nhan Dan*, 19 April 1996, pp. 1, 4.

28. "Da Can Ban Hoan Thanh Dai Hoi Dang Bo Co So: 90–95% So Dang Vien Du Cac Dai Hoi," *Nhan Dan*, 23 March 1996, pp. 1, 4.

29. Phan Loi, "Dai Hoi Dang Bo Huyen Mo Duc (Quang Ngai): Bon Chong Trinh Kinh Te O Mot Huyen Thuan Nong," *Nhan Dan*, 20 March 1996, pp. 1, 4; and Vu Kiem, Van Xuyen, and Tu Uyen, "Tai Dai Hoi Dang Bo Huyen Tieu Hai Dong Chi Le Phuoc Tho: Tien Hai Nhanh Chong Chuyen Dich Co Can Kinh Te Theo Huong Cong Nghiep Hoa, Hien Dai Hoa Nong Thon," *Nhan Dan*, 29 March 1996, pp. 1, 2.

30. Lam Hue Nu, "Dai Hoi Dang Bo Huyen Nhon Trach: Xay Dung Huyen Cong Nghiep Gan Voi Cong Nghiep Hoa Nong Thon," *Nhan Dan*, 22 March 1996, pp. 1, 2. Also see Ngu Phong, "Dai Hoi Dang Bo Hoi Dong Trung Uong Lien Minh Cac Hop Tac Xa Viet Nam Tang Cuong Su Lanh Dao Cua Dang Trong Doi Moi, Phat Trien Kinh Te Hop Tac; Dong Chi Nguyen Ha Phan Lam Viec Voi Dang Doan Cua Hoi Dong," *Nhan Dan*, 31 March 1996,

pp. 1, 4; "Dai Hoi Dang Bo Huyen Ninh Phuoc: Phat Trien Cac Vung Kinh Te Trong Diem," *Nhan Dan*, 5 March 1996, pp. 1, 2; Nguyen Ke Nghiep and Le Hoang, "Dai Hoi Dang Bo Huyen Tam Thanh: Chu Truong Dua Co Khi Vao Nong Nghiep, Nong Thon; Dai Hoi Dang Bo Huyen Huu Long: Phat Trien Non Thon Vung Nui Cao Theo Huong Cong Nghiep Hoa," *Nhan Dan*, 6 March 1996, pp. 1, 3; Nguyen Khoi, "Moc Chau Phan Dau Cho Su Dong Deu," *Nhan Dan*, 6 March 1996, p. 3; Hai Duong, "Tai Dai Hoi Dang Bo Huyen Hung Ha: Dong Chi Dao Duy Tung: Thay Ro Hon Huong Di Vao Cong Nghiep Hoa Nong Nghiep, Xay Dung Nong Thon Moi," *Nhan Dan*, 7 March 1996, pp. 1, 4; Hai Duong, Duy Phuc, and Kim Quy, "Dai Hoi Dang Bo Huyen Duc Trong (Lam Dong) Tap Trung Moi Nguon Von De Chuyen Dich Co Cau Kinh Te Theo Huong Tang Ty Trong Cong Nghiep," *Nhan Dan*, 16 March 1996, pp. 1, 3; The Nghia, "Tai Dai Hoi Dang Bo Huyen Tho Xuan: Dong Chi Dao Duy Tung: Can Coi Giai Phap Cu The De Di Vao Cong Nghiep Hoa Nong Nghiep, Nong Thon," *Nhan Dan*, 25 March 1996, pp. 1, 4; and Vo Nang Nhan, "Dai Hoi Dang Bo Huyen Dac Ha Tap Trung Suc Phat Trien Kinh Te Theo Huong San Xuat Hang Hoa," *Nhan Dan*, 21 March 1996, pp. 1, 4.

31. Nguyen Thao, "Dai Hoi Dang Bo TP Viet Tri: Dong Chi Le Phuoc Tho: Xay Dung Va Phat Trien Thanh Pho Viet Tri Ngang Tam Yeu Cau Day Manh Cong Nghiep Hoa, Hien Dai Hoa Dat Nuoc," *Nhan Dan*, 8 March 1996, pp. 1, 3; Thanh Phong, "Dai Hoi Dang Bo TP Nha Trang: Phat Huy The Manh Du Lich, Phan Dau Giai Quyet Viec Lam Cho Hon 20 Nghin Lao Dong," *Nhan Dan*, 9 March 1996, pp. 1, 4; Phan Loi, "Dai Hoi Dang Bo TP Da Nang: Phan Dau Tro Thanh Trung Tam Kinh Te Mien Trung," *Nhan Dan*, 18 March 1996, pp. 1, 3; P.V., "Dai Hoi Dang Bo TP Thai Nguyen: Phan Dau Tro Thanh Trung Tam Chinh Tri, Kinh Te-Xa Hoi Cua Bac Thai," *Nhan Dan*, 21 March 1996, pp. 1, 2; Vu Kiem, Van Xuyen, and Tu Uyen, "Tai Dai Hoi Dang Bo Thanh Pho Nam Dinh: Dong Chi Nguyen Ha Phan: Xay Dung Thanh Pho Giai Dep, Van Minh, Kong De Mot Nguoi Trong Do Tuoi Lao Dong Khong Coi Viec Lam," *Nhan Dan*, 29 March 1996, pp. 1, 2; TTXVN and Tran Quynh, "Tai Dai Hoi Dang Bo Thi Xa Son La Chu Tich Le Duc Anh: Nhanh Chong Dua Thi Xa Tro Thanh Mot Trung Nhung Do Thi Phon Vinh O Vung Tau Bac," *Nhan Dan*, 30 March 1996, pp. 1, 4; and TTXVN and Tran Quynh, "Dai Hoi Dang Bo Quan Hoan Kiem (Ha Noi): Phat Trien Kinh Te Dong Thoi Giu Gin, Ton Tao Cac Di San Van Hoa," *Nhan Dan*, 30 March 1996, pp. 1, 4.

32. Thinh Giang, "Tong Bi Thu Do Muoi Tham Khu Cong Nghiep Sai Dong (Ha Noi)," *Nhan Dan*, 11 March 1996, pp. 1, 4; Phan Loi, "Co Van Pham Van Dong Tham, Lam Viec Tai Quang Ngai Va Quang Nam-Da Nang," *Nhan Dan*, 13 March 1996, pp. 1, 4; and "Dong Chi Dao Duy Tung Kiem Tra Cong Tac Dai Hoi Dang Cac Cap Tai Lang Son," *Nhan Dan*, 20 March 1996, pp. 1,

4. Ha Dang, chairman of the Central Committee's Ideology and Culture Department, attended the party meeting of the Writer's Association, held 12–13 March, which focused on steps necessary to guarantee political stability in which cultural creativity could thrive, and an unwavering commitment to reform. See Song Ha, "Dai Hoi Dang Bo Hoi Nha Van Viet Nam: Tac Pham Se Minh Chung Su Lanh Dao Cua Dang, Tu Tuong Nhan Van Va Dien Mao Van Hoc," *Nhan Dan*, 14 March 1996, pp. 1, 2. The mid–March 9th National Assembly replayed some of the core themes that had become a litany during the basic-level congresses. See "Tong Hop Y Kien Cu Tri Ca Nuoc Tai Ky Hop Thu 9, Quoc Hoi Khoa IX," *Nhan Dan*, 13 March 1996, p. 3.

33. Hanoi Voice of Vietnam Network in Vietnamese, 1000 GMT, 4 February 1996, *FBIS-EAS* 96-026, 7 February 1996, pp. 52–53.

34. Duy Phuc, Pham Van Khanh, and Thao Lam, "Dai Hoi Dang Bo Giao Duc Va Dao Tao: Dao Tao Con Nguoi Cho Thoi Ky Phat Trien Moi," *Nhan Dan*, 2 February 1996, p. 4.

35. Nguyen Anh Dung, "Dai Hoi Dang Bo Co Quan Bo Tai Chinh: Khai Thac, Quan Ly, Su Dung Tot Hon Cac Nguon Tai Chinh," *Nhan Dan*, 14 February 1996, pp. 1, 4.

36. Nguyen Oanh and Nguyen Toan Thang, "Dai Hoi Dang Bo Bo Nong Nghiep Va Phat Trien Nong Thon: Chuyen Dich Manh Me Co Cau Kinh Te Nong-Lam Nghiep Va Kinh Te Nong Thon Theo Huong Cong Nghiep Hoa," *Nhan Dan*, 27 March 1996, pp. 1, 3.

37. See Tran Kham, "Dai Hoi Dang Bo Co Quan Bo Cong Nghiep Tham Muu Cho Dang, Nha Nuoc Va Di Dau Trong Cong Nghiep Hoa, Hien Dai Hoa," *Nhan Dan*, 7 April 1996, pp. 1, 4; and Nam An et al., "Dai Hoi Dang Bo Co Quan Bo Thuong Mai, Bo Lao Dong—Thuong Binh Va Xa Hoi, Tong Cuc Du Lich," *Nhan Dan*, 8 April 1996, pp. 1, 4.

38. D.T., "Dai Hoi Dang Bo Khoi Cac Co Quan Doi Ngoai Trung Uong; Nang Hoat Dong Doi Ngoai Len Tam Cao Moi," *Nhan Dan*, 28 March 1996, pp. 1, 4.

39. Pham Van Khanh, "Dai Hoi Dang Bo Tu Tuong-Van Hoa Trung Uong Nang Cao Chat Luong Cong Tac Tu Tuong Vuon To Tam Cao Moi," *Nhan Dan*, 6 April 1996, pp. 1, 2; and TTXVN, "Dang Bo Khoi Co Quan Trung Uong Va Dang Bo Khoi Co Quan Trung Uong Ve Cong Tac Tu Tuong Tien Hanh Dai Hoi," *Quan Doi Nhan Dan*, 26 April 1996, pp. 1, 4.

40. Hong Khanh, "Dai Hoi Dang Bo Khoi Cac Co Quan Kinh Te Trung Uong: Lanh Dao Bao Dam Thuc Hien Thang Loi Cac Duong Loi, Chinh Sach, Quan Diem Phat Trien Kinh Te-Xa Hoi," *Nhan Dan*, 28 April 1996, pp. 1, 4. Also see P.V., "Dai Hoi Dang Bo Khoi I Cac Co Quan Trung Uong: Vung Vang, Tri Tue, Tham Muu Giup Dang Va Nha Nuoc," *Nhan Dan*, 27 April 1996, pp. 1, 4.

41. *Quan Doi Nhan Dan*, 3 February 1996, editorial, p. 1.

42. Duy Phuc, Pham Van Khanh, and Thao Lam, "Dai Hoi Dang Bo Hai Quan," *Nhan Dan*, 2 February 1996, pp. 1, 4.

43. Doan Khue, "Xay Dung Dang Bo Ngang Tam Nhien Vu Hai Quan La Luc Luong Nong Cot Bao Ve Vung Chach Chu Quyen Vung Bien, Hai Dan Cua To Quoc," *Quan Doi Nhan Dan*, 5 February 1996, pp. 1, 4.

44. Tho Truat and Quoc Viet, "Dai Hoi Dang Bo Quan Su TP. Ho Chi Minh: Chu Trong Giao Duc Ren Luyen, Xay Dung Ban Linh Chinh Tri Cho Bo Doi; Dang Bo Cuc Van Tai: Tap Trung Co Trong Diem, Doi Moi Trang Bi Va Phuong Tien Van Tai," *Quan Doi Nhan Dan*, 10 February 1996, pp. 1, 4. Also see Van Huong, "Tap Trung Lanh Dao Thuc Hien Tot 6 Mat Cong Tac Ky Thuat," *Quan Doi Nhan Dan*, 5 February 1996, pp. 1, 4; Duc Thinh, "Xay Dung Su Doan Vung Manh Toan Dien, Tinh Nhue," *Quan Doi Nhan Dan*, 30 January 1996, p. 1; and To Thanh Tuyen, "Tap Trung Tri Tue Thong Qua Nghi Quyet Lanh Dao Su Doan Vung Manh Toan Dien," *Quan Doi Nhan Dan*, 2 February 1996, pp. 1, 4.

45. Vu Quang Huy, "Dang Bo Quan Chung Khong Quan: Tang Cuong Cong Tac Kiem Tra, Gop Phan Giam Ty Le Dang Vien Vi Pham Ky Luat," *Quan Doi Nhan Dan*, 26 February 1996, p. 1. On educational requirements as articulated by party organizations of military elements see Pham Quyet Thang, "Dang Vien Va Dai Hoi Dang," *Quan Doi Nhan Dan*, 26 February 1996, pp. 1, 4; Ngo Anh Thy, "Dang Bo Doan B09 Tang-Thiet Giap (Quan Khu I): Tang Cuong Quan Ly, Ren Luyen Doi Ngu Dang Vien," *Quan Doi Nhan Dan*, 22 February 1996, p. 1; "Quan Chung Khong Quan Ra Luan Huan Luyen," *Quan Doi Nhan Dan*, 3 March 1996, p. 1; Van Hoc and Tran Ho Bac, "Cac Don Vi Ra Quan Huyen Luyen," *Quan Doi Nhan Dan*, 4 March 1996, pp. 1, 4; Trong Bao, "Phu Nu Quan Doi: Day Manh Giao Duc Truyen Thong, Xay Dung Don Vi, Giup Nhau Lam Kinh Te Gia Dinh Va Cac Phong Trao Xa Hoi," *Quan Doi Nhan Dan*, 7 March 1996, p. 1; Ho Ba Vinh, "Binh Doan Tay Nguyen: Chuan Bi Tot Chu Ra Quan Huan Luyen Nam 1996," *Quan Doi Nhan Dan*, 8 March 1996, pp. 1, 4; Thu Hien, "Lam Dong: Hoan Thanh Cong Tac Giao Quan Dot 1 Nam 1996," *Quan Doi Nhan Dan*, 8 March 1996, p. 1; and Van Hoc, "Dang Bo Quan Khu I: 100% To Chuc Co So Dang Da Tien Hanh Dai Hoi Dat Ket Qua Cao," *Quan Doi Nhan Dan*, 23 February 1996, p. 1.

46. Nguyen Thanh and Duong Ngan, "Dai Hoi Dang Bo Quan Su Ha Bac, Dong Bo Quan Su Ha Giang: Nang Cao Suc Manh Tong Hop, Xay Dung The Tran Quoc Phong—An Ninh Gan Voi Phat Trien Kinh Te-Xa Hoi O Dia Phuong," *Quan Doi Nhan Dan*, 2 March 1996, p. 1.

47. Minh Tuan and Thu Hien, "Dai Hoi Dang Bo Quan Su Tinh Ninh Binh, Tinh Lam Dong: Xac Dinh Cac Muc Tieu Lanh Dao Xay Dung Nen

Quoc Phong Dia Phuong Vung Manh Toan Dien," *Quan Doi Nhan Dan,* 5 March 1996, pp. 1, 4.

48. Thu Long, "Dang Bo Quan Khu Thu Do: Hoan Thanh Ke Hoach Dai Hoi Dang Cap Co So Va Tren Truc Tiep Co So," *Quan Doi Nhan Dan,* 8 March 1996, p. 1.

49. Quoc Viet, "Tai Dai Hoi Dai Bieu Dang Bo Bo Tong Tham Muu–Co Quan Bo Quoc Phong: Doi Moi Sau Sac Tu Duy Ve Nhiem Vu Bao Ve To Quoc, De Lam Tot Chuc Nang Tham Muu Va Quan Ly Nha Nuoc," *Quan Doi Nhan Dan,* 9 March 1996, pp. 1, 4.

50. Doan Khue, "Xay Dung Quan Doi Chinh Quy, Tinh Nhue Trong Su Nghiep Cong Nghiep Hoa, Hien Dai Hoa Dat Nuoc," *Nhan Dan,* 23 March 1996, pp. 1, 4; Duy Phuc and Pham Van Khanh, "Phan Dau La Trung Tam Dao Luyen Tri Tue Quan Su," *Nhan Dan,* 23 March 1996, pp. 1, 3; and Le Kha Phieu, "Can Bo, Chien Si Luc Luong Vu Trang Kien Dinh Muc Tieu Doc Lap Dan Toc Va Chu Nghia Xa Hoi, Duong Loi Ket Hop Hai Nhiem Va Chien Luoc," *Nhan Dan,* 25 March 1996, pp. 1, 2.

51. Pham Van Khanh and Vu Hieu, "Dai Hoi Dang Bo Quan Khu 1 Nan Cao Chat Luong Luc Luong Vu Trang Lam Nong Cot Xay Dung The Tran Quoc Phong Toan Dan Vung Manh," *Nhan Dan,* 15 March 1996, pp. 1, 3; Quoc Viet, "Dai Hoi Dai Bieu Dang Bo Quan Khu 1: Phat Huy Suc Manh Tong Hop, Xay Dung Neu Quoc Phong Toan Dan, Bao Ve Vung Chac Bien Gioi Quoc Gia," *Quan Doi Nhan Dan,* 15 March 1996, pp. 1, 4.

52. "Dai Hoi Dang Bo Hoc Vien Chinh Tri-Quan Su Phan Dau Tro Thanh Trung Tam Khoa Hoc Xa Hoi Va Nhan Van Hang Dau Cua Quan Doi," *Nhan Dan,* 15 March 1996, p. 3; and To Thanh Tuyen and Mai Huong, "Dai Hoi Dang Bo Hoc Vien Chinh Tri-Quan Su: Tap Trung Xay Dung Hoc Vien Thanh Trung Tam Dao Tao Can Bo Chinh Tri, Nghien Cuu Khoa Hoc-Xa Hoi Va Nhan Van," *Quan Doi Nhan Dan,* 15 March 1996, pp. 1, 3.

53. "Dai Hoi Dang Bo Quan Khu 9: Xay Dung Doi Ngu Can Bo, Dang Vien Co Phan Chat, Trinh Do Nang Luc Dap Ung Yeu Cao Nhiem Vu," *Quan Doi Nhan Dan,* 29 March 1996, pp. 1, 2. Also see Do Trong Duc, "Quan Chung Phong Khong: Thi Dua Tap Trung Vao Cac Nhiem Vu Trong Tam," *Quan Doi Nhan Dan,* 28 March 1996, p. 1.

54. Tran The Tuyen, "Dai Hoi Dang Bo Quan Khu 7: Tap Trung Nang Cao Nang Luc, Quan Uy Nha Nuoc Ve Quoc Phong, Xay Dung Doi Ngu Vung Manh Dap Ung Tinh Hinh Moi," *Quan Doi Nhan Dan,* 2 April 1996, pp. 1, 4.

55. The Gia, "Dai Hoi Dang Bo Quan Khu 7: Xay Dung The Tran Quoc Phong Toan Dan Gan Voi The Trau An Ninh Nhan Dan," *Nhan Dan,* 5 April 1996, pp. 1, 4.

56. Duy Phuc, "Dai Hoi Dang Bo Quan Khu 3: Nang Chat Luong Ba

Thu Quan, Xay Dung Khu Vuc Phong Thu Va The Tran Quoc Phong-An Ninh Vung Chac," *Nhan Dan*, 8 April 1996, pp. 1, 4.

57. Xuan Phong, "Dai Hoi Dang Bo Co Quan Tong Cuc Chinh Tri: Tap Trung Nang Luc Tri Tue, Thuc Hien Tot Chuc Nang Tham Muu Tren Mat Tran Chinh Tri, Tu Tuong, Van Hoa," *Nhan Dan*, 6 April 1996, pp. 1, 4.

58. Duy Phuc and Xuan Thuy, "Dai Hoi Dang Bo Tong Cuc Cong Nghiep Quoc Phong Va Kinh Te: Tao Suc Manh Tong Hop Xay Dung, Phat Trien Cong Nghiep Quoc Phong Va Kinh Te Quan Doi," *Nhan Dan*, 12 April 1996, pp. 1, 4.

59. "Mai Mai La Niem Tin Yeu Cua Dang, Cua Nhan Dan, La Cho Dua Vung Chac, Bach Chien, Bach Thang Cua To Quoc," *Nhan Dan*, 7 May 1996, pp. 1, 2; Hanoi Voice of Vietnam Network in Vietnamese, 1400 GMT, 9 May 1996, *FBIS-EAS* 96-096, 15 May 1996, pp. 99–100; and "Giuong Cao Ngon Co Doc Lap Dan Toc Va Chu Nghia Xa Hoi, Dong Vien Toan Quan Buoc Vao Thoi Ky Moi, Gop Phan Tich Cuc Thuc Hien Su Nghiep Cong Nghiep Hoa, Hien Dai Hoa Dat Nuoc," *Quan Doi Nhan Dan*, 10 May 1996, pp. 1, 4.

60. Hanoi Voice of Vietnam Network in Vietnamese, 1400 GMT, 9 May 1996, *FBIS-EAS* 96-096, 15 May 1996, pp. 99–100. Also see Do Muoi, "Mai Mai La Niem Tin Yeu Cua Dang, Cua Nhan Dan, La Cho Dua Vung Chac, Bach Chien, Bach Thanh, Cua To Quoc," *Nhan Dan*, 7 May 1996, pp. 1, 2.

61. Dang Xuan Ky, "Vung Buoc Di Con Duong Xa Hoi Chu Nghia," *Tap Chi Cong San* (February 1996): 3–6; Bui Ngoc Thanh, "Khong Co Su Lua Chon Nao Khac," *Tap Chi Cong San* (February 1996): 7–11; Nguyen Khac Hien, "Kinh Te Thi Truong Va Dinh Huong Xa Hoi Chu Nghia Co Doi Lap Nhau Khong?" *Tap Chi Cong San* (February 1996): 12–15; Nguyen Van Oanh, "Ve Khai Niem Dinh Huong Xa Hoi Chu Nghia," *Tap Chi Cong San* (February 1996): 16–19; Vu Hien, "Cuc Dien Moi Va Dinh Huong Di Len Cua Dat Nuoc," *Tap Chi Cong San* (February 1996): 20–24; Nguyen Ngoc Khoa, "Bua Tien Moi Cua Dang Bo Huyen Thanh Oai," *Tap Chi Cong San* (February 1996): 50–54; and Nguyen Duy Quy, "Doc Lap Dan Toc Gan Lien Voi Chu Nghia Xa Hoi," *Tap Chi Cong San* (March 1996): 4–8.

62. Nguyen Phu Trong, "Dinh Huong Xa Hoi Chu Nghia Va Con Duong Di Len Chu Nghia Xa Hoi O Nuoc Ta," *Tap Chi Cong San* (March 1996): 9–14. Also see Phong Hai, "Nam Vung Dinh Huong Xa Hoi Chu Nghia-Thuoc Do Pham Chat, Nang Luc Cua Can Bo, Dang Vien Trong Su Nghiep Doi Moi Dat Nuoc," *Quan Doi Nhan Dan*, 27 May 1996, pp. 1, 4.

63. Ha Xuan Truong, "Dinh Huong Xa Hoi Chu Nghia Mot Khai Niem Khoa Hoc," *Tap Chi Cong San* (April 1996): 18.

64. Khong Doan Hoi, "Dinh Huong Xa Hoi Chu Nghia O Nuoc Ta," *Tap Chi Cong San* (March 1996): 15–17; Le Huu Nghia, "Vai Tro Cua Chinh Tri Trong Viec Bao Day Dinh Huong Xa Hoi Chu Nghia," *Tap Chi Cong San*

(March 1996): 18–20; To Huy Rua, "Con Duong Va Dieu Kien Bao Dam Dinh Huong Xa Hoi Chu Nghia O Nuoc Ta," *Tap Chi Cong San* (March 1996): 19–22; Nhat Tan, "Chu Nghia Mac-Le Nin Va Tu Tuong Ho Chi Minh Voi Dinh Huong Xa Hoi Chu Nghia O Nuoc Ta," *Tap Chi Cong San* (March 1996): 26–29; and Ha Xuan Truong, "Dinh Huong Xa Hoi Chu Nghia Mot Khai Niem Khoa Hoc," *Tap Chi Cong San* (April 1996): 18–22.

65. Rua, "Con Duong Va Dieu Kien Bao Dam Dinh Huong Xa Hoi Chu Nghia O Nuoc Ta," pp. 19–22.

66. Xuan Hai, "Hai Van De Duoc Thao Luan Soi Noi Tai Dai Hoi Cai Co So Va Tren Co So O Ha Noi," *Tap Chi Cong San* (April 1996): 32–35.

67. Quang Thong, "Dai Hoi Dang Bo Quan Khu 3: Dong Vien Moi No Luc Cua Quan Va Dan Tren Dia Ban, Xay Dung Quan Khu Thanh Pho Dai Phong Thu Vung Chac," *Quan Doi Nhan Dan*, 1 April 1996, pp. 1, 4. Also see Tran Nhung, "Tu Day Moi Ve Hoat Dong Doi Ngoai," *Quan Doi Nhan Dan*, 20 April 1996, pp. 1, 4; Nguyen Quoc Pham, "Tang Truong Kinh Te Gan Lien Voi Tien Bo Va Cong Bang Xa Hoi," *Quan Doi Nhan Dan*, 17 April 1996, pp. 1, 4; Nguyen Dinh Uoc, "Quoc Phong, An Ninh Voi Su On Dinh Chinh Tri Cua Dat Nuoc," *Quan Doi Nhan Dan*, 18 April 1996, pp. 1, 4; and Doan Chuong, "Gop Phan Tim Hien Du Thao Bao Cao Chinh Tri Dai Hoi VIII Cua Dang: Giu Vung Dinh Huong Xa Hoi Chu Nghia," *Quan Doi Nhan Dan*, 16 April 1996, pp. 1, 4. These *Quan Doi Nhan Dan* commentaries on the draft political report emphasized the threats posed by external and internal forces that had adopted a peaceful transformation approach to undermining the Vietnamese system of rule.

68. Xuan Hai, "Hai Van De Duoc Thao Luan Soi Noi Tai Dai Hoi Cai Co So Va Tren Co So O Ha Noi," pp. 32–35.

CHAPTER 3

1. Ha Dong, director of the Ideology and Culture Department, Deputy Foreign Minister Le Mai, deputy director of the External Relations Department Vo Van Tai, and deputy chief of the Office of the Central Committee Dinh Huu Khoa also attended the press conference. See Hanoi Voice of Vietnam Network in Vietnamese, 1100 GMT, 9 April 1996, *FBIS-EAS* 96-070, 10 April 1996, p. 66.

2. For the text of the Twelfth Plenary communiqué, see "Thong Bao Hoi Nghi Lan Thu Muoi Ban Chap Hanh Trung Uong Khoa VII," *Quan Doi Nhan Dan*, 22 April 1996, p. 1. For Do Muoi's opening and closing speeches see "Chung Ta Phai Tran Trong Va Nghiem Tuc Tiep Thu Y Kien Dong Gop Cua Nhan Dan De Tiep Tuc Hoan Chinh Du Thao Van Kien Trinh Dai Hoi," *Quan Doi Nhan Dan*, 22 April 1996, pp. 1, 4; and "Trong Trach Cua Dang Ta

La Phai Xay Dung Mot Ban Chap Hanh Trung Uong Vung Manh, Co Chat Luong Cao, Tieu Bieu Cho Pham Chat Va Tri Tue Cua Toan Dang Cua Ca Dan Toc," *Quan Doi Nhan Dan*, 22 April 1996, pp. 1, 4. Also see Hanoi Voice of Vietnam Network in Vietnamese, 2300 GMT, 9 May 1991, *FBIS-EAS* 91-104, 30 May 1991, pp. 68–69; and Hanoi Voice of Vietnam Network in Vietnamese, 1100 GMT, 21 April 1996, *FBIS-EAS* 96-078, 22 April 1996, pp. 100–101.

3. Western journalists rumored that Phan had been accused of divulging the names of several Vietnamese communist guerrillas during his 1959 to 1963 incarceration at the hands of the South Vietnamese government. Senior Vietnamese officials dismissed that speculation and argued that Phan's current views regarding the reforms led to his ouster, though it is entirely possible that accusations of wartime wrongdoings were trotted out by Phan's opponents to cinch his dismissal.

4. "Vietnam Ousts Official," *New York Times*, 28 April 1996, p. 3.

5. Hanoi Voice of Vietnam Network in Vietnamese, 1400 GMT, 16 January 1996, *FBIS-EAS* 96-016, 24 January 1996, pp. 100–102.

6. In mid–March 1996 Prime Minister Norodom Ranarith publicly appealed to General Secretary Do Muoi to intervene in the dispute, urged a meeting with Prime Minister Vo Van Kiet to resolve the problem, and agreed that the border technical working groups should convene. However, Ranarith argued that the issue in this instance had more to do with the continued implementation of the joint communiqué and less to do with questions that could be resolved on the basis of technical readings of authoritative maps, which was how the Vietnamese hoped the matter could be handled.

7. A small group of Vietnamese belonging to this organization sought asylum in the U.S. embassy in March 1996, but departed from the embassy grounds after being assured by the Cambodia Ministry of Interior that they would not be deported as long as they obeyed Cambodian laws.

8. The hand of Hong Ha, chairman of the party Central Committee's External Relations Department, was evident in the draft version of the report that was presented to the media on 9 April. The first section of the draft that summarized foreign policy plans and intentions accorded prominence to Hanoi's relations with communist and workers parties, independence movements, and progressive organizations, a subject that Ha signaled was very important to him personally, and a matter for which he bore special responsibility, during his August 1995 visit to the United States. At that time Hong Ha made it clear that though the External Relations Committee worked closely with the foreign ministry on issues of policy, on the matter of party-to-party relations the committee was the single authority responsible for managing links with 188 ruling parties and other national-level organizations worldwide.

9. Coincidentally, on 10 April — the date set aside for the distribution via the media of the draft political report — a joint press communiqué was issued following the visit to Cambodia by Vo Van Kiet, marking a joint agreement to promote bilateral cooperation in trade, transport, and communications; hold a third round of expert-level talks in Hanoi concerning Vietnamese residents in Cambodia; sign a consular agreement as soon as possible; and convene a meeting of the border experts' working group during the last week of April 1996. Hanoi Voice of Vietnam Network in Vietnamese, 2300 GMT, 10 April 1996, *FBIS-EAS* 96-071, 11 April 1996, pp. 93–94.

10. *Political Report of the Central Committee (VIIth Tenure) to the VIIIth National Congress*, 9 April 1996, issued by the VNCP Secretariat in Hanoi in English. Hereafter, bracketed textual citations of page numbers refer to this text. For the Vietnamese language version see "Du Thao Bao Cao Chinh Tri Cua Ban Chap Hanh Trung Uong Dang Khoa VII Trinh Dai Hoi Lan Thu VIII Cua Dang," n.d.

11. In response to the delegates who suggested that the takeoff point was an issue, the authoritative chairman's group argued that the country had in fact achieved the takeoff point, with no further explanation offered. "Bao Cao Cua Doan Chu Tich Ve Mot So Van De Trong Bao Cao Chinh Tri Qua Thao Luan Cua Hoi Nghi," pp. 73–74.

12. Ibid., pp. 74–75.

13. In 1994 the chairman's group made the case that agricultural modernization would catalyze industrialization. Ibid., pp. 75–76. Of the 621 delegates, 95.9 percent agreed with the course of industrialization and modernization defined by the party, while 13 delegates (2 percent) supported a course of industrialization only.

14. Quan Doi Nhan Dan Viet Nam, Tong Cuc Chinh Tri, *Quan Triet Va Thuc Hien Nghi Quyet Hoi Nghi Trung Uong Lan Thu 3 Ve Doi Moi Va Chinh Don Bang Trong Dang Bo Quan Doi*, Hanoi, August 1992, pp. 28–29.

15. Vu Kiem, "Lam Cho Tet Vui Muon Nha," *Nhan Dan*, 2 February 1994, p. 1; "Mat Tran To Quoc Viet Nam Phat Dong Phong Trao Cham Soc Thuong Binh, Gia Dinh Liet Si, Phung Duong Ba Me Viet Nam Anh Hung," *Nhan Dan*, 6 July 1995, pp. 1, 3; "Toan Dan Cham Soc Thuong Binh, Gia Dinh Liet Si Va Nguoi Co Cong Voi Nuoc," *Nhan Dan*, 6 July 1995, p. 1; "Huong Ung Loi Keu Goi Cua MTTQ Viet Nam," *Nhan Dan*, 15 July 1995, pp. 1, 3; "Ha Tay, Toan Dan Cham Soc Cac Doi Tuong Chinh Sac: Tong Cong Ty Buu Chinh Vien Thong Tang Moi Ba Me VNAH Trong Nganh 2 Trieu Dong," *Nhan Dan*, 16 July 1995, pp. 1, 4; "Thi Xa Long Xuyen Nang Cao Muc Song Thuong Binh, Gia Dinh Liet Si," *Nhan Dan*, 17 July 1995, pp. 1, 3; "Huong Uong Loi Keu Goai Cua MTTQ Viet Nam," *Nhan Dan*, 19 July 1995, p. 1; "Quang Ngai: Cac Xa, Phuong Tap Trung Suc Xoa Doi Ngheo Trong So

Gia Dinh Chinh Sach," *Nhan Dan*, 20 July 1995, p. 1; Tran Dinh Chinh, "Quang Tri: Nhieu Viec Lan Tinh Nghia Tri Gia Hang Ty Dong; Kon Tum: Cho Gia Dinh Chinh Sach Vay Von, Tao Viec Lam," *Nhan Dan*, 18 July 1995, p. 1; and "Nhieu Dia Phuong Mo Rong Phong Trao Phung Duong Ba Me Viet Nam Anh Hung, Tang Nha, So Tiet Kiem Tinh Nghia," *Nhan Dan*, 24 July 1995, pp. 1, 3.

16. Ministry of Foreign Affairs, Socialist Republic of Vietnam, "Statement by Mr. Hong Ha at the Press Conference on April 9, 1996"; and *Political Report of the Central Committee (VIIth Tenure) to the VIIIth National Congress*, pp. 1–57.

17. Viet An, "Dai Hoi Dai Bieu Dang Bo Ha Noi Thanh Cong Tot Dep: Thu Do—Vai Tro Trung Tam Trong Cong Nghiep Hoa, Hien Dai Hoa Dat Nuoc," *Quan Doi Nhan Dan*, 10 May 1996; and Tran Nguyen Trang, "Dai Hoi Dang Bo Thanh Pho Ho Chi Minh Lan Thu VI Thanh Cong Tot Dep: Day Manh Cong Nghiep Hoa, Hien Dai Hoa Vi Ca Nuoc, Cung Ca Nuoc," *Quan Doi Nhan Dan*, 12 May 1996, pp. 1, 3.

18. Duc Luong, "Tap Trung Chi Dao Dai Hoi Dang Bo Co So—Dac Lac: O Co So, Can Xay Dung Chuong Trinh Hanh Dong Tung Nam," *Nhan Dan*, 19 January 1996, pp. 1, 3; "Chu Tich Le Duc Anh Tham Va Lam Viec Tai Quang Ngai, Phu Yen, Binh Dinh, Thua Thien-Hue," *Nhan Dan*, 14 January 1996, pp. 1, 3; Vu Pham and Quyet Thanh, "Doi Dieu Ve Cong Nghiep Hoa, Hien Dai Hoa O Nuoc Ta," *Nhan Dan*, 12 January 1996, p. 3; Nguyen Anh Binh and Hong Nghia, "Xay Dung Dang: Dai Hoi Dang Bo Yen Phong-Mong Muon Va Su Bat Cap," *Nhan Dan*, 19 January 1996, p. 3; Huong Lien, "Song Be: Chuan Bi Dieu Kien De Buoc Vao Thoi Ky Cong Nghiep Hoa, Hien Dai Hoa," *Nhan Dan*, 17 January 1996, p. 3; and Nguyen Cong Tan, "Tao Ra Cac Dien Moi Vung Dong Bang Song Hong Trong Qua Trinh Cong Nghiep Hoa, Hien Dai Hoa," *Nhan Dan*, 23 January 1996, pp. 1, 4.

19. For example, see Manh Hung, "Gop Phan Tim Hieu Du Thao Bao Cao Chinh Tri Trinh Dai Hoi VIII Cua Dang: Xay Dung Nen Van Hoa Tien Tien Dam Ba Ban Sac Dan Toc," *Quan Doi Nhan Dan*, 23 April 1996, pp. 1, 2; Cao Thai, "Gop Phan Tim Hieu Du Thao Bao Cao Chinh Tri Trinh Dai Hoi VIII Cua Dang: Doi Moi Phuong Thuc Lanh Dao Cua Dang, Phat Huy Vai Tro Quan Ly Cua Nha Nuoc," *Quan Doi Nhan Dan*, 24 April 1996, pp. 1, 3; Doan Ngoc Hai, "Gop Phan Tim Hieu Du Thao Bao Cao Chinh Tri Trinh Dai Hoi VIII Cua Dang: Quan Diem Doc Lap Tu Chu, Sang Tao Cua Dang Trong Hoach Dinh Duong Loi Doi Moi," *Quan Doi Nhan Dan*, 25 April 1996, pp. 1, 3.

20. Tran Ba Khoa, "Nhan Thuc Dung Dang Thoi Dai Hien Nay," *Quan Doi Nhan Dan*, 15 April 1996, pp. 1, 2; Doan Chuong, "Gop Phan Tim Hieu Du Thao Bao Cao Chinh Tri Dai Hoi VIII Cua Dang," *Quan Doi Nhan Dan*,

16 April 1996, pp. 1, 4; Ngo Quoc Dat, "Ve Cac Doanh Nghiep Xay Dung Co Ban Cua Quan Doi," *Quan Doi Nhan Dan*, 16 April 1996, p. 3; Nguyen Dinh Loc, "Quoc Phong, An Ninh Voi Su On Dinh Chinh Tu Cua Dat Nuoc," *Quan Doi Nhan Dan*, 18 April 1996, pp. 1, 4; and Hoang Dung, "Nang Tam Tri Tue Cua Luc Luong Vu Trang Nhan Dan Trong Su Nghiep Day Manh Cong Nghiep Hoa, Hien Dai Hoa Nuoc Nha," *Quan Doi Nhan Dan*, 19 April 1996, pp. 1, 2. On cultural issues and the draft political report, see Phan Dang Nhat, "Ve Vi Tri Va Co Che Van Hanh Van Hoa," *Quan Doi Nhan Dan*, 25 April 1996, pp. 1, 4; and Hung, "Gop Phan Tim Hieu Du Thao Bao Cao Chinh Tri Trinh Dai Hoi VIII Cua Dang," pp. 1, 2. On party leadership and membership issues, see Hai, "Gop Phan Tim Hieu Du Thao Bao Cao Chinh Tri Thinh Dai Hoi VIII Cua Dang, pp. 1, 4; and Phong Hoi, "Nam Vung Dinh Huong Xa Hoi Chu Nghia — Thuoc Do Pham Chat, Nang Luc Cua Can Bo, Dang Vien Trong Su Nghiep Doi Moi Dat Nuoc," *Quan Doi Nhan Dan*, 27 May 1996, pp. 1, 4. On foreign policy, see Tran Nhung, "Tu Duy Moi Ve Hoat Dong Doi Ngoai," *Quan Doi Nhan Dan*, 20 April 1996, pp. 1, 4.

    21. Van Huong, "Binh Chung Dac Cong: Nang Cao Chat Luong Huan Luyen Va Giu Nghiem Ky Luat," *Quan Doi Nhan Dan*, 13 May 1996, p. 1; Nguyen Thi Binh, "Dao Tap Nhan Luc De Phuc Vu Su Nghiep Cong Nghiep Hoa, Hien Dai Hoa Dat Nuoc," *Quan Doi Nhan Dan*, 13 May 1996, pp. 1, 2; Le Kha Phieu, "May Van De Ve Xay Dung Dang Trong Quan Doi," *Tap Chi Cong San* (May 1996): 4–10; and N.D., "Danh Gia Tong Quat Ve Muoi Nam Doi Muoi," *Nhan Dan*, 11 April 1996, p. 1, 3, and 12 April 1996, pp. 1, 3; N.D., "Ve Van De Xay Dung Quan He San Xuat Va Chinh Sach Doi Voi Cac Thanh Phan Kinh Te," *Nhan Dan*, 15 April 1996, pp. 1, 3; N.D., "Day Manh Cong Nghiep Hoa, Hien Dai Hoa Theo Dinh Huong Xa Hoi Chu Nghia Va Noi Dung Cong Nghiep Hoa, Hien Dai Hoa Den Nam 2000," *Nhan Dan*, 19 April 1996, pp. 1, 3.

    22. Ngoc Lan, "Thuc Hien Nghiem Nguyen Tac Tap Trung Dan Chu," *Nhan Dan*, 6 May 1996, pp. 1, 3.

    23. N.D., "Xay Dung Dang Ngang Tam Doi Hoi Cua Thoi Ky Moi," *Nhan Dan*, 24 April, 25 April 1996, pp. 1, 3.

    24. N.D., "Chinh Sach Giai Quyet Mot So Van De Xa Hoi," *Nhan Dan*, 23 April 1996, pp. 1, 3; Nguyen Anh Binh, "Xay Dung Dang: Doi Ngu Va Trach Nhiem," *Nhan Dan*, 19 April 1996, p. 3; Le Doan Hop, "Trao Doi Y Kien: Cong Tac Tu Tuong Bam Sat Nhiem Vu Phat Trien Kinh Te-Xa Hoi," *Nhan Dan*, 19 April 1996, p. 3; and N.D., "Xay Dung Nen Van Hoa Tien Tien, Dam Da Ban Sac Dan Toc," *Nhan Dan*, 20 April 1996, pp. 1, 3.

    25. For example, see Le Xuan Luu, "Ve Moi Quan He Giua Xay Dung Va Bao Ve To Quoc Trong Giai Doan Cach Mang Moi," *Tap Chi Cong San* (May 1996): 7–10, 14; Nguyen Van Loc, "Xay Dung Dang Phai Gan Lien Voi

Bao Ve Dang," *Tap Chi Cong San* (May 1996): 11–14; Nguyen Duc Binh, "Phan Dau Vuon Len Ngang Tam Nhung Nhiem Vu Cong Tac Tu Tuong Trong Thoi Ky Moi," *Tap Chi Cong San* (May 1996): 3–6; and Van Tien Dung, "Doi Dien Rut Ra Tu Thuc Tien Lanh Dao Chien Tranh Cach Mang Cua Dang," *Tap Chi Cong San* (June 1996): 7–11.

26. N.D., "Danh Gia Tong Quat Ve Muoi Nam Doi Moi," pp. 1, 3.

27. Ho Ngoc Cu, "Mong Muon Co Dinh Luong Va Bien Phap Cu The," *Nhan Dan*, 10 May 1996, p. 4; and Ban Tai Doan, "Vung Cao Lam Cong Nghiep Hoa, Hien Dai Hoa Bang Cach Nao," *Nhan Dan*, 13 May 1996, p. 4.

28. Hanoi Vietnamese News Agency in English, 0732 GMT, 3 June 1996, *FBIS-EAS* 96-107, 3 June 1996, p. 95; and *Saigon Giai Phong*, 23 May 1996, p. 2.

29. Dao Tri Uc, "Can Mot Chien Luoc Xay Dung Phap Luat Ua Dua Phep Luat Vao Cuoc Song," *Nhan Dan*, 14 June 1996, pp. 1, 3; Nguyen Anh Lien, "Can Dat Dung Tam Muc Hon Nua Doi Voi Cong Tac Kien Tra Cua Dang Cam Quyen," *Nhan Dan*, 22 June 1996, pp. 1, 3; Hoang Trong Hanh, "Khong Nen Dung Thuat Ngu Viet Tat GDP Trong Van Kien Dang," *Nhan Dan*, 17 June 1996, p. 3; Nguyen Dang Quang, "Can Co Mot Chuong Trinh Ve Chong Quan Lieu," *Nhan Dan*, 17 June 1996, pp. 1, 3; and Vu Minh Khuong, "Mot So Xu The Phat Trien Kinh Te The Gioi Va Su Nghiep Cong Nghiep Hoa Nuoc Ta," *Nhan Dan*, 19 June 1996, pp. 1, 3.

30. For example, see Duc Luong, P.V., and Ngo Le Dan, "Dai Hoi Dang Bo Tinh Tuyen Quang, Ha Giang, Kon Tum, Dong Nai," *Nhan Dan*, 6 May 1996, pp. 1, 4; and Nguyen Dinh Khanh, et al., "Dai Hoi Dang Bo Cac Tinh Tay Ninh, Ha Bac, Khanh Hoa, Ha Tay, Lang Son," *Nhan Dan*, 29 April 1996, pp. 1, 4.

31. Nguyen Den et al., "Dai Hoi Dang Bo Cac Tinh Cao Bang, Quang Nam-Da Nang, Song Be, Ninh Binh, Thai Binh," *Nhan Dan*, 30 April 1996, pp. 1, 4.

32. Luu Quoc Thang et al., "Dai Hoi Dang Bo Cac Tinh Kien Giang, Binh Thuan, Ninh Thuan," *Nhan Dan*, 1 May 1996, pp. 1, 4.

33. Phan Huy and The Gia, "Dai Hoi Dang Bo Tinh Tra Vinh, Lam Dong," *Nhan Dan*, 4 May 1996, pp. 1, 4; Le Quang Thang et al., "Dai Hoi Dang Bo Cac Tinh Lai Chau, Ben Tre, Yen Bai, Lao Cai," *Nhan Dan*, 7 May 1996, pp. 1, 3; P.V. and Tan Thanh," Dai Hoi Dang Bo Khoi Co Quan Dan Van Trung Uong, Ba Ria-Vung Tau, Quang Tri, Son La," *Nhan Dan*, 10 May 1996, pp. 1, 2; and Phan Hung, et al., "Dai Hoi Dang Bo Cac Tinh, Thanh Pho Haiphong, Hoa Binh, Can Tho, Dac Lac, Tien Giang, va Hai Hung," *Nhan Dan*, 11 May 1996, pp. 1, 3.

34. Ban Chap Hanh Trung Uong Dang, "Thong Bao Hoi Nghi Lan Thu Muoi Mot Ban Chap Hanh Trung Uong Dang Khoa VII," *Nhan Dan*, 11 June 1996, p. 1.

35. Lai Ngoc Hai, "Tang Cuong Va Tro Quan Ly Cua Nha Nuoc," *Quan Doi Nhan Dan*, 8 June 1996, pp. 1, 2; Tran Bang, "Doanh Nghiep Quoc Phong Voi Cong Nghiep Hoa, Hien Dai Hoa," *Quan Doi Nhan Dan*, 9 June 1996, pp. 1, 4; Pham Tuyen, "Quan Triet Quan Diem Cong Nghiep Hoa, Hien Dai Hoa Vao Cong Tac Dao Tao Can Bo Quan Doi Trong Giai Doan Moi," *Quan Doi Nhan Dan*, 10 June 1996, p. 2; Hoang Van Hoa, "Ve Quan Ly Nha Nuoc Doi Voi Quoc Phong-An Ninh Trong Du Thao Bao Cao Chinh Tri," *Quan Doi Nhan Dan*, 11 June 1996, pp. 1, 2; Le Nam Phong, "Cong Tac Dao Tao Doi Ngu Can Bo Quan Doi-Yeu To Co Ban Nang Cao Chat Luong Cua Luc Luong Vu Trang," *Quan Doi Nhan Dan*, 10 June 1996, pp. 1, 2; and Dong Ngoc, "Ban Them Ve Ket Hoc Kinh Te Voi Quoc Phong, An Ninh," *Nhan Dan*, 28 May 1996, pp. 1, 3.

36. Thao Xuan Sung, "Van De Phat Trien Cua Cac Dan Toc Thieu So Va Mien Nui Trong Thoi Ky Cong Nghiep Hoa, Dien Dai Hoa Dat Nuoc," *Nhan Dan*, 24 May 1996, pp. 1, 2; Le Binh Vong, "Chong Tham Nhung—Nhiem Vu Quan Trong Cua Toan Dang, Toan Dan," *Nhan Dan*, 27 May 1996, pp. 1, 3; Do Nguyen Phuong, "Phat Trien Su Nghiep Y Te Va Nhiem Vu Cai Thien Suc Khoe Cua Dang," *Nhan Dan*, 5 June 1996, pp. 1, 3; "Thu Tuong Vo Van Kiet: Vi Cuoc Song Hom Nay Va Mai Sau, Tat Ca Chung Ta, Moi Nguoi Moi Ngan Han Lam Mot Viet Tot Cho Giu Gin Ve Sinh Moi Truong," *Nhan Dan*, 5 June 1996, pp. 1, 3; "Xa Luan: Bao Ve Moi Truong Muc Tieu Phat Trien Ben Vung," *Nhan Dan*, 5 June 1996, pp. 1, 2; Le Quy An, "Nhiem Vu Bao Ve Moi Truong Truoc Nhung Thach Thuc Va Thoi Co," *Nhan Dan*, 5 June 1996, p. 3; Dao Trong Thi, "Can Thay Ro Hon Vai Tro Cua Khoa Hoc-Cong Nghe, Giao Duc—Dao Tao Trong Su Nghiep Cong Nghiep Hoa, Hien Dai Hoa," *Nhan Dan*, 4 June 1996, pp. 1, 3; Dao Ngoc Dung, "Quan Ly Chat Che Va Khai Thac Dat Dai Co Hieu Qua," *Nhan Dan*, 6 June 1996, p. 3; Phong Ky Son, "Can Nang Cao Nang Luc Quan Ly Nha Nuoc Doi Voi Cac Thanh Phan Kinh Te," *Nhan Dan*, 7 June 1996, pp. 1, 3; Quach Dai Lanh, "Lam The Nao Co Du Can Bo Khoa Hoc Cong Nghe Cho Nong Thon, Vung Cao Vung Sau," *Nhan Dan*, 8 June 1996, pp. 1, 2; Ho Si Vinh, "Hien Dai Hoa Trong Van Hoa," *Nhan Dan*, 9 June 1996, pp. 1, 3; Le Trong and Le Thi Nham Tuyet, "Can Uu Tien Dau Tu Nang Cao Dan Tri Cho Cong Nghiep Hoa Nong Nghiep Va Phat Trien Nong Thon," *Nhan Dan*, 10 June 1996, pp. 1, 3; and Le The Tiem, "Phong, Chong Toi Pham De Thuc Hien Xa Hoi Cong Bang, Van Minh," *Nhan Dan*, 11 June 1996, pp. 1, 3.

37. Le Binh Vong, "Day Manh Hon Cai Cach Hanh Chinh Nha Nuoc De Gop Phan Xay Dung, Hoan Thien Bo May Nha Nuoc," *Nhan Dan*, 12 June 1996, p. 3; Nguyen Duc Thanh, "Cong Tac To Chuc Can Bo Trong He Thong Chinh Tri I Thoi Ky Moi," *Nhan Dan*, 11 June 1996, p. 3; Vu Hien, "Chinh Sach Doi Ngoai Doc Lap Tu Chu Rong Mo Cua Dang Va Nhan Nuoc Ta,"

Nhan Dan, 22 May 1996, pp. 1, 3; Vu Thi Duc Thoi, "Phat Huy Bai Hoc Ket Hoc Suc Manh Dan Toc Voi Suc Manh Thoi Dai Trong Giai Doan Hien Nay," *Nhan Dan*, 27 May 1996, pp. 1, 3; and Nguyen Manh Khue, "Cham Lo Hon Nua Ve Tien Bo Xa Hoi," *Nhan Dan*, 23 May 1996, p. 3.

38. Ban Xay Dung Dang, "Ba Van De Lon Ve Xay Dung Dang," *Nhan Dan*, 25 May 1996, p. 3; and Cung Chinh Doan, "Phat Trien Dang Nhieu Hon Trong Doi Ngu Tri Thuc, Dap Ung Nhu Cau Cong Nghiep Hoa, Hien Dai Hoa Dat Nuoc," *Nhan Dan*, 7 June 1996, p. 3.

CHAPTER 4

1. Hong Kong AFP in English, 0407 GMT 22 June 1996, *FBIS-EAS* 96-122. 24 June 1996, p. 88; Andy Solomon, "Party Delegates Said Unable to Agree on New Leadership," *Asia Times*, 24 June 1996, pp. 1, 2; Seth Mydans, "Vietnam to Retain Three Aged Leaders, For Now," *New York Times*, 29 June 1996, p. 3. General Le Kha Phieu, Director of the Defense Ministry's General Political Department, was named General Secretary of the Vietnamese Community Party at the 4th plenary session of the Central Committee that closed on 29 December 1997. Incumbent General Secretary Du Muoi, President Le Duc Anh (all but incapacitated by a stroke last year) and former Prime Minister Vo Van Kiet who was replaced at the November 1997 National Assembly session, retired from their Politburo positions and accepted appointment as Advisors to the Central Committee. Former General Secretary Nguyen Van Linh, former Prime Minister Pham Van Dong, and former Chairman of the Council of State Vo Chi Cong, stepped down from their advisory positions, to which they had been appointed in 1991, and reappointed at the Eighth National Party Congress in mid–1995. Linh passed away in May 1998.

2. Hanoi Voice of Vietnam Network in Vietnamese, 0500 GMT, 27 June 1996, *FBIS-EAS* 96-125, 27 June 1996, pp. 40–41; and Hanoi Voice of Vietnam Network in Vietnamese, 1100 GMT, 27 June 1996, *FBIS-EAS* 96-126, 28 June 1996, p. 43.

3. "Cac Dai Bieu Quoc Te Den Ha Noi Du Dai Hoi VIII Dang Ta: Hoi Dam Giai Hai Doan Dai Bieu Dang Cong San Viet Nam Va Dang Cong San Trung Quoc; Tong Bi Thu Do Muoi Tiep Vai Hoi Dam Voi Dong Chi Ly Bang," *Nhan Dan*, 28 July 1996, pp. 1, 4. Vietnamese officials later suggested that Li Peng had acted haughtily, breezed in and out of Hanoi without paying appropriate respect to his counterparts and pressed issues of importance to China with little mind to the agenda of the VNCP Congress.

4. Le Xuan Tung, "Ha Noi Phan Dau Cung Ca Nuoc Thuc Hien Thang Loi Su Nghiep Cong Nghiep Hoa, Hien Dai Hoa," *Nhan Dan*, 30 June 1996,

p. 7; "Phat Huy Tiem Nang Loi The Cua Cong Bien Gop Phan Xay Dung Va Bao Ve To Quoc Xa Hoi Cong Nhan: Trich Tham Luan Cua Dong Chi Le Danh Xuong, Dai Bieu Dang Bo Thanh Pho Hai Phong," *Nhan Dan*, 2 July 1996, p. 3; "Phat Trien Kinh Te-Xa Hoi Nong Thon O Trung Du Va Mien Nui: Trich Tham Luan Cua Dong Chi Bui Huu Hai, Dai Bieu Dang Bo Tinh Vinh Phu," *Nhan Dan*, 2 July 1996, p. 4; and "Mot So Van De Ke Hoach Phat Trien Kinh Te-Xa Hoi 5 Nam 1996–2000: Trich Tham Luan Cua Dong Chi Do Quoc Sam, Dai Bieu Dang Bo Tinh Lao Cai," *Nhan Dan*, 29 June 1996, p. 6. Do Quoc Sam was not reelected to the 8th Central Committee.

5. "Khai Mac Dai Hoi Lan Thi VIII Dang Cong San Viet Nam: Dai Hoi Tien Hanh Tu Ngay 28-6 Den 1-7," *Nhan Dan*, 28 June 1996, p. 1; "Dien Van Be Mac Do Dong Chi Do Muoi, Tong Bi Thu Ban Chap Hanh Trung Uong Dang Khoa VIII, Doc," *Tap Chi Cong San*, Number 13 (July 1996): 39; and "Nghi Quyet: Dai Hoi Dai Bieu Toan Quoc Lan Thu VIII, Dang Cong San Viet Nam," *Tap Chi Cong San*, Number 13 (July 1996): 38.

6. "Tong Bi Thu Do Muoi Doc Bao Cao Cua Bo Chinh Tri Trung Uong Dang Ve Cac Van Kien Dai Hoi: Tiep Tuc Su Nghiep Doi Moi, Day Manh Cong Nghiep Hoa, Hien Dai Hoa Vi Muc Tieu Dan Giau, Nuoc Manh, Xa Hoi Cong Bang, Van Minh, Vung Buoc Di Len Chi Nghi Xa Hoi," *Nhan Dan*, 29 June 1996, pp. 1–3.

7. Pham Van Dong, "Phuong Huong, Nhiem Vu va Nhung Muc Tieu Chu Yeu Ve Kinh Te Va Xa Hoi Trong Nam Nam (1981–1985) Va Nhung Nam 80," *Nhan Dan*, 30 March 1992, pp. 2–6; and Vo Van Kiet, "Phuong Huong, Muc Tieu Chu Yeu Phat Trien Kinh Te, Xa Hoi Trong 5 Nam 1986–1990)," *Nhan Dan*, 30 March 1992, pp. 2–5.

8. *Tap Chi Cong San* (July 1996): 3–40.

9. "Phuong Huong, Nhiem Vu Ke Hoach Phat Trien Kinh Te-Xa Hoi 5 Nam 1996–2000," *Nhan Dan*, 30 June 1996, pp. 4–6; and "Phuong Huong, Nhiem Vu Ke Hoach Phat Trien Kinh Te-Xa Hoi 5 Nam 1996–2000," *Nhan Dan*, 1 July 1996, p. 2.

10. "Bao Cao Chinh Tri Cua Ban Chap Hanh Trung Uong Dang Khoa VII Tai Dai Hoi Dai Bieu Toan Quoc Lan Thu VIII Cua Dang," *Nhan Dan*, 29 June 1996, pp. 4–5.

11. Andy Solomon, *Asia Times* (Bangkok) in English, 1 July 1996, pp. 1, 2, in *FBIS-EAS* 96-127, 1 July 1996, p. 55.

12. Section 4, article 20 of the 1996 revision dropped the 1991 requirement that the standing committees of party committee echelons report on "the general situation" and past work to the executive committee at regular meetings. Articles 18, 19 and 20 or chapter 4 of the 1996 version detailed the structure and responsibilities of local-level party organizations and paralleled the provisions in the 1991 laws. However, the 1996 revision eliminated

the requirement that the executive committee of the party organizations subordinate to the center or that the provinces report their activities to the next highest level.

13. For example, in the 1991 statute, article 11 of chapter 2 contained a provision for convening special congresses. The 1996 party laws moved that provision to chapter 3, article 15 on "The Party's Central Leading Organs," and added language reserving the right to convene extraordinary congresses of delegates for the Central Committee, reinforcing article 11 of the 1996 statute that stated that party committees convene congresses at the end of their tenure, eliminating the option of a midterm session for organizations below the level of the party center.

14. The 1996 statute, chapter 5 on basic party organizations, defined the terms according to which basic party organizations with fewer than 30 members must establish chapters or cells. In the 1991 party statute the formation of chapters and cells was left to the discretion of the basic organizations (article 24, chapter 5). Article 4 of the 1996 statute mandated that a party member sponsoring the application of a candidate member must have full membership status and have worked with the applicant for at least one year. The 1991 statute required that the sponsor had to have been a member for at least two years, a slightly stricter criterion that limited the number of potential sponsors. Essentially, at least one aspect of the application process was loosened by the 1996 Congress. However, article 5 of the 1996 text, on the party chapter's responsibilities in confirming a candidates' admission to the party, required that a chapter recommend to an "authorized party committee echelon" that the names of unqualified candidates be stricken from the list of probationary members. Article 5 of the 1991 statute required that a party committee echelon empowered to ratify membership admission was to be informed of the chapter-level decision to remove a name from the probationary list, suggesting that chapters had more leeway in rejecting candidates during the tenure of the 7th Central Committee than they would have under the terms defined by the 1996 statute.

15. Article 8 of the 1996 text vested some additional oversight authorities in higher echelon party committees by requiring party chapters — responsible for investigating errant and unredeemable party members — to report their findings to more senior party committees authorized to rule on membership status. The 1991 statute granted party chapters the authority to remove members who had failed to comply with regulations, skipped activities, or become delinquent in paying dues for more than three months. Similarly, while the 1996 article 8 required the party chapter to seek the views of echelons authorized to make decisions about membership status in an instance when a member requested to withdraw from the party, in the 1991

statute that decision was left up to the chapter, which was merely required to report the action to an appropriate higher-level committee for review. In the 1996 version of the party's laws the standing committee was given the power to make decisions on the punishment of certain classes of members (article 36). The 1996 statute made it somewhat easier to dissolve a party organization on the basis of a recommendation from a senior echelon party committee and a decision from the next higher level, dropping the requirement for the approval of two-thirds of the party committee or the endorsement of at least two-thirds of the regular party members in the case of chapters or organizations. The 1996 party laws also required that the Politburo, as opposed to the Central Committee, be the arbitrating authority in the event of a disagreement over the terms of discipline or judgments of party organization or member culpability.

16. Melbourne Radio, Australia, in English, 1000 GMT, 1 July 1996, *FBIS-EAS* 96-127, 1 July 1996, p. 54.

17. *Hanoi Moi*, 14 May 1996, pp. 1, 4.

18. Dang Lao Dong Viet Nam, *Dieu Le*, Hanoi: Ban Chap Hanh Trung Uong, 1968, p. 44.

19. *Nhan Dan*, 3 February 1977, pp. 2–5.

20. Hanoi Domestic Service in Vietnamese, 1430 GMT, 10 September 1987, *FBIS-EAS* , 87-176, 11 September 1987, p. 35.

21. Hanoi Voice of Vietnam Network in Vietnamese, 1400 GMT, 23 January 1996, *FBIS-EAS* 96-016, 24 January 1996, p. 104.

22. Ibid.

23. Nguyen Manh Cam's remarks at a 1 July 1996 press conference, Hanoi, Vietnam, from a Vietnamese Embassy summary, Washington, D.C., 18 July 1996.

Bibliography

Vietnamese Periodicals

Hanoi Moi
Lao Dong
Nhan Dan
Quan Doi Nhan Dan

Quan He Quoc Te
Saigon Giai Phong
Tap Chi Cong San
Tuoi Tre

Vietnamese-Language Papers
(published outside of Vietnam)

Hoa Thinh Don Viet Bao
Phu Nu Viet Nam
Thu Do Thoi Bao

Tu Do
Xay Dung

English-Language Periodicals

Asian Wall Street Journal
Far Eastern Economic Review
Foreign Broadcast Information
 Service — East Asian Service
Indochina Interchange

New York Times
Washington Post
Washington Times

Asia Times

Vietnamese Language Documents

Ban Tu Tuong-Van Hoa Trung Uong, *Tai Lieu Gioi Thieu Nghi Quyet Hoi Nghi Lan Thu 2 Ban Chap Hanh Trung Uong Dang Cong San Viet Nam, Ve Nhiem Vu Va Giai Phap On Dinh, Phat Trien Kinh Te Xa Hoi Trong Nam 1992-95,* Hanoi: Nha Xuat Ban Tu Tuong-Van Hoa, 1992.

_____, *Tiep Tuc Doi Moi va Phat Trien Kinh Te-Xa Hoi Nong Thong: Tai Lieu Hoc Tap Hghi Quyet Hoi Nghi Lan Thu Nam Ban Chap Hanh Trung Uong (Khoa VII) Dung Cho Co So Nong Thong*, Hanoi: Nha Xuat Ban Chinh Tri Quoc Gia, July 1993.

_____, *Tiep Tuc Xay Dung Va Hoan Thien Nha Nuoc Cong Hoa Xa Hoi Chu Nghia Viet Nam Trong Tam La Cai Cach Mot Buoc Nen Hanh Chinh: Tai Lieu Quan Triet Nghi Quyet Hoi Nghi Lan Thu 8 Ban Chap Hanh Trung Uong Dang Khoa VII*, Hanoi: Nha Xuat Ban Chinh Tri Quoc Gia, 1995.

Dang Cong San Viet Nam, *Van Kien: Hoi Nghi Lan Thu Hai Ban Chap Hanh Trung Uong (Khoa VII)*, Hanoi, November–December 1991.

_____, *Van Kien: Hoi Nghi Lan Thu Tu, Ban Chap Hanh Trung Uong, Khoa 7*, Luu Hanh Noi Bo, Hanoi, February 1993.

_____, *Van Kien: Hoi Nghi Lan Thu Nam Ban Chap Hanh Trung Uong (Khoa VII)*, Hanoi, 1993.

_____, *Van Kien: Hoi Nghi Dai Bieu Toan Quoc Giua Nhiem Ky Khoai VII*, Hanoi, January 1994.

_____, *Tai Lieu Tham Khao: Am Muu Va Hoat Dong "Dien Bien Hoa Binh" Cua Cac The Luc Thu Dich Tren Dat Nuoc Ta*, Hanoi, January 1994.

_____, *Van Kien: Hoi Nghi Lan Thu Bay Ban Chap Hanh Trung Uong, Khoa VII*, Hanoi, August 1994.

_____, *Van Kien: Dai Hoi Dai Bieu Toan Quoc Lan Thu VIII*, Hanoi: Nha Xuat Ban Chinh Tri Quoc Gia, 1996.

_____, *Dai Hoi Dai Bieu Toan Quoc Lan Thu VIII, Bao Cao Chinh Tri Cua Ban Chap Hanh Trung Uong Dang Khoa VII Tai Dai Hoi Dai Bieu Toan Quoc Lan Thu VIII Cua Dang*, Hanoi, June 1996.

Dang Lao Dong Viet Nam, *Dieu Le*, Hanoi: Ban Chap Hanh Trung Uong, 1968.

_____, *Dieu Le*, Hanoi: Nha Xuat Ban Su That, 1987.

_____, *Dieu Le*, Hanoi: Nha Xuat Ban Chinh Tri Quoc Gia, 1996.

"Dieu Le Dang Cong San Viet Nam," in *Van Kien: Dai Hoi VII Dang Cong San Viet Nam*, Hanoi, 1991, p. 44.

"Du Thao Bao Cao Chinh Tri Cua Ban Chap Hanh Trung Uong Dang Khoa VII Trinh Dai Hoi Lan Thu VIII Cua Dang," n.d.

Quan Doi Nhan Dan Viet Nam (Tong Cuc Chinh Tri), *Quan Triet Va Thuc Hien Nghi Quyet Hoi Nghi Trung Uong Lan Thu 3 Ve Doi Moi Va Chinh Don Dang Trong Bang Bo Quan Doi*, Hanoi, August 1992.

_____, *Thong Bao Noi Bo: Tinh Hinh The Gioi, Trong Nuoc Va Luc Luong Vu Trang*, January 1993.

_____, *Thong Bao Noi Bo: Tin The Gioi, Trong Nuoc Va Luc Luong Vu Trang*, March 1994.

Vietnamese Language Books

Ha, Hong, *Bac Ho O Phap*, Hanoi: Nha Xuat Ban Van Hoc, 1990.
———, *Thoi Thanh Nien Cua Bac Ho*, Hanoi: Nhan Xuat Ban Thanh Nien, 1994.
Han, Le Mau, *Dang Cong San Viet Nam: Cac Dai Hoi Va Hoi Nghi Trung Uong*, Hanoi: Nha Xuat Ban Chinh Tri Quoc Gia, 1995.
Muoi, Do, *Day Manh Su Nghiep Doi Moi V Chu Nghia Xa Hoi, vol. 3*, Hanoi: Nha Xuat Ban Chinh Tri Quoc Gia, 1993.
———, *Ve Xay Dung Dang*, Hanoi: Nha Xuat Ban Chinh Tri Quoc Gia, 1994.
———, *Day Manh Su Nghiep Doi Moi V Chu Nghia Xa Hoi, vol. 5*, Hanoi: Nha Xuat Ban Chinh Tri Quoc Gia, 1995.
Trinh, Le Xuan, *Kinh Te Xa Hoi Viet Nam 2000: Muc Tieu, Phuong Huong Va Giai Phap Chu Yeu — Tai Lieu Tham Khao Noi Bo*, Hanoi: Uy Ban Ke Hoach Nha Nuoc, December 1990.

Vietnamese Language Articles (Signed)

An, Le Quy, "Nhiem Vu Bao Ve Moi Truong Truoc Nhung Thach Thuc Va Thoi Co," *Nhan Dan*, 5 June 1996, p. 3.
An, Nam et al., "Dai Hoi Dang Bo Co Quan Bo Thuong Mai, Bo Lao Dong — Thuong Binh Va Xa Hoi, Tong Cuc Du Lich," *Nhan Dan*, 8 April 1996, pp. 1, 4.
An, Viet, "Dai Hoi Dai Bieu Dang Bo Ha Noi Thanh Cong Tot Dep: Thu Do — Vai Tro Trung Tam Trong Cong Nghiep Hoa, Hien Dai Hoa Dat Nuoc," *Quan Doi Nhan Dan*, 10 May 1996.
Ban Chap Hanh Trung Uong Dang, "Thong Bao Hoi Nghi Lan Thu Muoi Mot Ban Chap Hanh Trung Uong Dang Khoa VII," *Nhan Dan*, 11 June 1996, p. 1.
Ban Xay Dung Dang, "Ba Van De Lon Ve Xay Dung Dang," *Nhan Dan*, 25 May 1996, p. 3.
Bang, Tran, "Doanh Nghiep Quoc Phong Voi Cong Nghiep Hoa, Hien Dai Hoa," *Quan Doi Nhan Dan*, 9 June 1996, pp. 1, 4.
Bao, Trong, "Phu Nu Quan Doi: Day Manh Giao Duc Truyen Thong, Xay Dung Don Vi, Giup Nhau Lam Kinh Te Gia Dinh Va Cac Phong Trao Xa Hoi," *Quan Doi Nhan Dan*, 7 March 1996, p. 1.
Binh, Nguyen Anh, "Cau Hoi Truoc Dai Hoi Dang Bo Co So Nong Thon," *Nhan Dan*, 6 December 1995, pp. 1, 3.
———, "Dai Hoi Dang Bo Duong Sat Viet Nam: Phat Huy Truyen Thong Giai Cap Cong Nhan, Tang Cuong Cong Tac Xay Dung Dang, Xay Dung Doi

Ngu, Tung Buoc Hien Dai Hoa He Thong Duong Sat," *Nhan Dan*, 5 April 1996, pp. 1, 4.

———, "Xay Dung Dang: Doi Ngu Va Trach Nhiem," *Nhan Dan*, 19 April 1996, p. 3.

Binh, Nguyen Anh, and Hong Nghia, "Xay Dung Dang: Dai Hoi Dang Bo Yen Phong-Mong Muon Va Su Bat Cap," *Nhan Dan*, 19 January 1996, p. 3.

Binh, Nguyen Duc, "Phan Dau Vuon Len Ngang Tam Nhung Nhiem Vu Cong Tac Tu Tuong Trong Thoi Ky Moi," *Tap Chi Cong San* (May 1996): 3–6.

Binh, Nguyen Thi, "Suy Nghi, Ve Cong Nghiep Hoa, Hien Dai Hoa Dat Nuoc," *Nhan Dan*, 26 February 1996, pp. 1, 4.

———, "Dao Tap Nhan Luc De Phuc Vu Su Nghiep Cong Nghiep Hoa, Hien Dai Hoa Dat Nuoc," *Quan Doi Nhan Dan*, 13 May 1996, pp. 1, 2.

Bon, Bui Dinh, "Xay Dung Giai Cap Cong Nhan Viet Nam Ngang Tam Voi Su Nghiep Cong Nghiep Hoa, Hien Dai Hoa Dat Nuoc," *Quan Doi Nhan Dan*, 1 May 1996, pp. 1, 2.

Cam, Nguyen Manh, "Binh Thuong Hoa Kinh Te." Keynote speech to the U.S.–Vietnam Trade Forum conference on economic normalization, Washington, D.C., October 1995.

Canh, Nguyen Van, "Voi Y Nghi Ve Dai Hoi Dang," *Xay Dung* (California) (31 January 1996): 9–18.

Chinh, Tran Dinh, "Quang Tri: Nhieu Viec Lan Tinh Nghia Tri Gia Hang Ty Dong; Kon Tum: Cho Gia Dinh Chinh Sach Vay Von, Tao Viec Lam," *Nhan Dan*, 18 July 1995, p. 1.

Chuong, Doan, "Gop Phan Tim Hieu Du Thao Bao Cao Chinh Tri Dai Hoi VIII Cua Dang: Giu Vung Dinh Huong Xa Hoi Chu Nghia," *Quan Doi Nhan Dan*, 16 April 1996, pp. 1, 4.

Cu, Ho Ngoc, "Mong Muon Co Dinh Luong Va Bien Phap Cu The," *Nhan Dan*, 10 May 1996, p. 4.

Cuong, Nguyen The, "Minh Hai Su Chuyen Dong Bat Dau Tu Dai Hoi Dang Bo Co So," *Nhan Dan*, 10 January 1996, p. 3.

N.D., "Danh Gia Tong Quat Ve Muoi Nam Doi Muoi," *Nhan Dan*, 11 April and 12 April 1996, pp. 1, 3.

———, "Ve Van De Xay Dung Quan He San Xuat Va Chinh Sach Doi Voi Cac Thanh Phan Kinh Te," *Nhan Dan*, 15 April 1996, pp. 1, 3.

———, "Day Manh Cong Nghiep Hoa, Hien Dai Hoa Theo Dinh Huong Xa Hoi Chu Nghia Va Noi Dung Cong Nghiep Hoa, Hien Dai Hoa Den Nam 2000," *Nhan Dan*, 19 April 1996, pp. 1, 3.

———, "Xay Dung Nen Van Hoa Tien Tien, Dam Da Ban Sac Dan Toc," *Nhan Dan*, 20 April 1996, pp. 1, 3.

———, "Chinh Sach Giai Quyet Mot So Van De Xa Hoi," *Nhan Dan*, 23 April 1996, pp. 1, 3.

_____, "Xay Dung Dang Ngang Tam Doi Hoi Cua Thoi Ky Moi," *Nhan Dan*, 24 April, and 25 April 1996, pp. 1, 3.

Dan, Ngo Le, and TTXVN, "Chu Tich Le Duc Anh, Thu Tuong Vo Van Kiet Lam Viec Voi Mot So Tinh Phia Nam," *Nhan Dan*, 16 February 1996, pp. 1, 4.

Dang, Nguyen Van, "Ve Phuong Huong Tiep Tuc Doi Moi Co Che Quan Ly Kinh Te," *Tap Chi Cong San* 18 (December 1995): 18–24.

Dao, Le Quang, "Dai Doan Ket Toan Dan Trong Giai Doan Moi," *Nhan Dan*, 10 November 1995, p. 3.

Dao, Pham, et al., "65 Nam Doanh Thanh Nien Cong San Ho Chi Minh: Ngat 23–3, Khai Mac Dai Hoi Thanh Nien Tien Tien Toan Quoc," *Nhan Dan*, 20 March 1996, pp. 1, 3.

Dat, Ngo Quoc, "Ve Cac Doanh Nghiep Xay Dung Co Ban Cua Quan Doi," *Quan Doi Nhan Dan*, 16 April 1996, p. 3.

Den, Nguyen, et al., "Dai Hoi Dang Bo Cac Tinh Cao Bang, Quang Nam-Da Nang, Song Be, Ninh Binh, Thai Binh," *Nhan Dan*, 30 April 1996, pp. 1, 4.

Dien, Le Quang, "Phai Chang Khong Can Su Lanh Dao Cua Dang Cong San Khi Nuoc Ta Chuyen Sang Kinh Te Thi Truong," *Tap Chi Cong San* 10 (August 1995): 59–60.

Dieu, Vu, "Da Hoi Dang Bo Thanh Pho Ha Long: Khai Thac Loi The, Tang Nhanh Nhip Do Phat Trien," *Nhan Dan*, 11 February 1996, p. 1.

Do, Tran, "Gop Y Ve Dai Hoi VIII," *Xay Dung* (California) 74 (December 1995), pp. 29–36.

Doan, Ban Tai, "Vung Cao Lam Cong Nghiep Hoa, Hien Dai Hoa Bang Cach Nao," *Nhan Dan*, 13 May 1996, p. 4.

Doan, Cung Chinh, "Dang Bo Tong Cuc Hau Can: Xac Dinh Nhiem Vu Trong Tam Bao Dam Hau Can Quan Doi 1996," *Quan Doi Nhan Dan*, 12 December 1995, p. 1.

_____, "Phat Trien Dang Nhieu Hon Trong Doi Ngu Tri Thuc, Dap Ung Nhu Cau Cong Nghiep Hoa, Hien Dai Hoa Dat Nuoc," *Nhan Dan*, 7 June 1996, p. 3.

Dong, Pham Van, "Phuong Huong, Nhiem Vu Va Nhung Muc Tieu Chu Yeu Ve Kinh Te Va Xa Hoi Trong Nam Nam (1981–85) Va Nhung Nam 80," *Nhan Dan*, 30 March 1992, pp. 2–6.

_____, "Mot Su Kien Lon Va Dau An Cua No," *Nhan Dan*, 1 January 1996, pp. 1, 3.

Du, Nguyen Quang, "Tang Cuong Ban Chat Giai Cap Cong Nhan Va Tinh Tien Phong Cua Dang," *Tap Chi Cong San* 3 (February 1996): 36–38.

Duc, Do Trong, "Quan Chung Phong Khong: Thi Dua Tap Trung Vao Cac Nhiem Vu Trong Tam," *Quan Doi Nhan Dan*, 28 March 1996, p. 1.

Dung, Dao Ngoc, "Quan Ly Chat Che Va Khai Thac Dat Dai Co Hieu Qua," *Nhan Dan*, 6 June 1996, p. 3.

Dung, Hoang, "Nang Tam Tri Tue Cua Luc Luong Vu Trang *Nhan Dan* Trong Su Nghiep Day Manh Cong Nghiep Hoa, Hien Dai Hoa Nuoc Nha," *Quan Doi Nhan Dan*, 19 April 1996, pp. 1, 2.

Dung, Nguyen Anh, "Dai Hoi Dang Bo Co Quan Bo Tai Chinh: Khai Thac, Quan Ly, Su Dung Tot Hon Cac Nguon Tai Chinh," *Nhan Dan*, 14 February 1996, pp. 1, 4.

Dung, Van Tien, "Quan Doi Ta Mai Mai Xung Dang Voi Loi Tuyen Duong Cong Trang Cua Chu Tich Ho Chi Minh," *Tap Chi Cong San* 18 (December 1995): 13–17.

———, "Doi Dien Rut Ra Tu Thuc Tien Lanh Dao Chien Tran Cach Mang Cua Dang," *Tap Chi Cong San*, Number 11 (June 1996): 7–11.

Duong, Hai, "Truoc Dai Hoi Dang Bo Co So: Xuan Thuy Voi Cac Chuong Tring Trong Diem," *Nhan Dan*, 19 July 1995, p. 3.

———, "Dang Bo Quan Doi Chuan Bi Tien Hanh Dai Hoi Dang Bo Cac Cap," *Nhan Dan*, 9 October 1995, p. 1.

———, "Quoc Oai Chuan Bi Dai Hoi Dang Bo Co So: Nhung Lan Gio Moi," *Nhan Dan*, 27 October 1995, p. 3.

———, "Tai Dai Hoi Dang Bo Huyen Hung Ha: Dong Chi Dao Duy Tung: Thay Ro Hon Huong Di Vao Cong Nghiep Hoa Nong Nghiep, Xay Dung Nong Thon Moi," *Nhan Dan*, 7 March 1996, pp. 1, 4.

Duong, Hai, Duy Phuc, and Kim Quy, "Dai Hoi Dang Bo Huyen Duc Trong (Lam Dong) Tap Trung Moi Nguon Von De Chuyen Dich Co Cau Kinh Te Theo Huong Tang Ty Trong Cong Nghiep," *Nhan Dan*, 16 March 1996, pp. 1, 3.

Gia, The, "Tang Cuong Cong Tac Kiem Tra, Phuc Vu Dai Hoi Dang Cac Cap," *Nhan Dan*, 25 November 1995, pp. 1, 2.

———, "Khang Dinh Vai Tro Cua Chi Bo Trong Mo Hinh Kinh Te Moi," *Nhan Dan*, 6 December 1995, p. 3.

———, "Dai Hoi Dang Bo Huyen Hoc Mon: Chuyen Dich Co Can Kinh Te Nong Nghiep Hoa, Hien Dai Hoa," *Nhan Dan*, 12 February 1996, pp. 1, 4.

———, "Dai Hoi Dang Bo Quan Khu 7: Xay Dung The Tran Quoc Phong Toan Dan Gan Voi The Trau An Ninh Nhan Dan," *Nhan Dan*, 5 April 1996, pp. 1, 4.

Gia, The, and Thanh Phong, "TP Ho Chi Minh Va Ha Tinh Tong Ket Nam Nam Thuc Hien Nghi Quyet Trung Uong 8B," *Nhan Dan*, 25 September 1995, pp. 1, 3.

Giam, To Buu, "Nam Vung Dinh Huong Xa Hoi Chu Nghia Trong Viec Phat Trien Nen Kinh Te Nhieu Thanh Phan," *Nhan Dan*, 4 May 1996, pp. 1, 4.

Giang, Thanh, "Cong Nghiep Hoa Dat Nuoc The Hien Tu Tuong Va Mo Uoc Cua Chung Ta," *Nhan Dan*, 21 February 1996, pp. 1, 3.
Giang, Thinh, "Tong Bi Thu Do Muoi Tham Khu Cong Nghiep Sai Dong (Ha Noi)," *Nhan Dan*, 11 March 1996, pp. 1, 4.
Giao, Thuy, "Dang Cong San Viet Nam Gia Tang Khung Bop Doi Lap Xin Vao Tu," *Xay Dung* (California) 76 (31 January 1996): 3–5.
_____, "Tu Khai Tu Che Do Cong San Doi Sang Che Do Quan Phiet," *Xay Dung* (California) 69 (30 June 1996): 2–6.
T.H., "Hoat Dong Cong Tac Dang," *Nhan Dan*, 21 July 1995, p. 3.
_____, "Hoat Dong Cong Tac Dang," *Nhan Dan*, 15 September 1995, p. 3.
Ha, Nguyen Duc, "Cu The Hoa Cong Tac Xay Dung Co So Dang," *Nhan Dan*, 28 June 1995, p. 3.
_____, "Ket Qua Va Kinh Nghiem Doi Moi, Chinh Don Dang O Yen Bai," *Tap Chi Cong San* 16 (November 1995): 47–49.
_____, "Nhung Dieu Rut Ra Qua Dai Hoi Diem O Cac Co So," *Nhan Dan*, 8 December 1995, pp. 1, 3.
Ha, Song, "Dai Hoi Dang Bo Hoi Nha Van Viet Nam: Tac Pham Se Minh Chung Su Lanh Dao Cua Dang, Tu Tuong Nhan Van Va Dien Mao Van Hoc," *Nhan Dan*, 14 March 1996, pp. 1, 2.
Hai, Doan Ngoc, "Gop Phan Tim Hieu Du Thao Bao Cao Chinh Tri Trinh Dai Hoi VIII Cua Dang: Quan Diem Doc Lap Tu Chu, Sang Tao Cua Dang Trong Hoach Dinh Duong Loi Doi Moi," *Quan Doi Nhan Dan*, 25 April 1996, pp. 1, 3, 4.
Hai, Lai Ngoc, "Tang Cuong Va Tro Quan Ly Cua Nha Nuoc," *Quan Doi Nhan Dan*, 8 June 1996, pp. 1, 2.
Hai, Phong, "Nam Vung Dinh Huong Xa Hoi Chu Nghia — Thuoc Do Pham Chat, Nang Luc Cua Can Bo, Dang Vien Trong Su Nghiep Doi Moi Dat Nuoc," *Quan Doi Nhan Dan*, 27 May 1996, pp. 1, 4.
Hai, Xuan, "Moi Quan He Giui Doi Moi Chinh Don Va Tang Cuong Ban Chat Giai Cap Cong Nhan Cua Dang," *Tap Chi Cong San* 3 (February 1996): 39–41.
_____, "Hai Van De Duoc Thao Luan Soi Noi Tai Dai Hoi Cai Co So Va Tren Co So O Ha Noi," *Tap Chi Cong San* 7 (April 1996): 32–35.
Hanh, Hoang Trong, "Khong Nen Dung Thuat Ngu Viet Tat GDP Trong Van Kien Dang," *Nhan Dan*, 17 June 1996, p. 3.
Hien, Nguyen Khac, "Kinh Te Thi Truong Va Dinh Huong Xa Hoi Chu Nghia Co Doi Lap Nhau Khong?" *Tap Chi Cong San* 4 (February 1996): 12–15.
_____, "Hoan Thien He Thong Chinh Sach Thue," *Tap Chi Cong San* 11 (June 1996): 11–14.
Hien, Thu, "Lam Dong: Hoan Thanh Cong Tac Giao Quan Dot 1 Nam 1996," *Quan Doi Nhan Dan*, 8 March 1996, p. 1.

Hien, Vu, "Cuc Dien Moi Va Dinh Huong Di Len Cua Dat Nuoc," *Tap Chi Cong San* 4 (February 1996): 20–24.

———, "Chinh Sach Doi Ngoai Doc Lap Tu Chu Rong Mo Cua Dang Va Nhan Nuoc Ta," *Nhan Dan*, 22 May 1996, pp. 1, 3.

Hoa, Hoang Van, "Ve Quan Ly Nha Nuoc Doi Voi Quoc Phong-An Ninh Trong Du Thao Bao Cao Chinh Tri," *Quan Doi Nhan Dan*, 11 June 1996, pp. 1, 2.

Hoa, Pham Van, "To Chuc Tot Dai Hoi 3 Cap Dang Bo Thanh Pho Cho Chi Minh," *Saigon Giai Phong*, 16 October 1995, pp. 1, 5.

Hoang, Le, "Tinh Uy Lang Son Chuan Bi Dai Hoi Dang Cac Cap Gan Voi Tong Ket Cac Nghi Quyet Cua Trung Uong," *Nhan Dan*, 23 October 1995, p. 1.

Hoc, Van, "Dang Bo Quan Khu I: 100% To Chuc Co So Dang Da Tien Hanh Dai Hoi Dat Ket Qua Cao," *Quan Doi Nhan Dan*, 23 February 1996, p. 1.

Hoc, Van, and Tran Ho Bac, "Cac Don Vi Ra Quan Huyen Luyen," *Quan Doi Nhan Dan*, 4 March 1996, pp. 1, 4.

Hoi, Khong Doan, "Dinh Huong Xa Hoi Chu Nghia O Nuoc Ta," *Tap Chi Cong San* 5 (March 1996): 15–17.

Hoi, Phong, "Nam Vung Dinh Huong Xa Hoi Chu Nghia—Thuoc Do Pham Chat, Nang Luc Cua Can Bo, Dang Vien Trong Su Nghiep Doi Moi Dat Nuoc," *Quan Doi Nhan Dan*, 27 May 1996, pp. 1, 4.

Hop, Le Doan, "Trao Doi Y Kien: Cong Tac Tu Tuong Bam Sat Nhiem Vu Phat Trien Kinh Te-Xa Hoi," *Nhan Dan*, 19 April 1996, p. 3.

Hung, Manh, "Gop Phan Tim Hieu Du Thao Bao Cao Chinh Tri Trinh Dai Hoi VIII Cua Dang: Xay Dung Nen Van Hoa Tien Tien Dam Ba Ban Sac Dan Toc," *Quan Doi Nhan Dan*, 23 April 1996, pp. 1, 2.

Hung, Phan, et al., "Dai Hoi Dang Bo Cac Tinh, Thanh Pho Haiphong, Hoa Binh, Can Tho, Dac Lac, Tien Giang, Va Hai Hung," *Nhan Dan*, 11 May 1996, pp. 1, 3.

Huong, Van, "Tap Trung Lanh Dao Thuc Hien Tot 6 Mat Cong Tac Ky Thuat," *Quan Doi Nhan Dan*, 5 February 1996, pp. 1, 4.

———, "Binh Chung Dac Cong: Nang Cao Chat Luong Huan Luyen Va Giu Nghiem Ky Luat," *Quan Doi Nhan Dan*, 13 May 1996, p. 1.

Huy, Phan, "Tong Ket Cong Tac To Chuc Xay Dung Dang O Cac Tinh Phia Nam," *Nhan Dan*, 25 March 1995, pp. 1, 4.

———, "Can Tho Phat Dong Thi Dua Huong Toi Dai Hoi VIII Cua Dang," *Nhan Dan*, 25 January 1996, pp. 1, 4.

Huy, Phan, and The Gia, "Dai Hoi Dang Bo Tinh Tra Vinh, Lam Dong," *Nhan Dan*, 4 May 1996, pp. 1, 4.

Huy, Thuan, "Qua Mot So Dai Hoi Dang Bo Co Su O Cac Tinh Mien Trung:

Can Co Thoi Gian, Chuan Bi Tot Hon Ve Noi Dung Va Nhan Du," *Nhan Dan*, 5 December 1995, pp. 1, 4.

Huy, Vu Quang, "Dang Bo Quan Chung Khong Quan: Tang Cuong Cong Tac Kiem Tra, Gop Phan Giam Ty Le Dang Vien Vi Pham Ky Luat," *Quan Doi Nhan Dan*, 26 February 1996, p. 1.

Khai, Phan Van, "Phat Huy Da Tien Bo Moi, Phan Dau Thuc Hien Thang Loi Nhiem Vu Nam 1996 Theo Nghi Quyet Cua Quoc Hoi," *Nhan Dan*, 3 March, 4 March 1996, pp. 1, 3.

Kham, Tran, "Dai Hoi Dang Bo Co Quan Bo Cong Nghiep Tham Muu Cho Dang, Nha Nuoc Va Di Dau Trong Cong Nghiep Hoa, Hien Dai Hoa," *Nhan Dan*, 7 April 1996, pp. 1, 4.

Khanh, Hong, "Dai Hoi Dang Bo Khoi Cac Co Quan Kinh Te Trung Uong: Lanh Dao Bao Dam Thuc Hien Thang Loi Cac Duong Loi, Chinh Sach, Quan Diem Phat Trien Kinh Te-Xa Hoi," *Nhan Dan*, 28 April 1996, pp. 1, 4.

Khanh, Nguyen Dinh, and Nguyen Hong, "Kon Tum: Bat Dau Tu Cuoc Song Cua Dan," *Nhan Dan*, 3 November 1995, p. 3.

Khanh, Nguyen Dinh, et al., "Dai Hoi Dang Bo Cac Tinh Tay Ninh, Ha Bac, Khanh Hoa, Ha Tay, Lang Son," *Nhan Dan*, 29 April 1996, pp. 1, 4.

Khanh, Pham Van, "Tinh Uy Ha Tay: Tong Ket Thuc Hien Doi Moi, Chinh Don Dang Va Cong Tac Dan Van," *Nhan Dan*, 23 July 1995, pp. 1, 4.

———. "Doi Moi, Chinh Don Dang O Gia Lai: Giai Phap Dong Bo, Phu Hop Voi Tung Vung," *Nhan Dan*, 24 November 1995, p. 3.

———, "Ghi Nhan Tu Dai Hoi Diem Dang Bo Co So O Hai Hung," *Nhan Dan*, 7 December 1995, pp. 1, 4.

———, "Dai Hoi Dang Bo Thi Xa Hung Yen: Tap Trung Phat Trien Manh Cong Nghiep, Gan Lien Vo Do Thi Hoa," *Nhan Dan*, 10 February 1996, pp. 1, 4.

———, "Dai Hoi Dang Bo Tong Cuc Canh Sat Nhan Dan: Xay Dung Luc Luong Vung Manh, Bao Dam Trat Tu An Toan Xa Hoi," *Nhan Dan*, 29 February 1996, pp. 1, 4.

———, "Day Manh Toc Do Cong Nghiep Hoa Gan Voi Quy Hoach, Quan Ly Do Tho," *Nhan Dan*, 4 March 1996, pp. 1, 4.

———, "Dai Hoi Dang Bo Tu Tuong-Van Hoa Trung Uong: Nang Cao Chat Luong Cong Tac Tu Tuong Vuon To Tam Cao Moi," *Nhan Dan*, 6 April 1996, pp. 1, 2.

Khanh, Pham Van, and Vu Hieu, "Dai Hoi Dang Bo Quan Khu 1 Nan Cao Chat Luong Luc Luong Vu Trang Lam Nong Cot Xay Dung The Tran Quoc Phong Toan Dan Vung Manh," *Nhan Dan*, 15 March 1996, pp. 1, 3.

Khanh, Pham Van, and Nguyen Hong, "Kon Tum, Gia Lai, Dac Lac: Chuan Bi Dai Hoi Dang Cac Cap," *Nhan Dan*, 24 October 1995, pp. 1,2.

Khoa, Nguyen Ngoc, "Bua Tien Moi Cua Dang Bo Huyen Thanh Oai," *Tap Chi Cong San* 4 (February 1996): 50–54.

Khoa, Tran Ba, "Nhan Thuc Dung Dang Thoi Dai Hien Nay," *Quan Doi Nhan Dan*, 15 April 1996, pp. 1, 2.

Khoi, Nguyen, "Moc Chau Phan Dau Cho Su Dong Deu," *Nhan Dan*, 6 March 1996, p. 3.

Khue, Doan, "Xay Dung Dang Bo Ngang Tam Nhien Vu Hai Quan La Luc Luong Nong Cot Bao Ve Vung Chach Chu Quyen Vung Bien, Hai Dan Cua To Quoc," *Quan Doi Nhan Dan*, 5 February 1996, pp. 1, 4.

_____, "Xay Dung Quan Doi Chinh Quy, Tinh Nhue Trong Su Nghiep Cong Nghiep Hoa, Hien Dai Hoa Dat Nuoc," *Nhan Dan*, 23 March 1996, pp. 1, 4.

Khue, Nguyen Manh, "Cham Lo Hon Nua Ve Tien Bo Xa Hoi," *Nhan Dan*, 23 May 1996, p. 3.

Khuong, Vu Minh, "Mot So Xu The Phat Trien Kinh Te The Gioi Va Su Nghiep Cong Nghiep Hoa Nuoc Ta," *Nhan Dan*, 19 June 1996, pp. 1, 3.

Kiem, Vu, "Lam Cho Tet Vui Muon Nha," *Nhan Dan*, 2 February 1994, p. 1.

Kiem Vu, Van Xuyen, and Tu Uyen, "Tai Dai Hoi Dang Bo Huyen Tieu Hai Dong Chi Le Phuoc Tho: Tien Hai Nhanh Chong Chuyen Dich Co Can Kinh Te Theo Huong Cong Nghiep Hoa, Hien Dai Hoa Nong Thon," *Nhan Dan*, 29 March 1996, pp. 1, 2.

_____, "Tai Dai Hoi Dang Bo Thanh Pho Nam Dinh: Dong Chi Nguyen Ha Phan: Xay Dung Thanh Pho Giai Dep, Van Minh, Kong De Mot Nguoi Trong Do Tuoi Lao Dong Khong Coi Viec Lam," *Nham Dan*, 29 March 1996, pp. 1, 2.

Kiet, Vo Van, "Phuong Huong, Muc Tieu Chu Yeu Phat Trien Kinh Te, Xa Hoi Trong 5 Nam 1986–90," *Nhan Dan*, 30 March 1992, pp. 2–5.

_____, "Dong Luc Phat Trien Cua Tay Nguyen Nam Trong Tri Tue Va Ban Tay Cua Chung Ta," *Nhan Dan*, 20 March 1996, pp. 1, 3.

Ky, Dang Xuan, "Vung Buoc Di Con Duong Xa Hoi Chu Nghia," *Tap Chi Cong San* 4 (February 1996): 3–6.

T.B.L., "Ta Ca Cac Co So Dang Tien Hanh Dai Hoi Truoc Thang 12–1995," *Saigon Giai Phong*, 30 July 1995, pp. 1, 7.

_____, "Thanh Uy Chi Dao: Tiep Tuc Thi Diem, Rut Kinh Nghiem To Chuc Tot Dai Hoi Dang Bo Cac Cap," *Saigon Giai Phong*, 8 September 1995, pp. 1, 5.

Lan, Ngoc, "Thuc Hien Nghiem Nguyen Tac Tap Trung Dan Chu," *Nhan Dan*, 6 May 1996, pp. 1, 3.

Lanh, Quach Dai, "Lam The Nao Co Du Can Bo Khoa Hoc Cong Nghe Cho Nong Thon, Vung Cao Vung Sau," *Nhan Dan*, 8 June 1996, pp. 1, 2.

Lap, Duong Tu, "Ve Mot Buc Thu Bat Thuong," *Xay Dung* (California) 77 (29 February 1996): 38–40.

Lien, Huong, "Song Be: Chuan Bi Dieu Kien De Buoc Vao Thoi Ky Cong Nghiep Hoa, Hien Dai Hoa," *Nhan Dan*, 17 January 1996, p. 3.

Lien, Nguyen Anh, "Can Dat Dung Tam Muc Hon Nua Doi Voi Cong Tac Kien Tra Cua Dang Cam Quyen," *Nhan Dan*, 22 June 1996, pp. 1, 3.

Linh, Nguyen Van, "Dua Vao Nhan Dan, Tang Cuong Va Tro Lanh Dao Cua Dang, Tiep Tuc Dua Cong Cuoc Doi Moi Den Thang Loi Hoan Toan," *Tap Chi Cong San* 10 (August 1995): 5–8.

Loc, Nguyen Dinh, "Quoc Phong, An Ninh Voi Su On Dinh Chinh Tu Cua Dat Nuoc," *Quan Doi Nhan Dan*, 18 April 1996, pp. 1, 4.

Loc, Nguyen Van, "Xay Dung Dang Phai Gan Lien Voi Bao Ve Dang," *Tap Chi Cong San* 10 (May 1996): 11–14.

Loi, Phan, "Co Van Pham Van Dong Tham, Lam Viec Tai Quang Ngai Va Quang Nam-Da Nang," *Nhan Dan*, 13 March 1996, pp. 1, 4.

———, "Dai Hoi Dang Bo TP Da Nang: Phan Dau Tro Thanh Trung Tam Kinh Te Mien Trung," *Nhan Dan*, 18 March 1996, pp. 1, 3.

———, "Dai Hoi Dang Bo Huyen Mo Duc (Quang Ngai): Bon Chong Trinh Kinh Te O Mot Huyen Thuan Nong," *Nhan Dan*, 20 March 1996, pp. 1, 4.

Long, Thu, "Dang Bo Quan Khu Thu Do: Hoan Thanh Ke Hoach Dai Hoi Dang Cap Co So Va Tren Truc Tiep Co So," *Quan Doi Nhan Dan*, 8 March 1996, p. 1.

Luong, Duc, "Tap Trung Chi Dao Dai Hoi Dang Bo Co So," *Nhan Dan*, 16 January 1996, p. 1.

———, "Tap Trung Chi Dao Dai Hoi Dang Bo Co So—Dac Lac: O Co So, Can Xay Dung Chuong Trinh Hanhg Dong Tung Nam," *Nhan Dan*, 19 January 1996, pp. 1, 3.

———, "Tinh Uy Kon Tum Chuan Bi Dai Hoi Cap Tren Co So," *Nhan Dan*, 22 January 1996, pp. 1, 4.

———, "Be Mac Lop Can Bo Gioi Tri Thuc Nghien Cuu Duong Loi, Quan Diem Cua Dang," *Nhan Dan*, 27 January 1996, pp. 1, 4.

———, "Dai Hoi Dang Bo Cap Tren Co So O Tuyen Quang: Nhieu Dai Bieu Ung Cu Va Ban Chap Hanh Moi," *Nhan Dan*, 30 January 1996, pp. 1, 4.

Luong, Duc, and Mai Phong, "Xay Dung Dang: Nhung Dieu Rut Ra Qua Dai Hoi Diem Dang Bo Co So O Ninh Binh," *Nhan Dan*, 4 August 1995, p. 3.

Luong, Duc, P.V., and Ngo Le Dan, "Dai Hoi Dang Bo Tinh Tuyen Quang, Ha Giang, Kon Tum, Dong Nai," *Nhan Dan*, 6 May 1996, pp. 1, 4.

Luu, Le Xuan, "Ve Moi Quan He Giua Xay Dung Va Bao Ve To Quoc Trong Giai Doan Cach Manh Moi," *Tap Chi Cong San* 10 (May 1996): 7–10, 14.

Muoi, Ba, "Dai Hoi Dang Bo Huyen Ninh Phuoc: Phat Trien Cac Vung Kinh Te Trong Diem," *Nhan Dan*, 5 March 1996, pp. 1, 2.

Muoi, Do, "Cong Nghiep Hoa, Hien Dai Hoa Phai Duoc Quan Triet Trong Dai Hoi Dang Bo Cac Cap, Truoc Het Tu Co So," *Nhan Dan*, 11 January 1996, pp. 1, 4.

———, "Bien Quyet Tam Cua Dang, Cua Giai Cap Cong Nhan Thanh Suc Manh Cua Dong Bao Ca Nuoc De Tien Hanh Thang Loi Cong Cuoc Doi Moi, Cong Nghiep Hoa, Hien Dai Hoa Nuoc Nha," *Nhan Dan*, 24 February 1996, pp. 1, 4.

———, "Mai Mai La Niem Tin Yeu Cua Dang, Cua Nhan Dan, La Cho Dua Vung Chac, Bach Chien, Bach Thanh, Cua To Quoc," *Nhan Dan*, 7 May 1996, pp. 1, 2.

———, "Thu Do Hanoi La Bo Mat Cua Quoc Gia; Ca Nuoc Phai Vi Thu Do Va Thu Do Phai V Ca Nuoc," *Nhan Dan*, 8 May 1996, pp. 1, 3.

———, "Phan Dau De Xung Dang Voi Truyen Thong Cach Mang Cua Thanh Pho Mang Ten Bac Ho Kinh Yeu," *Nhan Dan*, 9 May 1996, pp. 1, 3.

Nghia, Le Huu, "Vai Tro Cua Chinh Tri Trong Viec Bao Day Dinh Huong Xa Hoi Chu Nghia," *Tap Chi Cong San* 5 (March 1996): 18–20.

Nghia, The, "Tai Dai Hoi Dang Bo Huyen Tho Xuan: Dong Chi Dao Duy Tung: Can Coi Giai Phap Cu The De Di Vao Cong Nghiep Hoa Nong Nghiep, Nong Thon," *Nhan Dan*, 25 March 1996, pp. 1, 4.

Nghiep, Nguyen Ke, and Le Hoang, "Dai Hoi Dang Bo Huyen Tam Thanh: Chu Truong Dua Co Khi Vao Nong Nghiep, Nong Thon; Dai Hoi Dang Bo Huyen Huu Long: Phat Trien Non Thon Vung Nui Cao Theo Huong Cong Nghiep Hoa," *Nhan Dan*, 6 March 1996, pp. 1, 3.

Ngoc, Dong, "Ban Them Ve Ket Hoc Kinh Te Voi Quoc Phong, An Ninh," *Nhan Dan*, 28 May 1996, pp. 1, 3.

Nguyen, Duc, "Dong Bang Song Cuu Long: Cong Nghiep Hoa Tu Dau?" *Quan Doi Nhan Dan*, 5 March 1996, p. 3.

Nhan, Vo Nang, "Dai Hoi Dang Bo Huyen Dac Ha Tap Trung Suc Phat Trien Kinh Te Theo Huong San Xuat Hang Hoa," *Nhan Dan*, 21 March 1996, pp. 1, 4.

Nhat, Phan Dang, "Ve Vi Tri Va Co Che Van Hanh Van Hoa," *Quan Doi Nhan Dan*, 25 April 1996, pp. 1, 4.

Nhom Phong Vien Chinh Tri-Xa Hoi, "Tien Toi Dai Hoi Lan Thu VIII Cua Dang: Mot Dien Hong Cua Thoi Ky Moi," *Nhan Dan*, 12 February, 13 February 1996, pp. 1, 4.

Nhung, Tran, "Tu Duy Moi Ve Hoat Dong Doi Ngoai," *Quan Doi Nhan Dan*, 20 April 1996, pp. 1, 4.

Nu, Lam Hue, "Dai Hoi Dang Bo Huyen Nhon Trach: Xay Dung Huyen Cong Nghiep Gan Voi Cong Nghiep Hoa Nong Thon," *Nhan Dan*, 22 March 1996, pp. 1, 2.

Oanh, Nguyen, and Nguyen Toan Thang, "Dai Hoi Dang Bo Bo Nong Nghiep

Va Phat Trien Nong Thon: Chuyen Dich Manh Me Co Cau Kinh Te Nong-Lam Nghiep Va Kinh Te Nong Thon Theo Huong Cong Nghiep Hoa," *Nhan Dan*, 27 March 1996, pp. 1, 3.

Oanh, Nguyen Van, "Ve Khai Niem Dinh Huong Xa Hoi Chu Nghia," *Tap Chi Cong San* 4 (February 1996): 16–19.

Oanh, Vu, "Cong Nghiep Hoa, Hien Dai Hoa La De Xay Dung Dat Nuoc Dang Hoang Non, To Dep Hon," *Nhan Dan*, 12 May 1995, p. 3.

———, "Day Manh Cong Tac Dan Van O Co So," *Nhan Dan*, 5 August 1995, p. 3.

———, "May Van De Ve Xay Dung Ly Tuong Cho Thanh Nien Nay," *Tap Chi Cong San* 11 (June 1996): 3–7.

Pham, Nguyen Quoc, "Tang Truong Kinh Te Gan Lien Voi Tien Bo Va Cong Bang Xa Hoi," *Quan Doi Nhan Dan*, 17 April 1996, pp. 1, 4.

Pham, Vu, and Quyet Thanh, "Doi Dieu Ve Cong Nghiep Hoa, Hien Dai Hoa O Nuoc Ta," *Nhan Dan*, 12 January 1996, p. 3.

Phat, Ngo Van, "Hoc Vien Hai Quan: Dai Hoi Dang Cac Cap Dat Chat Luong Tot," *Nhan Dan*, 3 January 1996, p. 3.

Phieu, Le Kha, "Can Bo, Chien Si Luc Luong Vu Trang Kien Dinh Muc Tieu Doc Lap Dan Toc Va Chu Nghia Xa Hoi, Duong Loi Ket Hop Hai Nhiem Va Chien Luoc," *Nhan Dan*, 25 March 1996, pp. 1, 2.

———, "May Van De Ve Xay Dung Dang Trong Quan Doi," *Tap Chi Cong San* 9 (May 1996): 4–12.

Phong, Le Nam, "Cong Tac Dao Tao Doi Ngu Can Bo Quan Doi-Yeu To Co Ban Nang Cao Chat Luong Cua Luc Luong Vu Trang," *Quan Doi Nhan Dan*, 10 June 1996, pp. 1, 2.

Phong, Ngu, "Dai Hoi Dang Bo Hoi Dong Trung Uong Lien Minh Cac Hop Tac Xa Viet Nam Tang Cuong Su Lanh Dao Cua Dang Trong Doi Moi, Phat Trien Kinh Te Hop Tac; Dong Chi Nguyen Ha Phan Lam Viec Voi Dang Doan Cua Hoi Dong," *Nhan Dan*, 31 March 1996, pp. 1, 4.

Phong, Thanh, "Cac Dong Chi Nguyen Duc Binh, Nguyen Ha Phan, Le Kha Phieu Kiem Tra Dai Hoi Dang Bo Cac Cap O Ha Tinh, Nghe An," *Nhan Dan*, 12 February 1996, pp. 1, 4.

———, "Dai Hoi Dang Bo TP Nha Trang: Phat Huy The Manh Du Lich, Phan Dau Giai Quyet Viec Lam Cho Hon 20 Nghin Lao Dong," *Nhan Dan*, 9 March 1996, pp. 1, 4.

Phong, Xuan, "Dai Hoi Dang Bo Co Quan Tong Cuc Chinh Tri: Tap Trung Nang Luc Tri Tue, Thuc Hien Tot Chuc Nang Tham Muu Tren Mat Tran Chinh Tri, Tu Tuong, Van Hoa," *Nhan Dan*, 6 April 1996, pp. 1, 4.

Phu, Do, "Xay Dung Doi Ngu O Dang Bo Co Quan Tong Cong Ty Dau Khi," *Nhan Dan*, 20 September 1995, p. 3.

Phuc, Duy, "Dai Hoi Dang Bo Quan Khu 3: Nang Chat Luong Ba Thu Quan,

Xay Dung Khu Vuc Phong Thu Va The Tran Quoc Phong-An Ninh Vung Chac," *Nhan Dan*, 8 April 1996, pp. 1, 4.

Phuc, Duy, and Pham Van Khanh, "Phan Dau La Trung Tam Dao Luyen Tri Tue Quan Su," *Nhan Dan*, 23 March 1996, pp. 1, 3.

Phuc, Duy, Pham Van Khanh, and Thao Lam, "Dai Hoi Dang Bo Giao Duc Va Dao Tao: Dao Tao Con Nguoi Cho Thoi Ky Phat Trien Moi," *Nhan Dan*, 2 February 1996, pp. 1, 4.

———, "Dai Hoi Dang Bo Hai Quan," *Nhan Dan*, 2 February 1996, pp. 1, 4.

Phuc, Duy, and Xuan Thuy, "Dai Hoi Dang Bo Tong Cuc Cong Nghiep Quoc Phong Va Kinh Te: Tao Suc Manh Tong Hop Xay Dung, Phat Trien Cong Nghiep Quoc Phong Va Kinh Te Quan Doi," *Nhan Dan*, 12 April 1996, pp. 1, 4.

Phuc, Nguyen Trong, "Dang Ta, Dang Cua Tinh Than Doc Lap, Tu Chu va Sang Tao," *Nhan Dan*, 4 December 1995, p. 3.

Phuc, Vu, "Hoc Vien Chinh Tri Quan Su: Gan Cong Tac Dang Voi Nang Cao Chot Luong Dao Tao," *Nhan Dan*, 20 June 1995, p. 1.

Phuoc, Nguyen Kien, "Dai Hoi Dang Bo Co So: Phai Tao Ra Su Chuyen Bien Manh Me Ve Chat," *Nhan Dan*, 15 January 1996, pp. 1, 3.

Phuong, Do Nguyen, "Phat Trien Su Nghiep Y Te Va Nhiem Vu Cai Thien Suc Khoe Cua Dang," *Nhan Dan*, 5 June 1996, pp. 1, 3.

Phuong, Ngoc, "Cuan Bi Dai Hoi Dang," *Xay Dung* (California) 76 (31 January 1996): 28–31.

T.Q., "Ha Noi Don Nhan Y Kien Dong Gop Vao Cac Van Kien Dai Hoi VIII," *Nhan Dan*, 4 January 1996, p. 1.

Quang, Nguyen Dang, "Can Co Mot Chuong Trinh Ve Chong Quan Lieu," *Nhan Dan*, 17 June 1996, pp. 1, 3.

Quy, Nguyen Duy, "Doc Lap Dan Toc Gan Lien Voi Chu Nghia Xa Hoi," *Tap Chi Cong San* 5 (March 1996): 4–8.

Rua, To Huy, "Con Duong Va Dieu Kien Bao Dam Dinh Huong Xa Hoi Chu Nghia O Nuoc Ta," *Tap Chi Cong San* 6 (March 1996): 19–22.

Son, Phong Ky, "Can Nang Cao Nang Luc Quan Ly Nha Nuoc Doi Voi Cac Thanh Phan Kinh Te," *Nhan Dan*, 7 June 1996, pp. 1, 3.

Sung, Thao Xuan, "Van De Phat Trien Cua Cac Dan Toc Thieu So Va Mien Nui Trong Thoi Ky Cong Nghiep Hoa, Dien Dai Hoa Dat Nuoc," *Nhan Dan*, 24 May 1996, pp. 1, 2.

C.T., "Thanh Uy Trien Khai Ke Hoach: Chuan Bi Tot To Chuc Dai Hoi Dang Bo Cac Cap," *Saigon Giai Phong*, 12 May 1995, pp. 1, 5.

D.T., "Dai Hoi Dang Bo Khoi Cac Co Quan Doi Ngoai Trung Uong; Nang Hoat Dong Doi Ngoai Len Tam Cao Moi," *Nhan Dan*, 28 March 1996, pp. 1, 4.

TTXVN, "Dang Bo Khoi Co Quan Trung Uong Va Dang Bo Khoi Co Quan

Trung Uong Ve Cong Tac Tu Tuong Tien Hanh Dai Hoi," *Quan Doi Nhan Dan*, 26 April 1996, pp. 1, 4.
TTXVN and Tran Quynh, "Dai Hoi Dang Bo Quan Hoan Kiem (Ha Noi): Phat Trien Kinh Te Dong Thoi Giu Gin, Ton Tao Cac Di San Van Hoa," *Nhan Dan*, 30 March 1996, pp. 1, 4.
———, "Tai Dai Hoi Dang Bo Thi Xa Son La Chu Tich Le Duc Anh: Nhanh Chong Dua Thi Xa Tro Thanh Mot Trung Nhung Do Thi Phon Vinh O Vung Tau Bac," *Nhan Dan*, 30 March 1996, pp. 1, 4.
Tan, Nguyen Cong, "Tao Ra Cac Dien Moi Vung Dong Bang Song Hong Trong Qua Trinh Cong Nghiep Hoa, Hien Dai Hoa," *Nhan Dan*, 23 January 1996, pp. 1, 4.
Tan, Nhat, "Chu Nghia Mac-Le Nin Va Tu Tuong Ho Chi Minh Voi Dinh Huong Xa Hoi Chu Nghia O Nuoc Ta," *Tap Chi Cong San* 6 (March 1996): 26–29.
Thai, Cao, "Gop Phan Tim Hieu Du Thao Bao Cao Chinh Tri Trinh Dai Hoi VIII Cua Dang: Doi Moi Phuong Thuc Lanh Dao Cua Dang, Phat Huy Vai Tro Quan Ly Cua Nha Nuoc," *Quan Doi Nhan Dan*, 24 April 1996, pp. 1, 3.
Thang, Le Quang, et al., "Dai Hoi Dang Bo Cac Tinh Lai Chau, Ben Tre, Yen Bai, Lao Cai," *Nhan Dan*, 7 May 1996, pp. 1, 3.
Thang, Luu Quoc, "Dai Hoi Dang Bo Huyen Go Quao: Dang Manh Chuyen Dich Co Can Kinh Te, Xay Dung Cap Xa Vung Manh," *Nhan Dan*, 22 February 1996, pp. 1, 4.
Thang, Luu Quoc, et al., "Dai Hoi Dang Bo Cac Tinh Kien Giang, Binh Thuan, Ninh Thuan," *Nhan Dan*, 1 May 1996, pp. 1, 4.
Thang, Pham Quyet, "Dang Vien Va Dai Hoi Dang," *Quan Doi Nhan Dan*, 26 February 1996, pp. 1, 4.
Thang, Vu Pham Quyet, "Dien Dan: Ban Linh Chinh Tri Cua Dang Vien Truoc Cac Ky Dai Hoi," *Nhan Dan*, 6 March 1996, pp. 1, 4.
Thanh, Bui Ngoc, "Khong Co Su Lua Chon Nao Khac," *Tap Chi Cong San* 4 (February 1996): 7–11.
Thanh, Nguyen Duc, "Cong Tac To Chuc Can Bo Trong He Thong Chinh Tri I Thoi Ky Moi," *Nhan Dan*, 11 June 1996, p. 3.
Thanh, Nguyen, and Duong Ngan, "Dai Hoi Dang Bo Quan Su Ha Bac, Dong Bo Quan Su Ha Giang: Nang Cao Suc Manh Tong Hop, Xay Dung The Tran Quoc Phong—An Ninh Gan Voi Phat Trien Kinh Te-Xa Hoi O Dia Phuong," *Quan Doi Nhan Dan*, 2 March 1996, p. 1.
Thao, Nguyen, "Dai Hoi Dang Bo TP Viet Tri: Dong Chi Le Phuoc Tho: Xay Dung Va Phat Trien Thanh Pho Viet Tri Ngang Tam Yeu Cau Day Manh Cong Nghiep Hoa, Hien Dai Hoa Dat Nuoc," *Nhan Dan*, 8 March 1996, pp. 1, 3.

Thi, Dao Trong, "Can Thay Ro Hon Vai Tro Cua Khoa Hoc—Cong Nghe, Giao Duc—Dao Tao Trong Su Nghiep Cong Nghiep Hoa, Hien Dai Hoa," *Nhan Dan*, 4 June 1996, pp. 1, 3.

Thinh, Duc, "Xay Dung Su Doan Vung Manh Toan Dien, Tinh Nhue," *Quan Doi Nhan Dan*, 30 January 1996, p. 1.

Thinh, Tan, and Phan Van Khanh, "Tinh Uy Ba Ria-Vung Tau: Gan Viec Chuan Bi Dai Hoi Dang Voi Thuc Hien Cac Nghi Quyet Cua Trung Uong," *Nhan Dan*, 18 July 1995, pp. 1, 3.

Thoi, Vu Thi Duc, "Phat Huy Bai Hoc Ket Hoc Suc Manh Dan Toc Voi Suc Manh Thoi Dai Trong Giai Doan Hien Nay," *Nhan Dan*, 27 May 1996, pp. 1, 3.

Thong, Quang, "Dai Hoi Dang Bo Quan Khu 3: Dong Vien Moi No Luc Cua Quan Va Dan Tren Dia Ban, Xay Dung Quan Khu Thanh Pho Dai Phong Thu Vung Chac," *Quan Doi Nhan Dan*, 1 April 1996, pp. 1, 4.

Thu, Kim, "Tung Buoc Tieu Chuan Hoa Can Bo, Cham Lo Xay Dung Con Nguoi," *Nhan Dan*, 8 November 1995, p. 3.

Thuy, Duy, "Dang Bo Co Quan TCCT: Lam Tot Cong Tac Doi Moi Va Chinh Don Dang, Cong Tac Van Dong Quan Chung," *Quan Doi Nhan Dan*, 18 December 1995, pp. 1, 2.

Thy, Ngo Anh, "Dang Bo Doan B09 Tang-Thiet Giap (Quan Khu I): Tang Cuong Quan Ly, Ren Luyen Doi Ngu Dang Vien," *Quan Doi Nhan Dan*, 22 February 1996, p. 1.

Tiem, Le The, "Phong, Chong Toi Pham De Thuc Hien Xa Hoi Cong Bang, Van Minh," *Nhan Dan*, 11 June 1996, pp. 1, 3.

Toan, Le Van, "Tong Quan Nen Kinh Te Viet Nam Qua 10 Nam Nam Doi Moi," *Tap Chi Cong San* 3 (February 1996): 26–30.

Ton, Le Van, "Ha Tinh Cung Co Co So Dang," *Nhan Dan*, 1 November 1995, p. 3.

Trang, Tran Ngoc, "Xay Dung Nen Kinh Te Nhieu Thanh Phan Theo Dinh Huong Xa Hoi Chu Nghia," *Nhan Dan*, 30 April 1996, pp. 1, 4.

Trang, Tran Nguyen, "Dai Hoi Dang Bo Thanh Pho Ho Chi Minh Lan Thu VI Thanh Cong Tot Dep: Day Manh Cong Nghiep Hoa, Hien Dai Hoa Vi Ca Nuoc, Cung Ca Nuoc," *Quan Doi Nhan Dan*, 12 May 1996, pp. 1, 3.

Tri, Nhom Phong Vien Chinh, "Dang Bo Cac Quan 3, 10 Mo Hoi Nghi Chuyen De Phuc Vu Viec Xay Dung Van Kien Dai Hoi," *Saigon Giai Phong*, 20 June 1995, pp. 1, 5.

Trong, Le, and Le Thi Nham Tuyet, "Can Uu Tien Dau Tu Nang Cao Dan Tri Cho Cong Nghiep Hoa Nong Nghiep Va Phat Trien Nong Thon," *Nhan Dan*, 10 June 1996, pp. 1, 3.

Trong, Nguyen Phu, "Cong Tac Xay Dung Dang: Nen Danh Gia The Nao Cho Dung?" *Tap Chi Cong San* 2 (January 1996): 24.

———, "Hieu The Nao Ve Ban Chat Cua Dang Ta?" *Tap Chi Cong San* 3 (February 1996): 31–35.

———, "Dinh Huong Xa Hoi Chu Nghia Va Con Duong Di Len Chu Nghia Xa Hoi O Nuoc Ta," *Tap Chi Cong San* 5 (March 1996): 9–14.

Truat, Tho, and Quoc Viet, "Dai Hoi Dang Bo Quan Su TP. Ho Chi Minh: Chu Trong Giao Duc Ren Luyen, Xay Dung Ban Linh Chinh Tri Cho Bo Doi; Dang Bo Cuc Van Tai: Tap Trung Co Trong Diem, Doi Moi Trang Bi Va Phuong Tien Van Tai," *Quan Doi Nhan Dan*, 10 February 1996, pp. 1, 4.

Truong, Ha Xuan, "Dinh Huong Xa Hoi Chu Nghia Mot Khai Niem Khoa Hoc," *Tap Chi Cong San* 7 (April 1996): 18.

Tuan, Le Minh, "Qua II Co So Dang O Binh Dinh Tien Hanh Dai Hoi Diem," *Nhan Dan*, 12 January 1996, p. 3.

Tuan, Minh, and Thu Hien, "Dai Hoi Dang Bo Quan Su Tinh Ninh Binh, Tinh Lam Dong: Xac Dinh Cac Muc Tieu Lanh Dao Xay Dung Nen Quoc Phong Dia Phuong Vung Manh Toan Dien," *Quan Doi Nhan Dan*, 5 March 1996, pp. 1, 4.

Tung, Le Xuan, "Ha Noi Phan Dau Cung Ca Nuoc Thuc Hien Thang Loi Su Nghiep Cong Nghiep Hoa, Hien Dai Hoa," *Nhan Dan*, 30 June 1996, p. 7.

Tuyen, Pham, "Quan Triet Quan Diem Cong Nghiep Hoa, Hien Dai Hoa Vao Cong Tac Dao Tao Can Bo Quan Doi Trong Giai Doan Moi," *Quan Doi Nhan Dan*, 10 June 1996, p. 2.

Tuyen, To Thanh, "Tap Trung Tri Tue Thong Qua Nghi Quyet Lanh Dao Su Doan Vung Manh Toan Dien," *Quan Doi Nhan Dan*, 2 February 1996, pp. 1, 4.

Tuyen, To Thanh, and Mai Huong, "Dai Hoi Dang Bo Hoc Vien Chinh Tri-Quan Su: Tap Trung Xay Dung Hoc Vien Thanh Trung Tam Dao Tao Can Bo Chinh Tri, Nghien Cuu Khoa Hoc-Xa Hoi Va Nhan Van," *Quan Doi Nhan Dan*, 15 March 1996, pp. 1, 3.

Tuyen, Tran The, "Dai Hoi Dang Bo Quan Khu 7: Tap Trung Nang Cao Nang Luc, Quan Uy Nha Nuoc Ve Quoc Phong, Xay Dung Doi Ngu Vung Manh Dap Ung Tinh Hinh Moi," *Quan Doi Nhan Dan*, 2 April 1996, pp. 1, 4.

Uc, Dao Tri, "Can Mot Chien Luoc Xay Dung Phap Luat Ua Dua Phep Luat Vao Cuoc Song," *Nhan Dan*, 14 June 1996, pp. 1, 3.

Uoc, Nguyen Dinh, "Quoc Phong, An Ninh Voi Su On Dinh Chinh Tri Cua Dat Nuoc," *Quan Doi Nhan Dan*, 18 April 1996, pp. 1, 4.

P.V., "Hai Hung: Chuan Bi Dai Hoi Dang, Cap Huyen, Thi Va Co So," *Nhan Dan*, 17 June 1995, pp. 1, 4.

———, "Tong Ket Doi Moi Chinh Don Dang Chuan Bi Dai Hoi Dang Bo Co So Cac Cap," *Nhan Dan*, 8 August 1995, p. 1.

———, "Lop Nghien Cuu Duong Loi, Quan Diem Cua Dang Cho Can Bo Cac Cap," *Nhan Dan*, 12 September 1995, pp. 1, 3.

_____, "Dot Hai Lop Can Bo Cao Cap Nghien Cuu Dong Loi, Quan Diem Cua Dang," *Nhan Dan*, 3 October 1995, pp. 1, 2.

_____, "5 Nam Thuc Hien Nghi Quyet Trung Uong 8B O Yen Bai," *Nhan Dan*, 3 December 1995, pp. 1, 4.

_____, "TP Ho Chi Minh: Mot So Kinh Nghiem Qua Dai Hoi Cac Co So Dang Duoc Chon Thi Diem," *Nhan Dan*, 18 December 1995, pp. 1, 3.

_____, "Dai Hoi Dang Bo C13 (Tong Cuc Can Sat *Nhan Dan*): Giu Vung Trat Tu An Toan Xa Hoi, Tao Moi Truong Thuan Loi Cho Dat Nuoc Phat Trien," *Nhan Dan*, 7 January 1996, pp. 1, 4.

_____, "Dai Hoi Dang Bo TP Thai Nguyen: Phan Dau Tro Thanh Trung Tam Chinh Tri, Kinh Te-Xa Hoi Cua Bac Thai," *Nhan Dan*, 21 March 1996, pp. 1, 2.

_____, "Dai Hoi Dang Bo Khoi I Cac Co Quan Trung Uong: Vung Vang, Tri Tue, Tham Muu Giup Dang Va Nha Nuoc," *Nhan Dan*, 27 April 1996, pp. 1, 4.

P.V. and Do Ngoc Dang, "Ha Tay: Cu Them Can Bo Giup Chi Dao Dai Hoi Co So," *Nhan Dan*, 6 January 1996, pp. 1, 3.

P.V. and TTXVN, "Chu Tich Le Duc Anh Tham Va Chuc Tet Can Bo, Phong Vien Bao *Nhan Dan*, Can Bo, Cong Nhan Cong Ty In Tien Bo," *Nhan Dan*, 17 February 1996, pp. 1, 4.

P.V. and Tan Thanh, "Dai Hoi Dang Bo Khoi Co Quan Dan Van Trung Uong, Ba Ria-Vung Tau, Quang Tri, Son La," *Nhan Dan*, 10 May 1996, pp. 1, 2.

Van, Le, "Xay Dung Dang: Dang Bo Manh Khong Phai La Phep Cong Nhieu Co So," *Nhan Dan*, 8 November 1995, p. 3.

Viet, Quoc, "Tai Hoi Dang Bo Trung Doan 141 (Su Doan 312): Phat Huy Tri Tue Cua Dang Vien, Tap Trung Dong Gop Y Kien Vao Noi Dung Chu Yeu Du Thao Cac Van Kien Cua Dang," *Quan Doi Nhan Dan*, 25 December 1995, pp. 1, 4.

_____, "Tai Dai Hoi Dai Bieu Dang Bo Bo Tong Tham Muu-Co Quan Bo Quoc Phong: Doi Moi Sau Sac Tu Duy Ve Nhiem Vu Bao Ve To Quoc, De Lam Tot Chuc Nang Tham Muu Va Quan Ly Nha Nuoc," *Quan Doi Nhan Dan*, 9 March 1996, pp. 1, 4.

_____, "Dai Hoi Dai Bieu Dang Bo Quan Khu 1: Phat Huy Suc Manh Tong Hop, Xay Dung Neu Quoc Phong Toan Dan, Bao Ve Vung Chac Bien Gioi Quoc Gia," *Quan Doi Nhan Dan*, 15 March 1996, pp. 1, 4.

Vinh, Ho Ba, "Binh Doan Tay Nguyen: Chuan Bi Tot Chu Ra Quan Huan Luyen Nam 1996," *Quan Doi Nhan Dan*, 8 March 1996, pp. 1, 4.

Vinh, Ho Si, "Hien Dai Hoa Trong Van Hoa," *Nhan Dan*, 9 June 1996, pp. 1, 3.

Vong, Le Binh, "Chong Tham Nhung—Nhiem Vu Quan Trong Cua Toan Dang, Toan Dan," *Nhan Dan*, 27 May 1996, pp. 1, 3.

___, "Day Manh Hon Cai Cach Hanh Chinh Nha Nuoc De Gop Phan Xay Dung, Hoan Thien Bo May Nha Nuoc," *Nhan Dan*, 12 June 1996, p. 3.

Vu, Nguyen Nghia, "Doi Moi Va Chinh Don Dang, Nhan To Quyet Dinh Qua Trinh Phat Trien O Lao Cai," *Nhan Dan*, 1 November 1995, p. 3.

VIETNAMESE LANGUAGE ARTICLES (UNSIGNED)

"Ban Bi Thu T.U. Dang Chi Thi: Phat Dong Phong Trao Thi Du Lap Thanh Tich Chao Mung Dai Hoi Lan Thi VIII Cua Dang," *Nhan Dan*, 29 December 1995, pp. 1, 3.

"Ban Bi Thu To Chuc Dang Gop Y Kien Nang Cao Chat Luong Dai Hoi Dang Boi Cac Tinh Dong Bang, Song Cuu Long," *Nhan Dan*, 15 February 1996, pp. 1, 4.

"Ban Bi Thu To Chuc Y Kien Nang Cao Chat Luong Dao Hoi Dang Bo Cac Tinh Dong Bang Song Cuu Long," *Quan Doi Nhan Dan*, 15 February 1996, pp. 1, 4.

"Bao Cao Chinh Tri Cua Ban Chap Hanh Trung Uong Dang Khoa VII Tai Dai Hoi Dai Bieu Toan Quoc Lan Thu VIII Cua Dang," *Nhan Dan*, 29 June 1996, pp. 4–5.

"Bao Cao Chinh Tri Cua Ban Chap Hanh Trung Uong Dang Khoa VII Tai Dai Hoi Dai Bieu Toan Quoc Lan Thu VIII Cua Dang," *Nhan Dan*, 30 June 1996, p. 2.

"Be Mac Lop Can Bo Cao Cap Nghien Cuu Duong Loi, Quan Diem Cua Dang (Dot Ba)," *Nhan Dan*, 10 November 1995, p. 4.

"Bo Chinh Tri Ban Hanh Nghi Quyet Ve Tiep Tuc Doi Moi To Chuc Va Hoat Dong Thuong Nghiep, Phat Trien Thi Truong Theo Dinh Huong Xa Hoi Chu Nghia," *Nhan Dan*, 19 January 1996, pp. 1, 3.

"Cac Dai Bieu Quoc Te Den Ha Noi Du Dai Hoi VIII Dang Ta: Hoi Dam Giai Hai Doan Dai Bieu Dang Cong San Viet Nam Va Dang Cong San Trung Quoc; Tong Bi Thu Do Muoi Tiep Vai Hoi Dam Voi Dong Chi Ly Bang," *Nhan Dan*, 28 July 1996, pp. 1, 4.

"Cac Dong Chi Dao Duy Tung, Nong Duc Manh, Hong Ha Lam Viec Voi Cac Tinh Uy Hoa Binh, Son La Va Lai Chau Ve Chuan Bi Dai Hoi Dang Cac Cap," *Nhan Dan*, 17 February 1996, pp. 1, 4.

"Cac Tinh: Thai Binh, Yen Bai, Quang Nam-Da Nang Co Tu 63 Den 87% Dang Bo Co So Dai Hoi Xong," *Quan Doi Nhan Dan*, 5 February 1996, p. 1.

"Chu Tich Le Duc Anh Tham Va Lam Viec Tai Quang Ngai, Phu Yen, Binh Dinh, Thua Thien-Hue," *Nhan Dan*, 14 January 1966, pp. 1, 3.

"Chung Ta Phai Tran Trong Va Nghiem Tuc Tiep Thu Y Kien Dong Gop Cua

Nhan Dan De Tiep Tuc Hoan Chinh Du Thao Van Kien Trinh Dai Hoi," *Quan Doi Nhan Dan*, 22 April 1996, pp. 1, 4.

"Cong Tac Tu Tuong Nam 1996 Tap Trung Tuyen Truyen, Co Dong Ve Dai Hoi VIII Cua Dang," *Nhan Dan*, 7 January 1996, pp. 1, 2.

"Da Can Ban Hoan Thanh Dai Hoi Dang Bo Co So: 90–95% So Dang Vien Du Cac Dai Hoi," *Nhan Dan*, 23 March 1996, pp. 1, 4.

"Dai Hoi Dang Bo Hoc Vien Chinh Tri-Quan Su Phan Dau Tro Thanh Trung Tam Khoa Hoc Xa Hoi Va Nhan Van Hang Dau Cua Quan Doi," *Nhan Dan*, 15 March 1996, p. 3.

"Dai Hoi Dang Bo Huyen Ninh Phuoc: Phat Trien Cac Vung Kinh Te Trong Diem," *Nhan Dan*, 5 March 1996, pp. 1, 2.

"Dai Hoi Dang Bo Quan Khu 9: Xay Dung Doi Ngu Can Bo, Dang Vien Co Phan Chat, Trinh Do Nang Luc Dap Ung Yeu Cao Nhiem Vu," *Quan Doi Nhan Dan*, 29 March 1996, pp. 1, 2.

"Dai Hoi Dang Bo Trung Doan 141 (Su Doan 312): Phat Huy Dan Chu, Dong Gop Nhieu Y Kien Vao Cac Van Kien Dai Hoi Dang VIII," *Quan Doi Nhan Dan*, 18 December 1995, p. 1.

"Dien Dan: Tong Ket La De Vuon Len Tam Cao Moi," *Nhan Dan*, 2 January 1996, pp. 1, 3.

"Dien Van Be Mac Do Dong Chi Do Muoi, Tong Bi Thu Ban Chap Hanh Trung Vong Dang Khoa VIII, Doc," *Tap Chi Cong San* 13 (July 1996): 39.

"Dong Chi Dao Duy Tung Du Va Noi Chuyen Tai Dai Hoi Dang Bo Huyen Cam Binh," *Nhan Dan*, 29 January 1996, pp. 1, 4.

"Dong Chi Dao Duy Tung Kiem Tra Cong Tac Dai Hoi Dang Cac Cap Tai Lang Son," *Nhan Dan*, 20 March 1996, pp. 1, 4.

"Dong Chi Nguyen Manh Cam Lam Viec Voi Tinh Thanh Hoa," *Nhan Dan*, 30 January 1996, p. 1.

"Du Thao: Bao Cao Chinh Tri Tai Dai Hoi Dai Bien Dang Bo Thanh Pho Hanoi Lan Thu XII," *Hanoi Moi*, 28 November 1995, pp. 1–4.

"80% Dang Bo Cac Truong Dai Hoc, Cac Dang O Ha Noi Xay Dung Quy Che Cong Tac," *Nhan Dan*, 22 May 1995, p. 1

"Giuong Cao Ngon Co Doc Lap Dan Toc Va Chu Nghia Xa Hoi, Dong Vien Toan Quan Buoc Vao Thoi Ky Moi, Gop Phan Tich Cuc Thuc Hien Su Nghiep Cong Nghiep Hoa, Hien Dai Hoa Dat Nuoc," *Quan Doi Nhan Dan*, 10 May 1996, pp. 1, 4.

"Ha Tay, Toan Dan Cham Soc Cac Doi Tuong Chinh Sac: Tong Cong Ty Buu Chinh Vien Thong Tang Moi Ba Me VNAH Trong Nganh 2 Trieu Dong," *Nhan Dan*, 16 July 1995, pp. 1, 4.

"Hanoi Tiep Tuc Doi Moi Cong Tac Van Dong Quan Chung," *Nhan Dan*, 25 November 1995, p. 1.

"Hoat Dong Cua Lanh Dao Dang, Nha Nuoc: Cac Dong Chi Nguyen Duc Binh, Vu Oanh, Nguyen Ha Phan, Do Quang Thanh, Truong My Hoa Tham Va Lam Viec Voi Cac Dia Phuong," *Nhan Dan*, 15 May 1995, pp. 1, 2.

"Hoat Dong Cua Lanh Dao Dang Va Nha Nuoc," *Nhan Dan*, 14 June 1995, p. 1.

"Hoi Nghi Can Bo Toan Quan Nghien Cuu Cac Dinh Huong Trong Cong Tac Tu Tuong Va Chuan Bi Dai Hoi Dang Cac Cap," *Nhan Dan*, 6 October 1995, pp. 1, 4.

"Huong Ung Loi Keu Goi Cua MTTQ Viet Nam," *Nhan Dan*, 15 July 1995, pp. 1, 3.

"Huong Vong Loi Keu Goai Cua MTTQ Viet Nam," *Nhan Dan*, 19 July 1995, p. 1.

"Khai Mac Dai Hoi Lan Thi VIII Dang Cong San Viet Nam: Dai Hoi Tien Hanh Tu Ngay 28-6 Den 1-7," *Nhan Dan*, 28 June 1996, p. 1.

"Khoi Co Quan T.U. Ve Cong Tac Tu Tuong Gop Y Kien Cho Du Thao Bao Cao Chinh Tri," *Nhan Dan*, 30 October 1993, pp. 1, 4.

"Mai Mai La Niem Tin Yeu Cua Dang, Cua *Nhan Dan*, La Cho Dua Vung Chac, Bach Chien, Bach Thang Cua To Quoc," *Nhan Dan*, 7 May 1996, pp. 1, 2.

"Mat Tran To Quoc Viet Nam Phat Dong Phong Trao Cham Soc Thuong Binh, Gia Dinh Liet Si, Phung Duong Ba Me Viet Nam Anh Hung," *Nhan Dan*, 6 July 1995, pp. 1, 3.

"Mot So Van De Ke Hoach Phat Trien Kinh Te-Xa 5 Nam 1996–2000: Trich Tham Luan Cua Dong Chi Do Quoc Sam, Dai Bieu Dang Bo Tinh Lao Cai," *Nhan Dan*, 29 June 1996, p. 6.

"MTTQ Viet Nam Phat Dong Thi Dua Mung Dai Hoi Lan Thu VIII Cua Dang," *Nhan Dan*, 14 January 1996, pp. 1, 3.

"Nghi Quyet: Dai Hoi Dai Bieu Toan Quoc Lan Thu VIII, Dang Cong San Viet Nam," *Tap Chi Cong San* 13 (July 1996): 38.

"Nhieu Dia Phuong Mo Rong Phong Trao Phung Duong Ba Me Viet Nam Anh Hung, Tang Nha, So Tiet Kiem Tinh Nghia," *Nhan Dan*, 24 July 1995, pp. 1, 3.

"Noi Dung Bai Phat Bieu Be Mac Hoi Nghi Lan Thu 9," pp. 5, 6.

"Phat Huy Tiem Nang Loi The Cua Cong Bien Gop Phan Xay Dung Va Bao Ve To Quoc Xa Hoi Cong Nhan: Trich Tham Luan Cua Dong Chi Le Danh Xuong, Dai Bieu Dang Bo Thanh Pho Hai Phong," *Nhan Dan*, 2 July 1996, p. 3.

"Phat Trien Kinh Te-Xa Hoi Nong Thon O Trung Du Va Mien Nui: Trich Tham Luan Cua Dong Chi Bui Huu Hai, Dai Bieu Dang Bo Tinh Vinh Phu," *Nhan Dan*, 2 July 1996, p. 4.

"Phuong Huong, Nhiem Vu Ke Hoach Phat Trien Kinh Te-Xa Hoi 5 Nam 1996–2000," *Nhan Dan*, 30 June 1996, pp. 4–6.

"Phuong Huong, Nhiem Vu Ke Hoach Phat Trien Kinh Te-Xa Hoi 5 Nam 1996–2000," *Nhan Dan*, 1 July 1996, p. 2.

"Quan Chung Khong Quan Ra Luan Huan Luyen," *Quan Doi Nhan Dan*, 3 March 1996, p. 1.

"Quang Ngai: Cac Xa, Phuong Tap Trung Suc Xoa Doi Ngheo Trong So Gia Dinh Chinh Sach," *Nhan Dan*, 20 July 1995, p. 1.

"Thi Xa Long Xuyen Nang Cao Muc Song Thuong Binh, Gia Dinh Liet Si," *Nhan Dan*, 17 July 1995, pp. 1, 3.

"Thong Bao Hoi Nghi Lan Thu Chin BCHTU (Khoa VII)," *Tap Chi Cong San*, Number 17 (December 1995): 3.

"Thong Bao Hoi Nghi Lan Thu Muoi Ban Chap Hanh Trung Uong Khoa VII," *Quan Doi Nhan Dan*, 22 April 1996, p. 1.

"Thu Thuong Vo Van Kiet Lam Viec Voi Tinh Lam Dong Ve Kinh Te-Xa Hoi Va Cong Tact Chuan Bi Dai Hoi Dang," *Quan Doi Nhan Nhan*, 16 February 1996, pp. 1, 4.

"Thu Truong Vo Van Kiet Lam Viec Voi Tinh Kien Giang Va Du Hoi Nghi So Ket 'Chuong Trinh Bao Dam Nuoc Sach Va Sinh Moi Truong' Cua Tinh Soc Trang," *Nhan Dan*, 11 May 1995, pp. 1, 4.

"Thu Tuong Vo Van Kiet Lam Viec Voi Ba Tinh Tay Nguyen Ve Kinh Te-Xa Hoi Va Cong Tac Chuan Bi Dai Hoi Dang," *Nhan Dan*, 15 February 1996, pp. 1, 3; *Quan Doi Nhan Dan*, 15 February 1996, pp. 1, 3.

"Thu Tuong Vo Van Kiet: Vi Cuoc Song Hom Nay Va Mai Sau, Tat Ca Chung Ta, Moi Nguoi Moi Ngan Han Lam Mot Viet Tot Cho Giu Gin Ve Sinh Moi Truong," *Nhan Dan*, 5 June 1996, pp. 1, 3.

"Tien Toi Dai Hoi Lan Thu VIII Cua Dang: Khang Dinh Huong Xa Hoi Chu Nghia O Nuoc Ta," *Nhan Dan*, 31 January 1996, pp. 1, 4.

"Tim Loi Giai Cho Buoc Di Cong Nghiep Hoa," *Nhan Dan*, 1 March 1996, pp. 1, 3.

"To Chuc Lay Y Kien Va Tong Hop Y Kien Nhan Dan Gop Vao Ban Du Thao Bao Cao Chinh Tri Trinh Dai Hoi VIII," *Quan Doi Nhan Dan*, 19 April 1996, pp. 1, 4.

"Toan Dan Cham Soc Thuong Binh, Gia Dinh Liet Si Va Nguoi Co Cong Voi Nuoc," *Nhan Dan*, 6 July 1995, p. 1.

"Thong Bao Hoi Nghi Lan Thu Chin BCHTU (Koa VII)," *Tap Chi Cong San* 17 (December 1995): 3, 4.

"Tong Bi Thu Do Muoi Doc Bao Cao Cua Bo Chinh Tri Trung Uong Dang Ve Cac Van Kien Dai Hoi: Tiep Tuc Su Nghiep Doi Moi, Day Manh Cong Nghiep Hoa, Hien Dai Hoa Vi Muc Tieu Dan Giau, Nuoc Manh, Xa Hoi Cong Bang, Van Minh, Vung Buoc Di Len Chi Nghi Xa Hoi," *Nhan Dan*, 29 June 1996, pp. 1–3.

"Tong Bi Thu Do Muoi Lam Viec Boi Bon Tinh Tay Nguyen," *Nhan Dan*, 16 June 1995, pp. 1, 3.
"Tong Bi Thu Do Muoi Lam Viec Vo 14 Tinh, Thanh Pho Ve Chuan Bi Cho Dai Hoi Dang Bo Cac Cap," *Nhan Dan*, 1 March 1996, p. 3.
"Tong Bi Thu Do Muoi Lam Viec Voi Mot So Giam Doc Doanh Nghiep O Ha Noi," *Nhan Dan*, 12 May 1995, pp. 1, 4.
"Tong Bi Thu Do Muoi Tham Va Lam Viec Tai TP Ho Chi Minh, Cac Tinh Can Tho, Dong Nai, Ba Ria-Vung Tau," *Nhan Dan*, 12 January 1996, pp. 1,2.
"Tong Hop Y Kien Cu Tri Ca Nuoc Tai Ky Hop Thu 9, Quoc Hoi Khoa IX," *Nhan Dan*, 13 March 1996, p. 3.
"Trao Doi Kinh Nghiem Ve Than Tra, Xac Minh Trong Cong Tac Kiem Tra Cua Dang," *Nhan Dan*, 10 June 1995, pp. 1, 2.
"Trong Trach Cua Dang Ta La Phai Xay Dung Mot Ban Chap Hanh Trung Uong Vung Manh, Co Chat Luong Cao, Tieu Bieu Cho Pham Chat Va Tri Tue Cua Toan Dang Cua Ca Dan Toc," *Quan Doi Nhan Dan*, 22 April 1996, pp. 1, 4.
"20 Dong Chi Duoc Bau Bo Sung BCH T.U. Dang (Khoa 7)," *Nhan Dan*, 26 January 1994, p. 1.
"Ve Dai Hoi Dang Bo Cac Cap," *Nhan Dan*, 11 December 1995, p. 3.
"Xa Luan: Bao Ve Moi Truong Muc Tieu Phat Trien Ben Vung," *Nhan Dan*, 5 June 1996, pp. 1, 2.
"Xa Luan: Dai Hoi Dang Bo Co So Can Ban Nhung Van De Cu The, Thiet Thuc," *Nhan Dan*, 27 December 1995, pp. 1, 4.
"Xa Luan: Tich Cuc Chuan Bi, Bao Dam Cho Dai Hoi VIII Cua Dang Thanh Cong Tot Dep," *Tap Chi Cong San* 17 (December 1995): 7.
"Xa Luan: To Chuc That Tot Dai Hoi Dang Co So," *Nhan Dan*, 5 December 1995, pp. 1, 2, 3.
"Xa Luan: To Chuc Tot Dai Hoi Dang Cac Cap Trong Toan Quan, Tien Toi Dai Hoi Dai Bieu Toan Quoc Lan Thi VIII Cua Dang," *Tap Chi Quoc Phong Toan Dan*, October 1995, pp. 1–4.
Xa Luan: Toan Dang Ta Tien Va Dai Hoi VIII," *Nhan Dan*, 4 December 1995, pp. 1, 2.

ENGLISH LANGUAGE BOOKS

Beresford, Melanie, *Vietnam: Politics, Economics and Society*, London: Pinter, 1988.
Frost, Frank, *Vietnam's Foreign Relations: Dynamics of Change*, Singapore: Institute of Southeast Asian Studies, Regional Strategic Studies Program, 1993.

Marr, David, and Christine P. White, editors, *Postwar Vietnam: Dilemmas in Socialist Development*, Ithaca, N.Y.: Southeast Asian Program, Cornell University Press, 1988.
Porter, Gareth, *Vietnam: The Politics of Bureaucratic Socialism*, Ithaca, N.Y.: Cornell University Press, 1993.
Stern, Lewis M., *Renovating the Vietnamese Communist Party: Nguyen Van Linh and the Programme for Organizational Reform, 1987–91*, Singapore: Institute of Southeast Asian Studies, 1993.
Turley, William, and Mark Selden, editors, *Reinventing Vietnamese Socialism: Doi Moi in Comparative Perspective*, Boulder, Colo.: Westview, 1993.
Williams, Michael C., *Vietnam at the Crossroads*, London: Pinter, 1992.

English Language Articles and Papers

Avery, Dorothy, "Vietnam in 1992: Win Some, Lose Some," *Asian Survey*, January 1993.
Doanh, Le Dang, "The Role of the State in Turning the Vietnamese Economy to a Market Economy," paper presented to the International Workshop of the SIDA, Stockholm, Sweden, 9–11 June 1992.
Dollar, David, "Vietnam: The Economy," presented to conference on Vietnam after the June 1991 Party Congress: Political and Economic Outlook, Department of State, Washington, D.C., 13 September 1991.
Duiker, William, *The Communist Road to Power in Vietnam*, Boulder, Colo.: Westview, 1981, pp. 141, 176–80, 187–90, 193–95, 221–24.
Elliott, David, "Vietnam Faces the Future," *Current History* (December 1995), pp. 412–19.
Fahey, Stephanie, "Vietnam 1993: Pivotal Year," *Southeast Asian Affairs 1994*, Singapore: Institute of Southeast Asian Studies, 1994, pp. 337–50.
Fforde, Adam, "The Political Economy of Reform in Vietnam: Some Reflections," manuscript, March 1991.
Hiebert, Murray, "Unhealed Wounds: Party Plenum Dominated by Concerns over China," *Far Eastern Economic Review*, 16 July 1992, pp. 20–21.
———, "Pandora's Box: Party Split Over Social, Financial Problems," *Far Eastern Economic Review*, 4 February 1993, p. 27.
Hung, Ly Thai, "Secret Document Issued Regarding Nguyen Ha Phan's Ousting," *VinSight* (NetCom), 5 May 1996.
———, Who Won the VCP Eight Congress," *VinSight* (NetCom), July 1996.
Huynh, Frank C. H., "Vietnam 1991: Still in Transition," *Southeast Asian Affairs 1992*, Singapore: Institute of Southeast Asian Studies, 1993.

Khng, Russell Heng Hiang, "Leadership in Vietnam: Pressures for Reform and Their Limits," *Contemporary Southeast Asia* 15, no. 1 (June 1993): 98–110.

Ljunggren, Borge, "Market Economies Under Communist Regimes: Reform in Vietnam, Laos and Cambodia — Beyond Socialist Renovation," Harvard Institute for International Development, 3 April 1991.

Mio, Tadashi, "Vietnam After the 7th Party Congress," *Vietnam Generation Journal* 4, nos. 3–4 (November 1992).

Mydans, Seth, "Vietnam to Retain Three Aged Leaders, for Now," *New York Times*, 29 June 1996, p. 3.

Porter, Gareth, "The Politics of 'Renovation' in Vietnam," *Problems of Communism* 39, no. 3 (1990): 72–88.

Saigonese, The, "Former Politburo Member in Coma," *VinSight* (NetCom), 2 June 1996.

Sidel, Mark, "Vietnam's America Watchers in a New Era," *SAIS Review* #16, no. 2 (Summer-Fall 1996): 43-69.

Solomon, Andy, "Party Delegates Said Unable to Agree on New Leadership," *Asia Times*, 24 June 1996, pp. 1, 2.

Suphaphon, Kanwirayothin, "Vietnam Party Leaders in Search of New Directions," *Bangkok Post*, 30 September 1993, p. 4.

Timmer, C. Peter, "Food Policy and Economic Reform in Vietnam," Harvard Institute for International Development, November 1990.

Turley, William, "Vietnam: The Political Environment," presented to Conference on Vietnam After the June 1991 Party Congress: Political and Economic Outlook, Department of State, Washington, D.C., 13 September 1991.

———, "Post–Cold War Security: Vietnam and Indochina," prepared for the National Bureau of Asian Research, Seattle, Wash., 15 March 1993.

"Vietnam Ousts Official," *New York Times*, 28 April 1996, p. 3.

Yeong, Mike, "New Thinking in Vietnamese Foreign Policy," *Contemporary Southeast Asia* 14, no. 3 (December 1992): 257–268.

Miscellaneous

Hanoi Domestic Service in Vietnamese.
Hanoi Vietnamese News Agency in English.
Hanoi Voice of Vietnam in English.
Hanoi Voice of Vietnam Network in Vietnamese.
Hong Kong AFP in English.

Melbourne Radio, Australia, in English.
Ministry of Foreign Affairs, Socialist Republic of Vietnam, "Statement by Mr. Hong Ha at the Press Conference on April 9, 1996."
Political Report of the Central Committee (VIIth Tenure) to the VIIIth National Congress, pp. 1–57 (photocopied).

Index

administrative reform 12, 67, 78, 79
Africa, 53, 77
agricultural sector 12, 24, 32, 38, 39, 45, 52, 54
All-Army Party Organization Congress 43
All-People National Defense System 43
An, Do Van 93
Anh, Le Duc 35, 69, 71, 73, 90
arms race 78
Association of Southeast Asian Nations (ASEAN), 39, 53, 55

Ba Ria–Vung Tau 64, 98
Bac Thai Province 64
banking 54
basic party committee meetings 9–14, 32, 34–37, 46
Binh, Nguyen Duc 32, 86
Binh Dinh Province 23
Binh Thuan Province 15, 32

cadre development 27, 39
Cam, Nguyen Manh 33, 85, 98
Cambodia 53, 76–77, 129, 130
Can Tho 33, 35, 64
Cao Bang Province 15
Capital Military Region 41
capitalism 27
Central Committee 10, 24, 33, 34, 71–72, 92–97

Central Committee blocs 106–107
Central Committee Inspection Committee 18
Central Executive Committee 66
Central Internal Protection Committee 81
Central Military Committee Resolution 79 19
Central Office for Guidance 37
Chi, Vo Tran 85
China 44, 45–46, 53, 62
Circular 11 34
Circular 9 16
Circular 266 16
class struggle 55
collective leadership 52
college officials 92
Communist party organizations in enterprises 31, 39
Cong, Vo Chi 71, 72
Confederation of Independent States 53, 77
conservative results 7
consumer goods production 52
contradictions 55
Control Committee 71–77, 87
cooperatives 29, 35, 38, 52, 78, 79
corruption 22, 26, 27, 31, 40, 54, 57, 60, 62, 63
credit fund collapse 52
cultural policy 75
Cuong, Vo Van 100
Cuu Long Delta 30

Dac, Tran Huu 87
Dac Lac Province 12, 23, 35
Dang, Ha 18
defense policies 59, 60
delegates, nomination of 10–11
democracy 76
democratic centralism 52
department directors 92
deputy ministers 92, 95
deputy party secretaries 93–94
development plans 33
Directive 51 11
Directive 07 11
discipline, Communist party 82, 87
district-level congresses 14, 23, 25, 31, 46
district party committee drafting committees 13
district party meetings 10
Division 312 19
Dong, Pham Van 72, 73
Dong Nai Province 32
draft documents 10, 18–19, 20, 23, 25, 30–34, 44–46, 48–51, 58–62
draft political report 11, 13, 14, 46, 47–48, 51–58
"dual hatted" officials 92, 93
Dung, Nguyen Tan 89
Duong, Tran Thi 99–100
Duyet, Pham The 85, 93

economic and political renovation, combining of 47
economic growth 21
"economic ministries" 96
economic reform 5, 20, 21, 51–52, 70
economic "take off" point 54
education policy 54, 56, 58, 74
Eighth Plenary Resolution 12
Eleventh Plenary 49, 66–67
expanded district conferences 10
elections, Community party 82
embargo 52, 53
employment issues 38, 52
environment 38, 63
equitization 56, 80

Europe 55, 62
External Relations Department 129
finances, Community party 81
financial policy 51, 54, 73
first round congresses, limiting number of 10
foreign investment sources 64
Foreign Ministry 59
foreign policy 11, 53, 55, 65, 72–73
foreign relations bloc 39
foreign trade 74
former party secretaries 93
former revolutionary bases 48
"four dangers" 78
Fourth Plenary 56
Free Vietnam 53

General Department for National Defense Industry and Economics 43
general department heads 92
General Political Department 18, 42
General Staff Congress 41
General Technical Department 13
generational change 6
Gia Lai Province 23, 35, 93
grassroots party organizations 9, 10, 11, 23, 24
guidance committees 12, 15

Ha, Hong 34, 35, 47, 53, 69, 129
Ha Bac Province 41, 64
Ha Giang Province 41 64
Ha Long City 34
Ha Tay Province 13, 14, 26, 34
Ha Tinh Province 35, 93
Hai, Bui Huu 71
Hai Hung Province 13, 26, 33
Hai Phong City 12, 26
Hanoi 26, 31, 89, 93
Hanoi Commercial College 97
Hanoi Moi 89
Hanoi National University 97
Hanoi Party Committee 100
Hanoi Polytechnic College 97
harbor development 71

health policy 54, 58, 62–63, 74
Hien, Nguyen Ngoc 98
Ho Chi Minh City 15, 29, 30; Military Party Committee 40
Ho Chi Minh National Political Institute 16, 32, 87, 97
Ho Chi Minh thought 44, 45, 60, 72, 78
Ho Chi Minh University 97
Hoa Binh 35, 64
Hoang Lien Son Province 98
hostile forces 43, 76
Hung, Pham 98
Hung, Vu Quoc 87
Huong, Le Minh 85

ideological issues 6, 45
Ideology and Culture Department 34, 37, 39
illegal trade activities 80
income distribution 54
incumbents, Central Committee 92, 93
industrialization and modernization 22, 26, 27, 30, 31, 35, 42, 45, 54, 60, 72, 74
inflation 52, 74
inspectors, Communist party 18
Institute of Economics 97
Institute of Science 97
Interim Party Conference 5, 30, 54, 109
investment law 74

joint ventures 30, 77
journalists 69

key cadre conferences 9, 14, 18
Khai, Phan Van 86
Khanh Hoa Province 13, 23, 64
Khue, Doan 40, 42, 71, 85
Kien, Le Van 87
Kiet, Vo Van 35, 69, 71, 73, 129, 130
Kon Tum 120

labor force policies 32, 56
Lai Chau Province 35, 64
Lam Dong Province 32, 35
land use issues 30, 55, 64
Lang Son Province 64
Lao Cai Province 71
Laos 53
Latin America 77
leadership change 5
Linh, Nguyen Van 71, 72
local congress political reports 10
local defense strategies 41
local experimental congresses 10
local leadership selection 11
local party congresses 14, 17
local party elections 24, 33–34, 37
Luong, Tran Duc 86
Luyen, Dao Dinh 18, 41

Manh, Nong Duc 35, 85
market-based economy 6
market mechanisms, development of 30, 52, 56, 72
Marxism-Leninism 44, 60, 61, 62, 72, 78
Marxist-Leninist Institute 97
mass mobilization 12
mass organizations 97
Mekong Delta economic center 64
membership recruitment 13, 14, 23, 24, 43, 47, 50, 67, 82, 84
membership standards and discipline, review of 10, 81
Middle East 53
military: appraisal of party members 115; congresses 18–20, 40–43; council system 43; development projects 41; Party Committee 18; regions 40, 42, 45; training 40
Military Committee 18, 84
military officers 92, 93, 94–95
Minh Tuan Province 64
Minister: of Agriculture and Rural Development 96; of Building 96; of Commerce 95; of Communications and Transportation 96; of Culture and Information 96; of

Defense 95; of Education and Training 96; of Finance 95; of Foreign Affairs 95; of Industry 96; of Interior 95; of Justice 98; of Labor, War Invalids and Social Welfare 96; of Marine Products 96; of Public Health 96; of Science, Technology and Environment 96; of Trade and Planning 96; of Youth and Sports 96
Ministry: of Education and Training 38; of Finance 39; of Industry 39; of Planning 96
ministry congresses 38–40
minorities 34, 48, 54, 64, 67, 71
modernization *see* industrialization and modernization
monetary policy 52, 54, 73, 78
mountainous area provinces 48, 71, 75
multisector economy 47, 52, 74
municipal party committee meetings 38
Muoi, Do 12, 22, 27, 30, 32, 33, 39–40, 43, 49, 50, 59–60, 66, 69, 70, 71–72, 73, 90, 100–102, 109–112, 119, 120, 129
My, Nguyen Thi Xuan 87

Nam Bo Khmer People's Representation 98
Nam Ha Province 13
National Assembly 96, 98, 99
National Center of Social Sciences and Humanities 97
National Defense Academy 40
Nationalities and Mountain Region Committee 99
Naval Party Congress 40
new leadership 69, 85, 88, 105
new members 92, 117
Nghe An Province 35
Nghi, Hoang Duc 99
Ngo, Bui Thien 85
Nguyen Ai Quoc Institute 87, 97
Nhan Dan 14, 22–23, 60, 62, 63, 66
Nien, Nguyen Minh 87

Ninh Binh Province 15, 41
Ninh Thuan Province 32, 64
Ninth Plenum 20–22

Oanh, Vu 18, 85, 122
obstacles to reform 6
office directors 92, 93
office managers 93
141st Regiment 19, 20
open economy 29
opening remarks 71, 72–73
Organization Department 6, 11, 12, 29, 49
outstanding members 10
outstanding party members 10
oversight sessions 10
overseas Vietnamese 53, 70

Party Commission for Science and Education 97
party committee system 43
party media representatives 93
party officials 93
PAVN *see* People's Army of Vietnam
peaceful evolution 76
peaceful transformation 20, 44, 46
Peng, Li 70, 135
People's Army of Vietnam (PAVN) 13, 42; *see also* military
People's Supreme Court 98
Personnel Subcommittee 49
Phan, Nguyen Ha 35, 50–51, 59, 85, 129
Phieu, Le Kha 18, 35, 42, 80
Phu, Lam 98
Phu Yen Province 23
Phuong, Do 88
pilot district congresses 12, 13, 15, 23
planning and market mechanisms, symbiotic relationship 56
planning work 51, 73
Pleiku 35
pluralim, rejection of 70
Politburo: 71, 85–86; inspection

visits 12–13, 122; Resolution Number Twelve 30
political degeneration of party cadre 57
political participation 30
political report 69, 75–81
precinct-level congresses 12
precinct party congresses 23, 25
preparatory process: meetings 9–27, 103–104; Party Center control over 7, 10, 14–15, 16–18, 31–32, 35–36
private capitalist economic activities, party members and 80–81, 101
private enterprise 29, 30, 47, 80
propaganda committees 36, 37
property ownership 57
provincial and municipal party secretaries, 92, 93, 94, 98
provincial military party committees 13
provincial party congresses 13, 64–66
public security committee 84

Quan, Tran Hong 39
Quan Doi Nhan Dan 19, 40, 60, 66
Quang Nam-Da Nang Province 23, 33, 64
Quang Ngai Province 23, 38
Quang Ninh Province 64
Quang Tri 64
Quy, Nguyen Duy 97

Ranarith, Norodom 129
reform process, national review of 5–6
regimental command meetings 19
regulations, Communist party 82
religious freedom 80
renovation, commitment to 70
research institute heads 92
Resolution 8B 12, 14, 19
Resolution 3 19

revised party statutes 21, 48, 81–84, 107–108, 136–138
rural development strategies 27, 31, 33, 45

Saigon Giai Phong 30
Sam, Do Quoc 71
science and technology policy 56, 59, 74
Secretariat 12, 13, 23, 25, 26, 29, 35, 47, 81, 83
secretaries, Communist party 19
"security ministries" 95
security policies 59
senior cadre course 15
senior officials, view of 6
Seventh National Congress 9–10, 48, 65
Seventh Plenary Resolution 12
Sixth National Congress 6, 34, 52, 65
smuggling 22
"social evils" 29, 59
social issues 5, 23, 36, 38, 54, 56, 65, 71, 73, 74, 76, 77, 78, 79
"social ministries" 96
socioeconomic plan 48, 50, 73–75
Son, Hoang Kim 87
Son, Pham Thi 98
Son La Province 35, 65, 93
South China Sea 40
Soviet Union 44, 45, 53, 55, 62, 77
special development projects 12
specialized economic zones 74
standard of living issues 61
Standing Committee 88–92, 106
state owned enterprises 29, 30, 47, 52, 54, 56, 59, 62, 65,; 72, 77, 78–80, 98, 100, 102
State Planning Committee 71
statutes, Communist party 35, 66
stock market 56
strategic issues 6

Tan, Tran Trong 88
Tap Chi Cong San 44, 73–74

Tap Chi Quoc Phong Toan Dan 18
taxation 22, 34
Tenth Plenary 48–51
Thai Binh Province 13, 26, 33, 38
Tham, Nguyen Van 87
Thang, Do Quang 87, 122
Thanh Hoa Province 33, 64
Thieu, Nguyen Duc 87
Third Plenary 11, 12, 55
Tho, Le Phuoc 12, 32, 33, 85
Thu, Nguyen Thi Hoai 99
Tien Giang Province 14, 15
Tra, Pham Van 85
Tra Vinh 64
training 60
"transparency" 69
Tri, Ha Minh 98
Trong, Truong Vinh 87
Trung, Ha Tuan 87
Tu, Nguyen Dinh 39, 85, 122
Tung, Dao Duy 12, 32, 33, 35, 59, 85, 86
Tung, Le Xuan 71, 89
Tuyen Quang Province 64, 65
Twelfth Plenary 48, 49, 50, 59

United States of America 53
university chancellors 92
urban issues 71

Viet Bac area 42
Viet Kieu 53
Vietnam Fatherland Front 22
Vietnam News Agency 88
Vinh Phu Province 65, 71
Voice of Vietnam 51
voting process, plenary meetings 48

weak party organizations 10
women 14, 19, 24, 80, 117
women's organizations 14

Xuong, Le Danh 71

Yen Bai Province 18, 33, 64
Yeu, Nguyen Van 98
youth organization secretaries 19